Inside the Sausage Factory

The illusion of evidence-based policymaking

HOBART PAPERBACK 226

Inside the Sausage Factory

The illusion of evidence-based policymaking

Christopher Snowdon

iea
Institute of
Economic Affairs

First published in Great Britain in 2026 by
The Institute of Economic Affairs
2 Lord North Street
Westminster
London SW1P 3LB
in association with London Publishing Partnership Ltd
www.londonpublishingpartnership.co.uk

The mission of the Institute of Economic Affairs is to improve understanding of the fundamental institutions of a free society by analysing and expounding the role of markets in solving economic and social problems.

A CIP catalogue record for this book is available from the British Library.

ISBN 978-1-918291-54-4

TABLE OF CONTENTS

ABOUT THE AUTHOR

Dr Christopher Snowdon is the Head of Lifestyle Economics at the Institute of Economic Affairs. He is a regular contributor to the Spectator, the Telegraph and the Critic and often appears on TV and radio discussing lifestyle regulation and policy-based evidence. He is the editor of the Nanny State Index and the author of six books: Polemics (2020), Killjoys (2017), Selfishness, Greed and Capitalism (2015), The Art of Suppression (2011), The Spirit Level Delusion (2010) and Velvet Glove, Iron Fist (2009). He has a PhD in economics from the University of Buckingham.

ACKNOWLEDGMENT

Sincere thanks to Philip Booth and Len Shackleton for their perceptive comments and constructive criticism and to the Institute of Economic Affairs for its support.

FOREWORD

"Laws are like sausages. It is better not to see them being made" is an apocryphal quote frequently attributed to Chancellor Otto von Bismarck. He probably did not literally say that, but the statement is Bismarckian enough in spirit, in that it expresses an unsentimental, unromantic attitude to politics: politics as a grubby business, not a high-minded pursuit of lofty ideals.

One interpretation of the statement is that if people could see how sausages are being made, they probably would not want to eat them anymore, and likewise, if they could see how laws are being made, they would be far less willing to cede greater powers over their lives to the state.

The analogy no longer works as well today as it did in the 19th century, because the idea that sausage-making is a particularly unhygienic process is no longer true. One can, in fact, find several educational YouTube videos filmed inside sausage factories, which show how sausages are made. There is nothing repellent about it: the only ones which show unhygienic practices are the ones which are meant to expose bad actors which fall short of normal industry standards.

Has the process of making laws been similarly cleaned up and sanitised?

At first sight, it may seem so. The process has never been as transparent and inclusive as it is today. Gone are the shady backroom deals of the Bismarck era. Today, it is possible for an interested observer to follow the trajectory of a law from start to finish, and even to take part in it. At any given time, there are multiple parliamentary consultations and select committee inquiries on major and minor legislative projects, where anyone who feels qualified is welcome to submit evidence. Any formal input that informs legislative outcomes is in the public domain.

In addition, over the past thirty years, there has also been a marked trend towards 'evidence-based policymaking'. Policymakers now actively seek out the best available evidence from the relevant disciplines that the legislation refers to (e.g. economics, medicine, criminology), in order to professionalise policymaking, and reduce the role of distorting influences.

And yet, even the most sympathetic observer of Westminster politics would struggle to argue that these trends have improved the quality of the political decision-making process. There is no shortage of reforms which fail even on their own terms, and much more so on a broader cost-benefit analysis, often in ways that critics predicted from the outset.

In this book, Dr Christopher Snowdon takes a closer look at what goes on inside the political sausage factory. In order to do so, he did not break into the Houses of Parliament to eavesdrop, and he did not wiretap the place either: he simply analyses information that is publicly available, but which, on its own, is just a meaningless heap of raw data.

He shows that while governments do indeed collect mountains of evidence, there is no reason to believe that the quality of the evidence is what ultimately drives the policy outcomes. Beneath the veneer of evidence-based, transparent and participatory policymaking, politics remains the same grubby old business it has always been.

Dr Snowdon's main area of interest is public health policy, but some of his insights are almost certainly transferable to other policy areas as well.

The general pattern he finds is that people who start out as public health researchers often turn into political activists lobbying for legislative changes to restrict consumer choices. These activists, aided by a sympathetic media landscape and a latently anti-capitalist *zeitgeist*, create a moral panic around an actual or perceived public health problem, and promote their preferred policy interventions as the solution. Politicians eager to avoid bad headlines then give those activists what they want, regardless of whether the policy makes much sense.

Dr Snowdon stands firmly in the tradition of the public choice school of economics, a school of thought which sees politics in decidedly unsentimental – we might almost say, Bismarckian – terms. They are not, as some of their critics claim, anti-politics cynics. They simply start from the presumption that politics does not turn us into better people.

But Dr Snowdon's work also goes beyond Public Choice Economics as conventionally defined. Traditionally, when proponents of the public choice school talk about how political actors use the political process to advance their self-interest, the self-interest they have in mind is financial gain (in the case of private industry), power (in the case of politicians), or prestige (in the case of bureaucracies). At first sight, public health activism seems to be a deviation from that pattern. The political changes public health activists lobby for will neither make them rich, nor powerful, nor prestigious. So where is the self-interest? Is this not a pure act of 'altruism', even if it is a misguided one?

Dr Snowdon does not doubt the sincerity of his opponents' convictions. They honestly believe that they are engaged in a noble struggle against manipulative, predatory industries which prey on people's weaknesses. Nonetheless, their brand of political activism has become professionalised: it is a state-subsidised career path. The people who have chosen that career path are never going to conclude that we now have enough public health legislation, and that their job is done. Indeed, although they have achieved sensational policy victories in recent years, they always quickly move on and find a new field of activism.

The political sausage factory is probably always going to be an unsavoury place. We will never find a way to clean it up properly. What we can vary, though, is its size and scope. We do not need to constantly expand the political sausage factory: it does not have to cover half of the country. We should scale it back to a minimum size, and limit its remit to its core business.

Read this book, and let it ruin your appetite for politics.

KRISTIAN NIEMIETZ
Editorial Director, Institute of Economic Affairs
London, April 2026

SUMMARY

In the classic model of evidence-based policymaking, the government identifies a problem, canvasses a range of potential policies to address it, and commissions high-quality evidence from impartial academics to find the most cost-effective solution. After implementation, the government commissions independent research to evaluate whether the policy has achieved its clearly stated goal.

It is widely acknowledged that real world policymaking rarely, if ever, follows this idealised model of a rational, linear process. In democracies, politicians do not necessarily get to decide which issues take priority. Problems and their purported solutions can be thrust upon them by emergencies, media pressure, the parliamentary opposition and lobbyists from business and civil society. Nevertheless, the United Kingdom has a system of public consultations, impact assessments and post-implementation reviews which, alongside the checks and balances of academic publishing, is designed to put evidence at the heart of policymaking.

The aim of this book is to examine the role of evidence in public health policymaking in the United Kingdom. It examines four case studies between 2008 and 2018: plain packaging for tobacco, the Soft Drinks Industry Levy, minimum pricing for alcohol, and the stake reduction for fixed odds betting terminals (FOBTs). With the exception of minimum pricing, which was introduced in Scotland but not England, the campaigns for all four policies succeeded and were said to be evidence-based.

To assess which pieces of evidence were most influential in each policy debate, a quantitative analysis was conducted to examine the documents cited by government departments and agencies, politicians and the media during the course of each campaign, using the online archives of five major media outlets and the transcripts of fourteen debates in the House of Commons. In each case (although more weakly in the FOBT debate) there were 'superstar' studies which dominated political and media attention. All of them supported the policy proposal and they combined to produce 'packages of evidence' which appeared to show (1) how the policy would work in theory, (2) how a similar policy had recently worked in another country, and (3) that experts believed the policy would succeed.

Following a qualitative analysis of the packages of evidence and a retrospective evaluation of the policies, I identify a series of significant deviations from the classic model of evidence-based policymaking which suggest that the decision to proceed with the policy (or abandon it) was, in every case, not primarily, or even largely, dictated by a dispassionate review of high-quality research evidence.

Further analysis indicates that, in contrast to many case studies in the political science literature, the policymaking process was dominated by small, paternalistic interest groups who achieved their policy aims in a relatively short period of time without having to make any major compromises. None of the policies were formulated within government and none of them had been priorities for the government or the electorate at the outset of the campaigns.

Using insights from public choice theory, I conclude that the behaviour of virtually all the policy actors, including politicians, the general public and professional lobby groups on both sides, can be explained by the pursuit of 'thick-rational' self-interest. Ambivalent policymakers responded to political pressure from concentrated interest groups who used research evidence as one of several devices to generate publicity for their campaigns. Consumers who would be adversely affected by the policies had insufficient incentive to mobilise in their collective interest and non-consumers had no obvious reason to oppose policies that offered the possibility of a marginal benefit. Seeing little public opposition, the government considered the reputational risks of inaction to be greater than the risks of proceeding with policies that were broadly revenue-neutral or, in the case of the sugar tax, revenue-raising.

... you change your laws so fast without enquiring of results past or present that this is all experiment, seesaw, doctrinaire; shuttlecock between battledores.

– Florence Nightingale

Laws are like sausages. It is better not to see them being made.

– Attributed to Otto von Bismarck

PART ONE

EVIDENCE

1 EVIDENCE-BASED POLICY

In 1972, Archie Cochrane wrote a short book titled *Effectiveness and Efficiency* which drew attention to the worryingly large number of unproven medical interventions being used in the National Health Service (NHS). The history of medicine is rife with quackery and, even in the mid-twentieth century, procedures and drugs were sometimes used on the basis of little more than tradition and intuition. The personal opinion of doctors often counted for more than empirical evidence which was, in any case, lacking. The mere fact that patients frequently recovered after being treated was not proof of a treatment's effectiveness. As Cochrane knew from his experience as a doctor, patients frequently recovered with or without medical intervention (Cochrane 1972: 5).

Recognising that clinicians were prone to bias and the *post hoc ergo propter hoc* fallacy, Cochrane ranked their opinion at the bottom of the evidence pyramid. Observational studies, in which one group of people are compared against another, were better, but were still 'thoroughly unsatisfactory', wrote Cochrane, because a self-selecting group of people who are defined by one characteristic (such as seeking out a particular treatment) will often share other characteristics which confound results (ibid.: 21). When individuals are not selected at random, differences in health outcomes cannot necessarily be attributed to the treatment.

At the top of the evidence pyramid, Cochrane put the double-blind randomised controlled trial (RCT) in which half the patients are randomly assigned to be treated while the other half are not. To prevent bias and to counter the placebo effect, neither the patient nor the researcher is told who has been given the treatment (hence double-blind). When conducted properly, RCTs greatly reduce the chance of useless remedies appearing to be effective as a result of confounding factors and bias, but they do not offer 100% protection against dumb luck. To test for fluke findings, the best practice is to test for statistical significance, and experiments should be rerun, preferably by independent researchers, with all the studies then compiled in a systematic review or meta-analysis.

Although RCTs had been used since the 1940s, Cochrane found many examples of NHS treatments that had never been put through them. Some of them, such as insulin for diabetes, were so obviously effective that an RCT would be unnecessary and unethical. Others, such as tonsillectomy and psychotherapy, were not. The need for thorough evidence became more urgent as the benefits of treatments became more marginal. As Baron (2018) argues, evidence-based medicine was not needed for most of human history because the impact of health interventions, such as penicillin in the treatment of bacterial infections, was too big to ignore. But in the modern world, many beneficial treatments have a more modest effect that may not be obvious due to confounding variables; variables that can be excluded in RCTs.

Cochrane argued that if RCTs were more widely used, the NHS would become both more effective and more efficient. Useless and harmful treatments would be abandoned and effective treatments would be used at the right time and in the right places (Cochrane noted that effective treatments were sometimes over-used and over-prescribed). He concluded with an appeal for more applied research into NHS treatments, in which the 'technique will nearly always be an RCT' (Cochrane 1972: 80). His book was highly influential in the UK and abroad. RCTs are now universally regarded as the gold standard of scientific evidence in health. The Cochrane Collaboration was founded in 1993 to produce systematic reviews of RCTs, and in 1999 the National Institute for Clinical Excellence was founded to evaluate both the effectiveness and efficiency of medical treatments in the UK.

From medicine to policy

The idea of transferring the lessons of evidence-based medicine to public policy led to the term 'evidence-based policy' coming into common use in the late twentieth century. Writing in the 1980s, Martin Bulmer (1986: 5–6) explained the five stages of 'the rational model' of policymaking:

1. A problem which requires action is identified. The goals, values and objectives related to the problem are set out.
2. All important possible ways of solving the problem or achieving the goals and objectives are listed. These are alternative strategies, courses of action or policies.

3. The important consequences which would follow from each alternative strategy are predicted and the probability of those consequences is estimated.
4. The consequences of each strategy are then compared to the goals and objectives identified under (2).
5. Finally, a policy or strategy is selected in which consequences most closely match goals and objectives, or the problem is most nearly solved.

Only a handful of RCTs were used in social policy before 1980, mostly in the USA, but they become more common in the 1980s and 1990s. Unlike in medicine, RCTs are often impractical or impossible in other areas of public policy. There is usually no equivalent of a placebo; we cannot, for example, make people think they are paying a tax or being given a house when they are not. We can try a policy out in one part of the country while leaving the rest of the country with the status quo, but the individuals involved are not truly randomised. Even when feasible, RCTs tend to be expensive and so, in their absence, 'softer' forms of evidence have to be accepted. From the outset, therefore, 'evidence-based policy'had a looser definition than evidence-based medicine and some saw the term as little more than a marketing device for traditional policymaking.

The phrase 'evidence-based policy' became prominent in Britain in the late 1990s after the Labour Party won the 1997 general election under Tony Blair. The Labour manifesto declared that 'New Labour is a party of ideas and ideals but not of outdated ideology. What counts is what works. The objectives are radical. The means will be modern' (Dale 2000: 348). As a political slogan, 'what counts is what works' had a particular appeal to a party that was eager to convince the public that it had abandoned socialist dogma. The statement is difficult to disagree with (who does not want things to work?) and it allows those who use it to present themselves as open-minded pragmatists while subtly implying that their opponents are led by blind ideology. Other politicians on the centre-left have since echoed the same refrain. In 2008, for example, Australia's new Prime Minister, Kevin Rudd, promised that his government would deliver 'a robust, evidence-based policymaking process' that would be 'driven by analysis of all the available options, and not by ideology' (Rudd 2008). Barack Obama, in his inaugural address of 2009, said 'the question that we ask is not whether our government is too big or too small, but whether it works ... Where the answer is yes, we intend to move forward. Where the answer is no, programs will end' (Obama 2009).

In 1999, the Cabinet Office produced a white paper titled *Modernising Government* which is often cited as the origin of the evidence-based policy movement in Britain (Parsons 2002; Wyatt 2002). The document does not actually mention the phrase 'evidence-based policy', and even the word 'evidence' only appears three times, but it does say that the government 'must be willing constantly to re-evaluate what it is doing so as to produce policies that really deal with problems; that are forward-looking and shaped by the evidence rather than a response to short-term pressures'. It adds that the government 'will improve our use of evidence and research so that we understand better the problems we are trying to address' (Cabinet Office 1999a: 15–17).

1999 was a big year for evidence-based policy. In addition to founding the UK Centre for Evidence Based Policy and Practice – created with a £1.3 million grant from the Economic and Social Research Council – the government set up the (short-lived) Centre for Management and Policy Studies to 'capture and absorb the best research evidence and management practice wherever they may be found' (Wyatt 2002: 13). Away from government, the Campbell Collaboration was also founded in 1999, based on the Cochrane Collaboration, to assess social policy.

Modernising Government was followed by *Professional Policy Making for the Twenty First Century*, also published in 1999 by the Cabinet Office. The report noted that government departments spent over £350 million on 'policy-related research' in 1998/99 (Cabinet Office 1999b: 36) and provided three case studies: warning labels on solvents which were shown to groups of parents, teachers and young people over a period of two years to find the most effective message; the Sure Start scheme which was based on a cross-departmental review showing that 'early, sustained, comprehensive interventions were the most effective in preventing later social exclusion'; and efforts to eradicate Potato Brown Rot based on a cost-benefit analysis and a pilot scheme (ibid.: 33–35).

It was telling that none of the case studies in *Professional Policy Making for the Twenty First Century* involved RCTs or even peer-reviewed studies. Although evidence was utilised, it fell short of the gold standard and there was little to suggest a fundamental change in the workings of government. Scientists, including social scientists, do not generally view mere 'information' as evidence *per se* and yet the Cabinet Office explicitly rejected the idea that they would confine themselves to academic research.

> ... there is a tendency to think of evidence as something that is only generated by major pieces of research. In any policy area there is a great deal of critical evidence held in the minds of both front-line staff in departments, agencies and local authorities and those to whom the policy is directed. Very often they will have a clearer idea than the policy makers about why a situation is as it is and why previous initiatives have failed. Gathering that evidence through interviews or surveys can provide a very valuable input to the policy making process and can often be done much more quickly than more conventional research (ibid.: 43).

The obvious question is, if personal anecdote and opinion count as evidence, how is evidence-based policymaking different to traditional policymaking? This speaks to a long-running conflict between academics and lawmakers. As Lomas and Brown (2009: 913–4) write:

> For researchers and, to a lesser extent, for evidence-based medicine proponents, the word *evidence* is synonymous with *research*, whereas for these civil servants, *evidence* is more synonymous with *data*, *analysis*, or *investigation* (emphasis in the original).

Academics prefer evidence that has been generated through the scientific method and published in journals (of which they are the gatekeepers) whereas politicians will accept mere 'information'. Academics complain about policymakers ignoring their research while policymakers complain about academics pursuing obscure subjects that have no practical policy implications ('policy-free evidence'). Academics complain about a lack of funding but also complain that funding from the government creates pressure to produce research that fits the government's agenda.

These tensions existed long before 1999. In an article published at the start of that year, Graham Leicester wondered whether researchers like himself had 'become so used to the term "evidence-based policy" that perhaps we now miss its ironic tone' (Leicester 1999: 5). The debate about how academic research is used in policymaking had changed little since the 1970s when American academics such as Carol Weiss were writing about 'research utilisation'. She described the 'most common concept of research utilisation' as being when 'research provides empirical evidence and conclusions that help to solve a policy problem' (Weiss 1979: 427). This is evidence-based policy by any other name, and the USA was in many respects its pioneer. Its (privately funded) Coalition for Evidence Based Policy was established in 1978 and the US government has been spending money on social research since the 1880s. It has carried out dozens, if not hundreds, of RCTs in the areas of education, basic income, welfare, employment, poverty reduction and criminal justice since the 1960s. In 1976, the US government spent more than $1.8 billion on 'social research and development' (Lynn 1978: 1). At that time, there was so much research that one academic complained that 'the attempt to manufacture socially useful knowledge to order – to treat the acquisition of knowledge like any other government procurement – has flooded the market with shoddy products' (ibid.: 5–6). Politicians, meanwhile, complained about the amount of taxpayers' money being spent on academic theories which they considered irrelevant, if not subversive.

Disseminating research

Carol Weiss shared the cynicism of many subsequent critics about the ability of academic research to shape public policy. Academics want policymakers to be methodical and systematic. They expect them to identify a problem and then seek out research to solve it. In practice, the policymaking process is more chaotic. Politicians are lobbied by interest groups and only see evidence when it is pushed under their noses. 'It probably takes an extraordinary concatenation of circumstances for research to influence policy decisions directly', Weiss concluded (Weiss 1979: 428). Among the many boxes a piece of research must tick before it is acted upon by policymakers, she said, were being unambiguous, timely and not running counter to political interests.

Politicians are busy people who are bombarded with requests to tackle a wide range of issues. As Cairney and Oliver (2017: 3) argue, they employ time-saving heuristics to navigate a world in which perfect rationality and perfect knowledge are unattainable:

> ... policymakers do not have the ability to gather and consider all evidence relevant to policy problems. Instead, they employ two shortcuts – 'rational', pursuing clear goals and prioritising certain sources of information, and 'irrational', drawing on emotions, gut feelings, beliefs and habits to make decisions quickly.

Cairney and Oliver list several ways in which researchers can exploit the bounded rationality of policymakers to exert influence. These include 'combining facts with emotional appeals' and 'telling simple and easily understood stories which manipulate people's biases' (ibid.: 4).

In short, much of this literature tells academics how to be better lobbyists. The crucial first step in policymaking is getting an issue on the agenda. Research that is focused on narrow policy questions, such as the effectiveness of different warning labels on solvents, can be used at the second stage, but academics can also push broader issues up the policy agenda. They can use their work to encourage policymakers to focus on different political ends, and they are sometimes keen to do so. Some of the academics who are pessimistic about policy ever being truly evidence-based are more optimistic about academics influencing the wider climate of opinion and putting certain issues on the table.

DeLeon and Weible (2010: 26) argue that 'the biggest gain for democracy is likely through the *long-term* learning among [policymaking] practitioners from a series of study results' (emphasis in the original). Note that DeLeon and Weible assume that researchers' influence on policymakers will improve *democracy* rather than mere policymaking. This suggests something more far-reaching and ambitious than the use of best statistical practice. Note also that they emphasise repetition of research findings until the researcher's conclusions become established facts. Again, therefore, academics are being encouraged to become policy entrepreneurs themselves. They are urged to decide not only on the means but on the ends of public policy. This adds a new dynamic because once academics become activists there is a danger of existing biases being magnified by the incentives of getting a policy win and making the world a better place, as they see it. Social scientists are no different from anyone else in having biases, both political and self-serving, and can have strong views on subjects that are beyond their academic expertise. Focused on a single issue, they may think it is worth spending more money to solve a particular issue than the median taxpayer is prepared to pay.

When science becomes central to politics, it risks becoming politicised. Politically, academics have leant towards the liberal-left for decades (Weiss 1978: 25), particularly in the social sciences, and this tendency has become more pronounced over time (Carl 2017; Eagan et al. 2014). They usually work within an academic system that rewards eye-catching research which appeals to funders. The UK's Research Excellence Framework actively encourages researchers to produce work that has an impact outside of academia. There is pressure to 'publish or perish' in many university departments while journals want dramatic findings rather than confirmations of the null hypothesis or replication of earlier experiments. Academics naturally feel that their area of research is of special interest and that their perspective is particularly useful, but advocacy research may exaggerate the scale of the problem it is addressing to inspire political action (Gilbert 1997). Those who have staked their reputation on a hypothesis being correct may be reluctant to change their minds in the light of new evidence.

These biases would be of little account if RCTs were the norm in public policy analysis, but they are not. In the absence of RCTs, researchers in the social sciences turn to weaker methods, such as modelling, surveys, focus groups, observational studies, ecological studies and interrupted time series, which are more sensitive to chance, statistical adjustments and the interpretation and assumptions of the researcher. Clarence (2002) argues that politicians talk about 'the science' as if it were an immutable fact, free of bias and errors, but many controversies exist even in medicine and the 'hard sciences'. In the social sciences, where randomised controlled trials are often impossible and issues are more political, controversy is inevitable.

The concept of evidence-based policymaking has been criticised for being technocratic and handing excessive power to social scientists who are neither impartial nor democratically accountable. Politicians have been accused of using 'the science' to shield them from public debate:

> By seeking to utilise rational policy making, what is effectively being argued for is the depoliticisation of the policy process: policy decisions are no longer decisions based on political beliefs about the world but are instead based upon "rational" evidence. This is attractive to politicians who can outflank critics by insisting that policies are therefore 'above' political criticism. (ibid.: 4)

If findings from the scientific literature are instrumental in both putting a perceived problem on the agenda and dictating how it is solved, the question of what counts as evidence and who controls it is an important one. As Marston and Watts (2003: 145) note, it is a crucial question because 'far from being a neutral concept, evidence-based policy is a powerful metaphor in shaping what forms of knowledge are considered closest to the "truth" in decision-making processes and policy argument.' They warn of the danger of evidence-based policy becoming 'a means for policy elites [to] increase their strategic control over what constitutes knowledge' (ibid.: 158).

Who is the policymaker to believe? Friedrich Hayek, in his Nobel Prize lecture, noted that '[i]t is often difficult enough for the expert, and certainly in many instances impossible for the layman, to distinguish between legitimate and illegitimate claims advanced in the name of science' (Hayek 1974). In practice, policymakers have enough experience of being presented with conflicting scientific findings to know that 'following the science' is not as simple as it sounds. During the COVID-19 pandemic, for example, different governments implemented totally different policies on travel bans, school closures and face-masks, but all were able to point to studies and scientists who supported them.

The pandemic provided a good illustration of why 'evidence-based policy' is easier said than done. There were established facts (SARS-CoV-2 was a highly virulent disease with a much higher fatality rate than influenza), facts that appeared to be established until they were overturned (the World Health Organisation initially insisted that the virus was not airborne and face-masks offered no protection (Sample 2020; Chamary 2021)), and then there was policy, which had to weigh the harm caused by the virus against the economic and social costs caused by non-pharmaceutical interventions. Politicians not only had to make decisions based on evidence that was incomplete and sometimes wrong but also had to factor in public opinion and intangible factors such as the value of personal liberty and the value of a human life.

The classic criticism of evidence-based policy is that the evidence itself is often weak, conflicting and politicised, and that even when it is more robust it cannot dictate major policy decisions because there are often complex trade-offs and value judgements at work. Evidence can provide the means to an end, but it cannot say what the end should be. In evidence-based medicine, there is a consensus about the aim of reducing morbidity. We identify a range of treatments and pick the one that performs best in randomised controlled trials, subject to cost-effectiveness. There may be biases at play, for example from a drug's manufacturer, but these can be overcome through the use of sound scientific methods. In public policy, by contrast, methods are less robust and biases more pervasive. Policy entrepreneurs on both sides of the debate marshal their evidence and policymakers decide whose evidence is most compelling. Politicians often have strong views of their own and will select evidence that can be used as ammunition for their side of the debate. Whichever way they lean, they can usually claim to have based their decision on evidence of some sort. The resulting policy might be better described as evidence-decorated or evidence-garnished than evidence-based. Some commentators have preferred to use the more modest term 'evidence-informed' (Parkhurst et al. 2018: 222).

Nevertheless, the general acceptance that policy *should* be evidence-based encourages policymakers and policy entrepreneurs to cite evidence and debate it. Writing in 2001, Nick Black (2001: 275) observed that '[t]he need *to be seen* to be making evidence-based decisions has permeated all areas of British public policy' (emphasis added). The modern British infra-structure of evidence-based policy, such as public consultations, systematic reviews and impact assessments overseen by the Regulatory Policy Committee, is designed to force governments and bureaucrats to provide evidence to justify their decisions. The Blair government did not invent all of these processes,[1] but there is a more explicit focus on evidence – particularly peer-reviewed evidence – than there was in the past. Public consultations are often subtitled 'Call for evidence' and their questions frequently ask respondents to cite data rather than opinion. A system of evidence reviews, consultations and impact assessments does not guarantee that policy will be 'evidence-based', let alone perfect, but it erects a series of obstacles for policy entrepreneurs to overcome and it creates a presumption that political debates should at least be *grounded* in evidence – or, more bluntly, in reality.

[1] Compliance Cost Assessments had been used since 1985 and were replaced by Regulatory Impact Analyses in 1998 which, in turn, became Impact Assessments in 2007.

2 POLICYMAKING IN THE REAL WORLD

One thing that all researchers who have written about policymaking agree on is that it is never purely 'evidence-based' in practice. In theory, the policymaking process involves putting a problem that requires government action on the agenda, canvassing possible solutions and commissioning research to see which would work best. This is followed by 'policy formulation, decision making, implementation and finally, evaluation' (Embrett and Randall 2014: 148). In his classic study of policymaking in the USA, *Agendas, Alternatives, and Public Policies,* John W. Kingdon (1995: 77–8) describes the ideal system of evidence-based problem solving as follows:

> If policymakers were operating according to a rational, comprehensive model, they would first define their goals rather clearly and set their levels of achievement of those goals that would satisfy them. Then they would canvass many (really, all) alternatives that might achieve these goals. They would compare the alternatives systematically, assessing their costs and benefits, and then they would choose the alternatives that would achieve their goals at the least cost.

Kingdon immediately acknowledges that 'such a model does not very accurately describe reality' (ibid.: 78).

So how does policy-making work in reality? There is no simple answer, but there are three theoretical frameworks that are worth considering.

The science of muddling through

The first comes from Kingdon himself and is known as the multiple streams approach. Based on extensive interviews with people involved in US policymaking in the 1970s and 1980s, he identified three important 'streams' in the policy-making process:

- Problem stream: An issue rises up the agenda that is seen to need solving.
- Policy stream: As ideas evolve in the 'policy primeval soup', a long list of possible solutions is narrowed down to a short list on the basis of feasibility, affordability and public acceptability.
- Political stream: Policy entrepreneurs work to make the policy fit the prevailing mood of the nation and build consensus for change before the window of opportunity closes.

At first glance, this framework resembles the classic model of rational policymaking, but it differs in three crucial ways. Firstly, the streams represent criteria that must be fulfilled during a 'window of opportunity' but the process does not necessarily occur in the chronological order implied above. Secondly, the gap between problem identification and policy implementation is not necessarily filled with newly commissioned research and evidence reviews. Thirdly, a problem does not necessarily get on the agenda after calm deliberation by a policymaker. Politicians do not always get to decide which political issues take priority. Problems and their purported solutions can be thrust upon them by emergencies, lobbyists, the media, the opposition and pressure groups.

Charles E. Lindblom (1959) famously described policymaking as 'the science of muddling through', but while it may seem chaotic, it is not random. Politicians tend to respond to political pressure rationally and in their own self-interest – which, from their perspective, is synonymous with both their party's self-interest and the nation's self-interest. In the framework proposed by Kingdon, issues are put on the agenda as a result of 'focusing events', such as disasters, or by routine indicators, such as traffic fatalities, going in the wrong direction, or by government officials and the public telling politicians that something is not working, or by a change of government. Once the problem rises up the agenda, a 'policy window' opens and policy entrepreneurs propose solutions. Whether the proposed solution becomes policy before the window closes depends on politics in the narrow sense – bargaining, logrolling, building consensus – as well as on public opinion.

The multiple streams approach is more of a framework by which policymaking can be studied than a predictive model. Nevertheless, Kingdon observed several tendencies in his study of American health and transport policy in the 1970s that he and other political scientists subsequently identified in further case studies (Jones et al. 2016). The following observations are of particular relevance to our topic:

- elected officials and, above all, the president are the most powerful agenda setters (Kingdon 1995: 199).
- interest groups tend to block or water down reforms rather than initiate them (ibid.).
- change happens slowly and there is a 'long softening-up process' before an idea becomes a policy. Policy entrepreneurs often have to wait years for the right circumstances to emerge for their policy to be adopted (ibid.: 201).
- the process involves 'considerable doses of messiness, accident, fortuitous coupling, and dumb luck' (ibid.: 206).

In Kingdon's account, for a policy to be seriously considered it must be feasible, reasonably popular and either low cost or revenue raising. Evidence alone can be used as ammunition, but it is rarely central and is never the only factor in decision-making.

As Brian W. Head (2010: 88) puts it, 'the policy process is best understood as a patchwork quilt of arguments and persuasion in which various forms of evidence are deployed as part of political debate.' Lindblom and Cohen (1979: 64) argue that 'policy is not made by a policymaker but by interaction among a plurality of partisans'. This view of the system, which could be described as political realism, offers a role for research evidence, but does not depend on research evidence. The resulting policies could be calmly evidence-based or irrationally emotional. The process may pay lip service to the ideals and routines of evidence-based policymaking, but only because 'some people feel better if they make their decisions after the ceremonies of analysis' (Lindblom and Cohen 1979: 84).

The public health perspective

The multiple streams framework has been used in some public health policy analysis, but with a much greater focus on interest groups and lobbying. Broadly speaking, public health academics view policymaking in the field of lifestyle and 'non-communicable diseases' as a pitched battle between industry and health advocates. A substantial literature focuses on the tactics, strategies and arguments of 'unhealthy commodity industries'. One of the main conclusions is that tactics associated with the tobacco industry have been copied by the alcohol, food and gambling industries, and by 'commercial entities' in general.

In two systematic reviews of studies looking at industry responses to public consultations on tobacco and alcohol advertising laws, Savell et al. (2014; 2016) identified four main categories of argument:

- negative unintended consequences (e.g. loss of jobs)
- regulatory redundancy (e.g. a ban is unnecessary because of self-regulation)
- insufficient evidence (that the proposal will work)
- legal (e.g. that an advertising ban would be unconstitutional).

Looking specifically at tactics, Savell et al. (2014: 4) identified six policy-influencing approaches used by the tobacco industry:

- Information (direct and indirect lobbying; commissioning research; collaborating with government)
- Constituency building (forming alliances with other sectors; media advocacy; creating front groups)

- Policy substitution (developing alternatives to regulation, e.g. voluntary codes of conduct)
- Legal (threatening legal action)
- Constituency fragmentation (neutralising or discrediting opponents)
- Financial incentive (gifts, inducements and promising future employment to policymakers).

A study of submissions to an Australian government consultation on sports betting advertising regulation found all six of these strategies used by the gambling industry (Hancock et al. 2018). A systematic review of studies looking at alcohol industry lobbying against marketing restrictions found five of the six tactics, with only 'constituency fragmentation' missing (Savell et al. 2016). More recently, the taxonomy has been extended to the food, pharmaceutical, chemical, fossil fuel, automobile and soft drink industries, as well as Big Tech and the gig economy (WHO Europe 2024).

However, these tactics are not unique to industry and all of them are used by other pressure groups, including public health campaigners, as the following examples show.

- *Information (direct and indirect lobbying; commissioning research; collaborating with government)*

This is the bread and butter of any political campaign. Several articles in the public health literature recommend face-to-face meetings with policymakers as the single most effective form of persuasion, as do articles in the broader literature on research utilisation.

Groups such as Action on Smoking and Health and Action on Sugar hold meetings and other events in Parliament to engage with politicians. Such pressure groups often commission research from third parties.

- *Constituency building (forming alliances with other sectors; media advocacy; creating front groups)*

  Public health interest groups often form coalitions and alliances, such as the Alcohol Health Alliance, to maximise their lobbying potential and media advocacy. All of the main groups to be discussed in this book have an All-Party Parliamentary Group to advance their arguments.

- *Policy substitution (developing alternatives to regulation, e.g. voluntary codes of conduct)*

  Public health groups do this in reverse by proposing statutory regulation as a substitute for voluntary agreements. In some instances, 'softer' regulation proposed by government is 'gold-plated' by pressure groups.

- *Legal (threatening legal action)*

  This is less common in public health but is not unheard of. In 2005, while campaigning for the smoking ban, ASH sent a registered legal letter to employers in the hospitality trade and warned of an 'ever rising threat of legal action from employees whose health is damaged by secondhand smoke'.[2] Some academics have proposed using UN Human Rights legislation to mandate bans on 'junk food' marketing (Garde et al. 2018).

- *Constituency fragmentation (neutralising or discrediting opponents)*

  Ad hominem arguments against those who are perceived to be defending industry interests are common in the public health literature. A number of articles have sought to discredit individuals and organisations on the basis of real or imagined financial ties to industry (e.g. Horel and Keyzer 2021; Hawkins and Holden 2013; McCambridge et al. 2014). Bath University's Tobacco Control Research Group runs a website (www.tobaccotactics.org) which strongly implies that those who speak out against certain anti-smoking policies are part of a co-ordinated opposition controlled by the tobacco industry. The epidemiologist Katherine Flegal (2021) became 'the target of an aggressive campaign that included insults, errors, misinformation, social media posts, behind-the-scenes gossip and manoeuvres' from the public health community after she published research showing that being overweight is not associated with increased mortality.

- *Financial incentive (gifts, inducements and promising future employment to policymakers)*

[2] https://ash.org.uk/media-and-news/press-releases-media-and-news/hospitality-trade-warned-of-legal-risk-from-secondhand-smoke/

> Tobacco, alcohol, food and gambling industries have donated a great deal of money to politicians and political parties over the years. There is evidence that the size and quantity of donations increase when industry-relevant policies are under discussion (Kypri et al. 2019). Inducements are less common from the public health side, but they do exist in the form of jobs and awards. For example, the WHO hands out No Tobacco Day Awards every year to politicians who have introduced anti-smoking or anti-vaping policies, thereby offering prestige and favourable publicity. The UK's public health minister, Jane Ellison, won the WHO Director-General Special award in 2016 after legislating for plain packaging. After losing her seat in the 2017 general election, she secured a job at the WHO as its Executive Director for External Relations and Governance. Nicola Sturgeon, who was instrumental in bringing about minimum pricing in Scotland, was appointed to the billionaire Michael Bloomberg's Task Force on Fiscal Policy for Health in 2018.

In any policy campaign, both sides use similar tools, including press releases, drinks receptions, media engagement, coalition building, undermining the opposition, briefing journalists and producing newsworthy publications. But, as Parkhurst et al. (2018: 226) note, the public health lobby portrays these tactics as underhand when used by its opponents:

> ... in England, the public health community for many years collaborated effectively to influence government policy on tobacco control,

> strategically utilising scientific evidence to support their position. This was widely seen to be a legitimate use of evidence. Yet the tobacco industry also routinely engaged in strategic uses of evidence to support arguments in opposition to tobacco control measures, typically in ways judged to be biased by researchers and tobacco control advocates.

A limitation of the public health analysis is that it tends to present policymaking as a binary choice between the interests of public health and the interests of industry. The views of consumers, voters and politicians tend to be overlooked or, if these participants oppose the policy in question, explained by reference to industry influence. Although 'industry tactics' are often assumed to be the main reason why certain proposals do not become law, lobbying is very difficult to quantify and causation cannot be proved or, in many cases, even inferred.

The public choice perspective

Public choice theory recognises that rent-seeking industries influence policymaking, often for the worse, but that they are just one self-interested policy actor among many. Others include ideological special interest groups, bureaucrats, voters, political parties and politicians themselves.

In public choice theory, there is a nexus between politicians, bureaucrats and interest groups, sometimes known as the Iron Triangle, that is instrumental in shaping policy (Overman and Simanton 1986). It is assumed that politicians' primary interest is their own political survival and re-election and that bureaucrats are interested in safeguarding and expanding their department's budget and prestige (Niskanen 1968). Public choice economists agree with the scholars of research dissemination and political science that neither political conviction nor evidence is decisive in policymaking.

> In the rough-and-ready world of practical politics, policy is shaped in a maelstrom of idealism, activism, ignorance, time constraints, power struggles, and special-interest pressures. It would be genuinely shocking for real-world policies to resemble those imagined by hopeful academics. (Rizzo and Whitman 2020: 310)

For their part, voters are rationally self-interested but also *rationally ignorant* about most policy issues. Since there is almost no chance that their vote will be decisive in an election, they have little incentive to inform themselves about politics (Downs 1957). Bad policies have adverse consequences for the electorate, but these costs tend to be spread thinly across the population and often go unnoticed whereas the benefits of rent-seeking policies are bestowed on a small, concentrated minority who are thus highly motivated to educate themselves and take action. The costs *to the individual* of lobbying against a bad policy are often greater than the burden of the policy, and individuals cannot vote against *specific* policies because – with the exception of referendums – their choice is between candidates who present a basket of policies every few years. For this reason, the demands of concentrated interest groups – commercial or ideological – often prevail over the interests of the majority (Olson 1971).

One of the more depressing insights from public choice economics is that both voters and politicians bear relatively low costs from making poor choices, as compared to private decision-makers, and therefore tend to make poorer choices than they would if acting purely on their own behalf in the marketplace. Insights from *behavioural* public choice economics make for even grimmer reading because a number of cognitive biases leave politicians particularly prone to producing hasty, ineffective, costly and/or unnecessary legislation. These include *action bias* which Patt and Zeckhauser (2000: 50) define as a penchant for taking action for the sake of being *seen* to take action (by the electorate).

> From the waiter who stops by the table to ask whether everything is okay, to the politician who files a bill he can report to his constituency even though it is sure to lose, agents are continually trying to make their actions evident, because principals often have difficulty discerning consequences. (ibid.: 63)

As the examples in this quote show, action bias is not inherently irrational. On the contrary, it is perfectly rational for a politician to show voters that he is doing something. The problem comes when the actions themselves are not justifiable on other grounds. Moreover, there can be irrational reasons for action bias. One of these is *overconfidence*. Rozenbilt and Keil (2002) coined the term 'the illusion of explanatory depth' to describe the phenomenon of people believing that they have much greater understanding of complex issues than they do. Most people believe they are above average in many domains, although this is mathematically impossible. Highly incompetent people not only lack the ability to comprehend important issues but lack the ability to recognise their lack of comprehension. This leaves them especially prone to overconfidence. As Kruger and Dunning (1999: 1,122) have shown, incompetent people who 'gain insight about their shortcomings' downgrade their assessment of their own skills and abilities: the more they know, the more they recognise how little they know.

A possible counterweight to action bias is *status quo bias*: a preference for the status quo that encourages a politician to do nothing. It could be argued that conservatives are driven by status quo bias while progressives are driven by action bias. However, a bias towards the status quo may inspire action from politicians of any hue if societal trends are perceived to be moving away from the norm. If the number of problem gamblers or alcoholics is perceived to be rising, for example, a conservative policymaker might ditch the regulatory status quo in an effort to return to the societal status quo. Even when the prevalence of a problem is static or falling, politicians are unlikely to be sanguine about the status quo when it is framed in a certain way (e.g. '79,000 people are killed by smoking every year'). The status quo is an anchor, but it is not the only form of anchoring. Politicians might instead take zero risk as their anchor and work towards that. *Zero-risk bias* can lead to the economically irrational conclusion that a goal must be achieved at any cost.

Other mental shortcuts that can tip over into biases include the *availability heuristic* in which policymakers turn to familiar and established frameworks for dealing with problems and seek to emulate them. The availability heuristic might explain why a politician would copy a policy from another country if it is perceived to have worked there. The *intentions heuristic* makes politicians (and voters) display a 'tendency to judge a policy based on the intentions of its advocates rather than on the policy's actual consequences' (Lucas and Tasić 2015: 218). If the intention of the policy is to improve health, as in the case studies we shall examine, this can become a powerful bias, especially when advocates frame the intentions of their opponents as being to make a profit. As Lucas and Tasić (2015: 220) argue, prejudice against free market policies stems, in part, from the intentions heuristic.

> Firms are motivated by profit, so consumers conclude that they can charge exorbitant prices for low quality products. As Joseph Schumpeter noted, people suffer from an 'ineradicable prejudice that every action intended to serve the profit interest must be anti-social by virtue of this fact alone.'

All these biases can lead to *motivated reasoning*, with policymakers placing undue weight on weak evidence that supports their view and being unduly sceptical of stronger evidence which contradicts it. This can be further aggravated by what Parkhurst (2016: 386) calls 'levels of contestation' in which people are more likely to mangle, misrepresent or misinterpret the evidence when passions run high than when the stakes are low.

> One would hardly expect groups to start manipulating research or cherry-picking evidence to influence policy decisions over which colour to paint a new school, or to change the weekday that municipalities collect household waste, for instance. Yet when a policy debate revolves around an issue held to be of high importance, there is a much greater incentive for strategic technical bias. (ibid.)

Cognitive biases are extremely common across the population and are by no means confined to policymakers. However, as Rizzo and Whitman (2020: 348) (and others) argue, these biases are '*more* worrisome in the public sector than the private sector, because the public sector offers far worse incentives for people to curb their irrational tendencies and numerous opportunities to indulge pleasing beliefs and prejudices at low cost' (emphasis in the original). Moreover, politicians may be more likely to rely on heuristics than ordinary people because they have a large number of important decisions to make, often involving uncertainty, and are bombarded by so much conflicting evidence that they can suffer from information overload (Vis 2019: 44).

None of the theories about how policymaking is made are beyond criticism and public choice is no exception. Green and Shapiro (1994) accuse it of relying too much on theoretical analysis and lacking empirical support. They argue that when real world political outcomes do not fit the rational choice model, economists resort to *post hoc* justifications, blaming imperfect information or broadening the concept of self-interest in a way that produces no testable propositions and adds little or nothing to our understanding of political science. However, even critics of public choice theory concede that some of the insights into pressure group politics developed by Mancur Olson have much to commend them (ibid.: 80; Barry 1970: 46). Using self-interest to explain collective action (or the lack of it) is more compelling when interest groups are fighting over resources than over issues of principle or ideology, as Olson himself acknowledged (Olson 1971: 159). On the face of it, the public health pressure groups that are the focus of this book should not exist at all according to public choice theorists since their aims are essentially paternalistic and policy victories will not bestow obvious benefits on their members. This is a conundrum we shall return to in later chapters.

Finally, it should be noted that the various perspectives on policymaking are not necessarily mutually incompatible. The multiple streams approach can incorporate more rigid theories, including public choice, and aspects of the public health perspective can dovetail into both public choice and the multiple streams approach. And although advocates of every strand of political science agree that evidence-based policy in its pure form is a will o' the wisp, none of these approaches precludes the possibility of evidence playing a role.

PART TWO

THE CASE STUDIES

METHODOLOGY

The following chapters examine four case studies of lifestyle-related public health policymaking in the United Kingdom in the 2010s: plain packaging for tobacco, the Soft Drinks Industry Levy (commonly known as the sugar tax), minimum pricing for alcohol, and the stake reduction for fixed odds betting terminals (FOBTs). Each of these policies was introduced after hard-fought campaigns, although only partially in the case of minimum pricing, which was introduced in Scotland (and later Wales) but not in England. All of the policies were said to be 'evidence-based' and were introduced (or rejected) in Westminster by a Conservative-led government.

Upon what evidence were these political decisions made and how strong was it? To assess this, we will look at the evidence cited by government agencies, politicians and the media during the course of the campaigns, based on a quantitative analysis of evidence cited in five major British media outlets and evidence cited by MPs in relevant House of Commons (HoC) debates. This will be accompanied by a qualitative analysis of the most frequently cited sources of evidence to assess what *type* of evidence appeared to be most persuasive and how *strong* that evidence was. Was it objective? Did it meet the highest standards of scientific 'proof'? Did it accurately predict subsequent outcomes? In the final analysis, was the political decision evidence-*based*, evidence-*informed* or merely evidence-*decorated*? And if objective empirical evidence was not the primary driver of policymaking, what was?

What do we mean by evidence? For our purposes, it is any published empirical claim about the expected impact of a policy, including evidence reviews. Evidence showing the existence or scale of the problem is not included. In the plain packaging case study below, for example, we do not include the evidence that smoking is harmful to health or estimates of how many children start smoking each year. Evidence of this sort frames the problem rather than offers a solution. Framing is important in campaigning and will be discussed in a later chapter, but for now we are interested only in evidence that helps policymakers decide whether a policy will be effective, ineffective or counterproductive.

Anecdotal evidence and personal opinion are not included, nor are claims based on unpublished research. In a few instances, research was cited in public debate that seems to have been published but is no longer available online. These sources are not included in the summary statistics but will be mentioned when relevant.

Underlying the methodology is the assumption that if proponents of a policy cite particular studies or statistics it is because they find them persuasive and think that others will find them persuasive. If a media outlet reports the results of a particular study, we assume that the editor and/or journalist believes the findings to be of some importance. If a journalist cites a piece of evidence in an op-ed while making the case for or against a policy, we assume that they feel that this evidence is compelling. In the case of press coverage, the mere fact that the findings were reported gives them significance in the political debate because media coverage can influence public opinion and is often intended to do so.

The analysis of media coverage uses the online archives of the *BBC News* website, the *Daily Telegraph* (including the *Sunday Telegraph*), the *Mirror* (including the *Sunday People*), the *Daily Mail* (including the *Mail on Sunday*) and the *Guardian* (including the *Observer*). These outlets were selected to provide a politically and socio-economically representative sample of the British media, including the most viewed news website (*BBC*), a left-leaning tabloid (*Mirror*), a right-leaning tabloid (*Mail*), a left-leaning broadsheet (*Guardian*) and a right-leaning broadsheet (*Telegraph*). Relevant articles were identified via Google searches using the following terms:

> plain packaging/plain packs/standardised packaging minimum pricing alcohol/minimum unit pricing sugar tax/sugary drink tax/soft drink tax fixed odds betting terminals/FOBTs
>
> For example: "site:theguardian.com plain packaging".

Each web search is limited to a window of time starting before each campaign had begun and ending when the final decision had been made. For plain packaging, the search dates ranged from 1/1/08 to 10/03/15. For the sugar tax, the search dates ranged from 1/1/10 to 15/3/16. For minimum pricing, the search dates ranged from 1/1/07 to 14/11/17. For fixed odds betting terminals, the search dates ranged from 1/1/12 to 14/11/18.

Analysis of House of Commons debates uses Hansard transcriptions: (http://hansard.parliament.uk) to count how many MPs made a contribution from the floor, mentioning specific pieces of identifiable evidence. Where referenced evidence is no longer available online it has been retrieved, whenever possible, by the Wayback Machine (archive.org).

3 FIRST CASE STUDY: PLAIN PACKAGING FOR TOBACCO

Background

By the mid-1960s, following reports from the UK's Royal College of Physicians (1962) and the US Surgeon General (1964), the link between smoking and lung cancer was considered proven. Epidemiology later produced strong evidence that smoking causes other conditions such as chronic obstructive pulmonary disease, heart disease and laryngeal cancer.

The tobacco industry infamously sought to undermine the evidence linking smoking to ill health even as their own private research confirmed it. Advised by lawyers in the 1950s to neither confirm nor deny that smoking caused cancer, industry executives took no official position on what they called the 'smoking controversy' but paid sceptical scientists and spokespeople to cast doubt on the evidence. As this has been extensively documented elsewhere, the following summary by Coraiola and Derry (2019: 240–1) will suffice:

> First, the industry realised it was commercialising a routinely fatal product and did not stop in spite of the blatant evidence. When scientific

> research showed that cigarettes cause cancer, the industry responded with a public relations program to dissuade public opinion about the harms of tobacco. Second, they created a machine of public deception to disconfirm, silence, and discredit contrary voices. When evidence against tobacco began to mount, the industry promoted a campaign of disinformation to obliterate the knowledge of the harms and attack the science behind the evidence. Third, they systematically concealed, edited, and destroyed records of their wrongdoing while propagating a different history of the tobacco controversy and their involvement in acts of irresponsibility.

The scale of this deceit became public knowledge in the late 1990s when a large archive of hitherto private industry documents was sent to the American anti-smoking campaigner and academic Stanton Glantz by an anonymous source. By the end of the twentieth century, the industry's reputation was tarnished beyond repair and its story of 'doubt and delay' became *the* textbook example of corporate malfeasance. Scientific research funded by tobacco companies was treated with extreme scepticism and industry opposition to anti-smoking policies became almost a commendation.[3] This naturally benefited anti-smoking

[3] Judging a statement on the history of the person or source making it, rather than on its merits, is an *ad hominem* argument known as the genetic fallacy, but evidence shows that *ad hominem* arguments are effective. In a series of experiments, Barnes et al. (2018: 9) found that 'some strictly ad hominem attacks (specifically the conflict of interest and past misconduct attacks) are just as effective as attacks on the empirical foundation of a claim.'

campaigners who portrayed themselves as being on the side of the angels in a battle between good and evil.

In Britain, cigarette advertising was banned on television in 1965 and health warnings were applied to cigarette packs in 1971 (the latter as a result of a voluntary agreement with industry). Until the 1990s, the government's anti-smoking strategy revolved around education and incremental tax rises. That began to change in 1997 when Tony Blair's Labour Party was elected with a manifesto commitment to ban all tobacco advertising and sponsorship, the last of which was abolished in 2003.

The small charity Action on Smoking and Health (ASH) was founded in 1970 and was funded by the Department of Health from 1971 after its attempts at grassroots fundraising failed. It has long been the UK's primary anti-smoking pressure group. Its campaigns have been supported by the British Medical Association, which became more vocal on the issue in the 1980s, and two of the country's biggest charities, Cancer Research UK and the British Heart Foundation, adopted a more activist approach in the 2000s.

ASH scored its biggest win in 2006 when Parliament voted to ban smoking in virtually all indoor premises that are open to the public. This was far from inevitable. Ireland had gone 'smoke-free' only two years earlier and very few countries had followed suit. The Labour Party's 2005 manifesto explicitly promised to exclude private member's clubs and pubs which did not sell food. ASH succeeded by forming the Smoke-Free Action Coalition, an alliance of organisations who created a 'swarm effect' by drip-feeding reports, studies, comments and opinion polls into the media from 2003 until the final parliamentary vote in February 2006 (Arnott and Willmore 2006). The proposed exemption for 'wet pubs' and private member's clubs was a threat to the rest of the pub estate and ASH was able to 'split the hospitality trade from the tobacco industry' and pull them towards demanding a 'level playing field' (i.e. a total ban) (Arnott et al. 2007: 425). Interestingly, those who led the campaign recall that it was not the tobacco industry but the government who were their 'major opponents' in this campaign. Victory was only possible once politicians were persuaded that the ban would be popular (ibid.: 426).

Katherine Smith (2013: 392–3) argues that tobacco control proponents were able to convince governments to take a more coercive approach to the smoking issue because they changed the framing in three ways. Firstly, they emphasised the putative economic costs of smoking, particularly to the health service. Secondly, they focused on the 'harm to others' aspect of passive smoking, thereby de-emphasising the paternalistic intent of their policies. Thirdly, they made arguments about health inequalities which became increasingly important in public policy during the Blair years.

As Smith (2013: 386) also notes, much of the literature on tobacco policy succumbs to the 'seductive framing' of a 'heroes and villains' narrative. Resisting this temptation, she prefers to see loose and flexible coalitions of interest groups aligning around specific issues. At the centre are the anti-smoking pressure groups and activist-academics who are most effective when they find allies on certain policy proposals. At times, they may find themselves with unlikely bedfellows, including elements of the tobacco industry. At other times, they are opposed by natural supporters. On tobacco taxes, for example, some tobacco companies support specific tax rises while some in public health oppose higher taxes because of their concerns about inequality (ibid.: 389). The issue of e-cigarettes as smoking cessation devices has been particularly divisive, with both the 'pro' and 'anti' sides able to wield evidence to support their diametrically opposed viewpoints.

On the core issue of cigarette smoking, however, the tobacco control movement is united and the tobacco control literature is unusually homogenous. There is very little disagreement about the need for policies such as smoking bans, plain packaging, graphic warnings, etc. Ethical questions are occasionally raised (e.g. Voigt 2012), but the unintended consequences of anti-smoking policies are typically dismissed, denied or treated as a price worth paying for the greater prize of a 'tobacco-free world'.

This unity of purpose stems from the perception that the issue is, at heart, a simple one; that smoking is an unhealthy addiction with no redeeming features; that there is no safe level of tobacco consumption; that the optimum amount of smoking in society is zero, and that any demand-side or supply-side policy that reduces smoking prevalence is to be welcomed. The logical conclusion to the tobacco control campaign is prohibition. That aim began to be stated explicitly in the 2010s as smoking rates dropped and the possibility of a full ban on tobacco or cigarette sales became more realistic. Public health academics then openly began talking about 'endgame strategies' and 'phasing out cigarette sales' (Smith and Malone 2020), a policy endorsed by the British government in 2023.

In tobacco control, activism merges with academia to an unusual extent. Evidence for policies is often constructed and evaluated by those who campaign for them. As Mair and Kierans (2007: 104–5) note, 'tobacco research has come to represent as much a moral activity as an investigative one, a weapon used by the "researcher-activist" in the "fight against tobacco"'. Campaigners, such as ASH's Deborah Arnott and Martin Dockrell, publish in public health journals while academics, such as Anna Gilmore and Linda Bauld, have sat on the board of ASH. Several senior figures in tobacco control, such as Stanton Glantz in the USA and Simon Chapman in Australia, were members of anti-smoking groups before they worked in public health academia. Professional activism is not considered a conflict of interest. In the 'financial & competing interests disclosure' section of an article attacking media criticism of a second-hand smoke study, Martin Dockrell of Action on Smoking and Health wrote:

> The author considers that his employment with Action on Smoking & Health does not constitute a conflict of interest as their goal of minimising the harm from smoking is served best by even-handedly assessing the effectiveness of public health interventions. (Dockrell 2009: 26)

In his discussion of the historiography of drug policy, David T. Courtright (2004) divided writers into 'policy hots' and 'historical cools'. Policy hots write indignant articles criticising current policy and attacking policy entrepreneurs on the other side of the debate. They openly endorse particular framings and specific policies, often using emotional language. By contrast, historical cools, such as the historian Virginia Berridge, set out the facts without giving the reader any sense of their own opinion. The field of tobacco control academia is dominated by policy hots.

The smoking ban was the most notable victory in a series of political wins for the anti-smoking coalition. It was preceded by larger health warnings in 2003 and followed by graphic warnings in 2008, a ban on cigarette vending machines in 2011 and a ban on tobacco being displayed in large shops in 2012. ASH had first proposed plain packaging in 2008 ,but the Labour government decided against including it when drawing up the Health Act (2009), citing a lack of evidence. In December 2012, Australia became the first country to introduce plain packaging and the policy became the next primary objective of the tobacco control movement in the UK.

The policy

Plain packaging (or 'standardised packaging') of tobacco bans all logos, colours and branding on cigarette and rolling tobacco packs apart from the brand name which, in the UK, can only be displayed in a plain black font on an olive-green background accompanied by a large graphic warning. The policy is designed to deter nonsmokers, especially children, from buying tobacco and to encourage existing smokers to quit. It was first introduced in Australia in December 2012 and was introduced in the UK in May 2016 with a twelve-month grace period during which cigarettes could be sold, but not manufactured, in conventional packs.

Timeline

31 May 2008: *Consultation on the Future of Tobacco Control* is published by the Department of Health (2008). It includes a

question about whether 'plain packaging of tobacco products has merit as an initiative to reduce smoking uptake by young people'.

October 2008: Graphic warnings on cigarette packs become mandatory in the UK.

December 2008: Summary report of the consultation is published. It shows that 98% of those who answered the question about plain packaging were in favour. Health Secretary Alan Johnson tells the House of Commons that 'there is no evidence base that it [plain packaging] actually reduces the number of young children smoking' but agrees to keep the policy 'under review'.[4]

April 2010: Australian Prime Minister Kevin Rudd announces plans to introduce plain packaging.

November 2010: UK Health Minister Andrew Lansley says he wants to 'look at the idea of plain packaging' as part of a 'radical new approach to public health'.[5]

March 2011: A white paper titled *Healthy Lives, Healthy People: A Tobacco Control Plan for England* announces that the government will gather evidence on the likely impact of plain packaging.

1 December 2011: The Tobacco Plain Packaging Act (2011) is signed into law in Australia, to come into force one year later.

16 April 2012: The first plain packaging consultation is launched in the UK. It is originally due to close on 10 July, but the deadline is extended by a month to allow more people to respond. It ultimately receives 668,000 responses.

---

[4] https://hansard.parliament.uk/commons/2008-12-16/debates/08121646000017/Smoking

[5] https://www.bbc.co.uk/news/health-11796903

1 December 2012: Plain packaging comes into force in Australia.

12 July 2013: Summary report of the first UK consultation is published. Of those who submitted a detailed response, 53% agreed with plain packaging and 43% were opposed. A press release from the Department of Health announces that 'the Government has decided to wait until the emerging impact of the decision in Australia can be measured before making a final decision on this policy.'

28 November 2013: The government is reported to have renewed its interest in plain packaging. Sir Cyril Chantler, a paediatrician, is commissioned to carry out an independent review.

3 April 2014: The Chantler Review is published. It concludes that plain packaging 'is very likely to lead to a modest but important reduction over time in the uptake and prevalence of smoking'. Public Health Minister Jane Ellison says she is 'currently minded to proceed with introducing regulations to provide for standardised packaging'.[6]

29 May 2014: The BBC broadcasts the first episode of *Burning Desire*, a two-part documentary about the tobacco industry which strongly promotes plain packaging.

26 June 2014: A second public consultation is launched, along with draft regulations, to run for six weeks until 7 August.

21 January 2015: The government says it will go ahead with the policy subject to a free vote in the House of Commons.

February 2015: Summary report of the second consultation is published.

[6] https://www.gov.uk/government/speeches/chantler-report-on-standardised-packaging-of-tobacco-products

11 March 2015: MPs vote in favour of plain packaging by 367 votes to 113. The policy is due to come into force in two stages in May 2016 and May 2017.

The evidence

There were 70 references to relevant, identifiable evidence in the media and 38 references in the HoC. Of the 28 pieces of evidence cited, 14 were cited once and only by the BBC or the *Guardian*. The debate about what happened in Australia led to relatively frequent references to the Australian Bureau of Statistics' tobacco sales data, the Australian Institute of Health and Welfare's smoking prevalence data, two KPMG reports commissioned by the tobacco industry about illicit tobacco sales (classified together in Figure 1), and a study by Kaul and Wolf (2014) which used an interrupted time-series methodology and concluded that plain packaging in Australia had little or no impact on smoking prevalence. Kaul and Wolf's study was funded by a tobacco company and was criticised by Laverty et al. (2015) which is one of several peer-reviewed articles that rebutted 'industry' claims during the campaign. The KPMG reports, released in quick succession in 2013 and 2014, claimed that there had been a rise in illicit tobacco sales in Australia after plain packaging was introduced.

As Figure 1 shows, three pieces of evidence stand out for being very heavily cited in the media and in the parliamentary debates. The Chantler Review and the Stirling Reviews collated and summarised the available research, making it accessible to policymakers. Most of the pieces of evidence in Figure 1 were discussed in one or both of these reports. By far the most heavily cited study was by

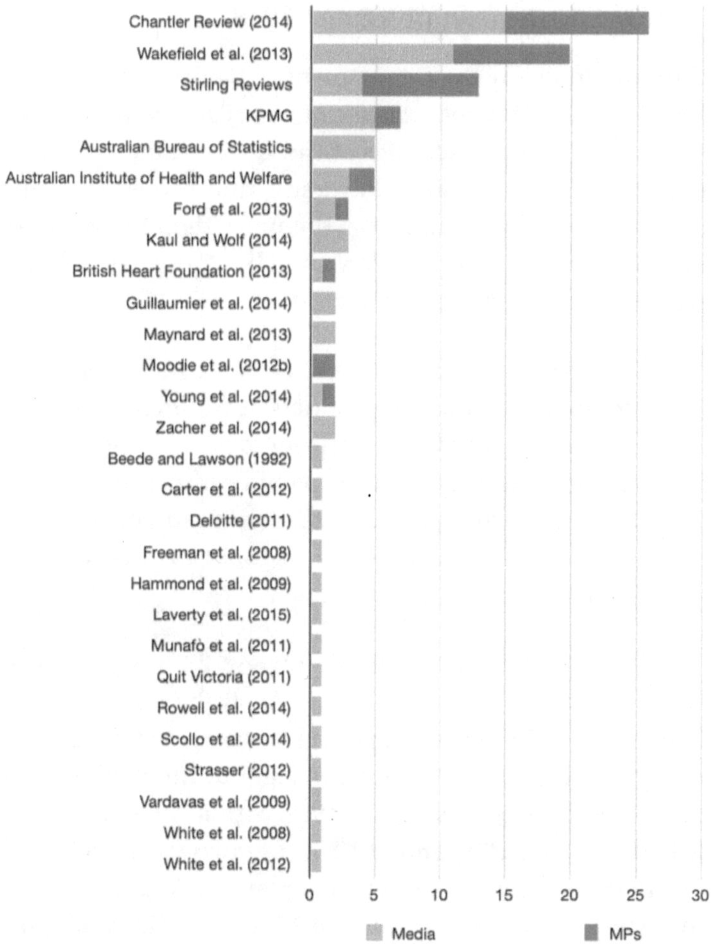

Figure 1. Number of references to evidence in the media and House of Commons

Wakefield et al. (2013), a team of academics in Australia who claimed to have the first 'real world' evidence of plain packaging's efficacy.

The Stirling Reviews (2012 and 2013)

Commissioned by the Department of Health, the first Stirling Review (‘*Plain tobacco packaging: A systematic review*’) was produced by academics at the UK Centre for Tobacco Control Studies (Stirling University) and the EPPI-Centre (University of London). It was the most significant source of evidence at the time, widely cited by supporters of plain packaging. It concluded that:

> ...plain packaging would reduce the attractiveness and appeal of tobacco products, it would increase the noticeability and effectiveness of health warnings and messages, and it would reduce the use of design techniques that may mislead consumers about the harmfulness of tobacco products (Moodie et al. 2012: v).

Of the 37 documents in the review, 23 were based on surveys. Most of them came from Australia and New Zealand, with six from the UK. Only five were rated ‘high’ quality by the authors of the review. Nine of the studies were published between 1990 and 1997 with a further 27 published between 2008 and 2012. These two waves reflected two periods of political interest in plain packaging. In 2011, there was a spike in interest and 14 new studies were published. There were no relevant studies published between 1998 and 2007 except a simple survey of Sydney residents who were asked about various potential tobacco control measures and gave ‘qualified support’ to plain packaging (Carter and Chapman 2006). This was one of three studies in the review which simply asked people whether they would support the idea.

The Stirling Review included several (unpublished) university theses, conference presentations and government reports. Of the 37 documents included, only 19 had been published in peer-reviewed journals. Two of these contained no new primary research (Carter and Chapman 2006; Freeman et al. 2010) and one looked at retail transaction times (Carter et al. 2012), leaving 16 peer-reviewed studies looking at the impact of plain packaging on smokers and nonsmokers in experimental conditions. One researcher (David Hammond) was a co-author of six of these studies while the lead author of the Stirling Review (Crawford Moodie) was a co-author of five.

The oldest of the studies was a thesis written by two academics from the Department of Marketing at New Zealand's University of Otago. It was later published in the journal *Public Health* and set the standard for the literature that followed (Beede and Lawson 1992). Over the course of 80 focus groups, 568 adolescents were shown cigarette packs with ten different health warnings on them. Half the cigarette packs were totally plain (i.e. no colours or branding and with the brand name printed in a simple black font). Asked afterwards to recall the health warnings, the adolescents were more likely to remember the warnings if they had seen them on a plain pack (74%) than on a branded pack (64%).

Broadly speaking, this was the same methodology used in most of the other studies. Groups of people, usually teenagers or young adults, were asked to give their reaction to plain packs and branded packs, with particular attention paid to whether they noticed health warnings, perceived greater health risks or simply found them ugly. The studies consistently found that plain packs were considered to be less attractive and that cigarettes in plain packs were perceived to be of lower quality. Of the seven studies that asked about health warnings, four found that plain packs made the warnings more salient.

The first Stirling Review gave a thorough overview of the state of the evidence at the start of 2012. Indeed, with the inclusion of unpublished Master's theses, opinion polls and conference presentations, it cast its net wider than typical systematic reviews in public health, which tend to ignore the 'grey' literature.

The second Stirling Review ('*Plain tobacco packaging research: an update*') added 17 studies that had been produced since the original publication and focused only on peer-reviewed research. The authors concluded that 'the evidence summarised in this update of the literature, in general, provides further support for the proposed benefits of plain packaging' (Moodie et al. 2013: 14). As before, the most common type of study in the review used a survey-based methodology. Of the 17 new studies, eight were based on surveys, mostly conducted online. Six of them were similar to previous studies in which participants were shown plain packs and asked how they felt about them. Five of the other studies used focus groups, although two of these were general discussions about tobacco policy and only briefly touched on plain packaging (Uppal et al. 2013; Edwards et al. 2012). Both of them revealed mixed views and a good deal of scepticism towards the idea. The other three studies based on focus groups asked participants to give their view of plain packs as compared to conventional packs, with particular reference to appeal, attractiveness, warnings and harm. Responses tended to be similar to those from the online surveys.

Two studies used eye-tracking technology to measure how much attention participants paid to health warnings on cigarette packs. Ramunno et al. (2012) found that people spent longer looking at the warnings when there was no branding on the pack, but Maynard et al. (2013) found this was only true of occasional smokers, not of daily smokers or people who had never smoked. This replicated the findings of a slightly earlier study by Munafò et al. (2011).

One study took the form of a 'naturalistic experiment' in which female smokers in Scotland were given cigarettes in dark brown plain packs for one week and were given their usual brand in another week. The authors found that 'plain packaging was associated with more negative perceptions and feelings about the pack and about smoking' and that 'participants reported looking more closely at the warnings on plain packs and also thinking more about what the warnings were telling them' (Moodie and MacKintosh 2013: 1). There were '[n]o significant overall differences in salience, seriousness or believability of health warnings' between the pack types but participants using the plain packs reported being more likely to hide or cover the pack, more likely to think about quitting and to have slightly reduced their cigarette consumption (ibid.).

Finally, a study by Pechey et al. (2013) involved asking 33 tobacco control experts by telephone how much they thought smoking rates would drop by if plain packaging were introduced. The mean predictions were 1% for adults and 3% for children. These estimates would later be used in the government's Impact Assessment.

The Chantler Review (April 2014)

By the autumn of 2013, the government was under significant political pressure to introduce plain packaging. In July, following the first public consultation, it had decided not to proceed with the policy and instead await evidence from Australia, where plain packaging had been in force since December 2012. Public health campaigners portrayed this as a U-turn and the government was accused by Labour ministers and sections of the media of capitulating to pressure from the tobacco industry. In November, the government suddenly announced that it had commissioned the paediatrician Sir Cyril Chantler to carry out an evidence review. To a large extent, this took the decision out of the government's hands. If Chantler had judged that the policy was unlikely to be successful and was pregnant with unintended consequences, it is possible that political pressures would still have forced the government into introducing plain packaging, but it is hard to imagine the government ditching the policy once an independent review had concluded that it was 'highly likely that standardised packaging would serve to reduce the rate of children taking up smoking' (Chantler 2014: 6).

The Chantler Review contained no new empirical research. Instead, Chantler consulted with academics, industry representatives and other stakeholders and made his judgement of the evidence. He steered clear of non-health issues, such as the legal and economic implications of plain packaging, although he did comment on the argument that plain packaging would fuel the illicit trade in tobacco. In summary, Chantler felt there was a strong association between tobacco advertising and smoking initiation and that packaging was part of the marketing matrix. He was impressed by the consistency of the findings in the studies covered by the Stirling Reviews and whilst he accepted that these findings were 'essentially indirect and "speculative"' (ibid.: 29), he considered it very likely that negative perceptions of plain packaged cigarettes would 'feed through into reduced tobacco consumption'. He cited 'emerging evidence from Australian studies' which showed 'behaviour change, including increased calls to quitting helplines, hiding packs in social situations, smoking less around others, and smoking fewer cigarettes overall' (ibid.: 30).

In the absence of randomised controlled trials, which he said would be unethical, Chantler felt there was sufficient evidence to assume that plain packaging would lead to a reduction in smoking initiation by children and a reduction in tobacco consumption overall. With regards to claims that the policy would fuel the illicit tobacco trade, he cited government sources in Australia (whom he visited while conducting the review) criticising the methodology of an industry-funded report from KPMG (2013) which had reported a rise in illicit tobacco sales after plain packaging was introduced. He referenced official customs data which, he claimed, 'shows no significant effect on illicit tobacco following the introduction of plain packaging' (Chantler 2014: 33).

Acknowledging his limitations as a paediatrician in evaluating all the evidence and arguments, he commissioned three academics to evaluate the Stirling Reviews, two of whom were experts in medical statistics. They confirmed that the reviews were well conducted and that most of the studies within them were of good quality. Chantler acknowledged that the studies in question were not perfect, but said the criticisms made of them by opponents of plain packaging 'rarely go beyond the limitations recognised and described by the authors' (ibid.: 26).

> Few research studies are without limitations, and undoubtedly many could be improved with insights from related fields, but this does not seem a reasonable basis on which completely to discount the findings of over 50 peer-reviewed, published studies. (ibid.: 27)

Having established that the impact of plain packaging on consumer perceptions was real, the big question was whether this would translate into changes in behaviour. In the final analysis, this came down to a subjective value judgement. Chantler's view was that it would. He did not give an estimate of how much plain packaging would impact smoking rates, but in comments that were reported in the HoC by the public health minister Jane Ellison, he said that *if* plain packaging reduced smoking by children by 2%, 'it would mean 4,000 fewer children taking up smoking each year'.[7] This figure was not derived from any modelling and seems to have been entirely illustrative.

Wakefield et al. (2013)

Of the dozens of studies looking specifically at plain packaging between 2008 and early 2015, only Wakefield et al. (2013) was heavily cited by politicians and journalists (n = 20). Using surveys to gauge the impact of plain packaging on smokers' perceptions of taste, attractiveness and harm was well-trodden ground by the time it was published. Melanie Wakefield herself had published a similar study five years earlier (Wakefield et al. 2008), but what her

[7] https://www.gov.uk/government/speeches/chantler-report-on-standardised-packaging-of-tobacco-products

new research lacked in originality it gained from its timing of publication – ten days after the government had put plain packaging on hold – and from the sense that it was the first 'real world' evidence to surface. The researchers interviewed smokers by telephone while plain packaging was being rolled out in Australia in late 2012 at a time when some were buying plain packs and others were still buying traditional packs (Wakefield et al. 2013).

This survey had the advantage of interviewing smokers who were using real plain packs as opposed to looking at mock-ups or photos. As in many earlier studies of its kind, respondents tended to feel that the plain packs were less attractive, that the cigarettes within were of lower quality, and that the health warnings were more prominent. But the most widely reported finding from the survey was that plain packaged cigarettes made smokers 81% more likely to think about quitting.

Discussion

As Figure 2 shows, evidence reviews and peer-reviewed studies were the most widely cited sources in the media and the HoC, although there was also some interest in the raw data on smoking prevalence and tobacco sales emerging from Australia. In this chart, the Chantler Review, which was not peer-reviewed, is classified as 'non-academic'. The category of 'other' includes illicit trade estimates from KPMG, estimates of the impact on retail serving times from Deloitte (who concluded that plain packaging would increase serving times), the study by Kaul and Wolf (which was not peer-reviewed), and a survey from the British Heart Foundation (2013) which found that Australian

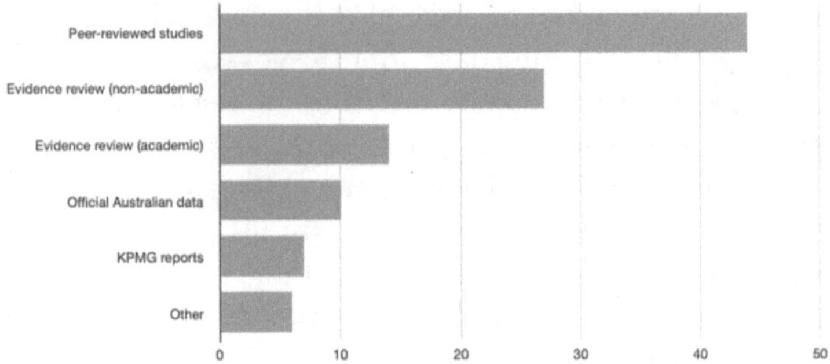

Figure 2. Type of evidence cited (by number of references)

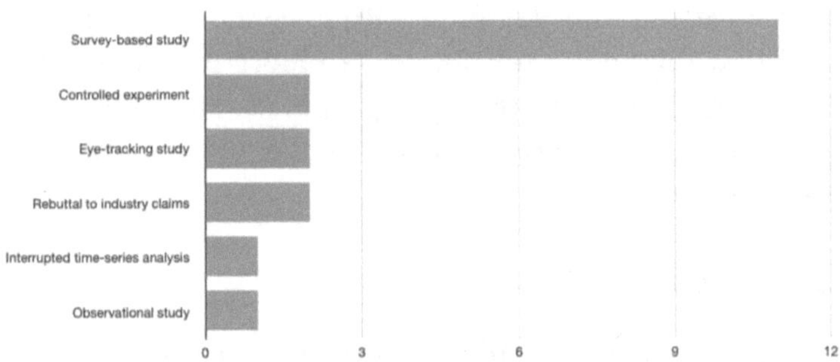

Figure 3. Methodology of peer-reviewed studies

teenagers were more likely than British teenagers to say that they were deterred from smoking by cigarette packs.

Figure 3 shows the methodologies used in the peer-reviewed studies cited (n = 19). Survey-based studies were the most common and covered a range of issues, including the salience of graphic warnings, intention to quit smoking and general support for the policy. Some were online, some were conducted by telephone and others in person.

Controlled experiments included a simulation experiment by Carter et al. (2012) which claimed that retail serving times were reduced by plain packaging. Two studies used eye-tracking technology to infer the salience of health warnings, both of which concluded that non-smokers and weekly smokers paid more attention to health warnings on plain packs, but daily smokers did not (Maynard et al. 2013, Munafò et al. 2011).

Only one peer-reviewed study used an interrupted time-series: Young et al. (2014) looked at calls to a smoking cessation phone line before and after plain packaging was introduced and concluded that plain packaging was associated with an increase in calls. Like several other studies, it included a direct appeal to policymakers:

> Australia has taken a lead on mandating plain packaging, now supported by evidence of an immediate impact of this legislation. This should encourage other countries that are preparing similar legislation. (ibid.: 31)

Figure 4 uses the same data as Figure 3 to show how often each type of study was referenced in the media and in the HoC debates. Survey-based studies, which made up the majority of peer-reviewed articles, received an even greater majority of references from the media and MPs. This was driven by the frequent mentions of Wakefield et al. (2013). Of the 44 references to peer-reviewed articles, 32 referred to survey-based studies, including 20 references to Wakefield et al. (2013).

Before turning to the qualitative review of the evidence in Chapter 7, a few observations can be made. Firstly, the

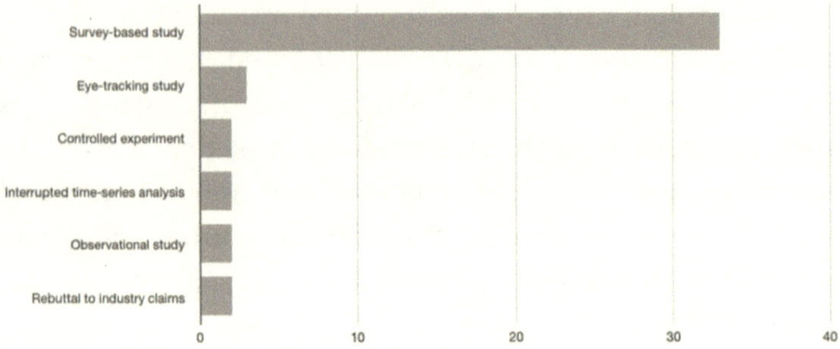

Figure 4. Type of peer-reviewed study cited (by number of references)

evidence cited was overwhelmingly in favour of plain packaging. Only a few pieces of evidence utilised by opponents of plain packaging were cited by the media and in the HoC debates: the KPMG reports, the study by Kaul and Wolf (2014) and the Deloitte (2011) report, which was briefly mentioned and dismissed in a *Guardian* article. All had been commissioned by the tobacco industry.

Opponents of plain packaging tended to rely on arguments, intuition and assumptions rather than academic studies. Their main argument was that smokers' negative response to plain packs in surveys would not translate into behavioural change, but this was difficult to prove. Once hard data on smoking prevalence and tobacco sales became available from Australia, a debate about the real-world evidence began. This was reflected in the five mentions of Australian Bureau of Statistics data on tobacco consumption in 2014 and 2015, as well as two mentions of a KPMG report in the HoC. However, this data – like the data on smoking prevalence – was open to interpretation and did not categorically support either side.

Secondly, it is notable that activist-academics worked quickly throughout the campaign to plug knowledge gaps and ease the concerns of policymakers. Central to this was Melanie Wakefield and her team at Cancer Council Victoria, who produced a slew of timely studies between 2011 and 2015. In 2014 and 2015 alone, Wakefield co-authored no fewer than 21 peer-reviewed studies related to plain packaging. They addressed the question of whether plain packs had an impact on consumer perceptions (Wakefield et al. 2013; White et al. 2015) but also addressed the concerns of policymakers that the policy would inconvenience retailers (Bayly et al. 2015) and lead to an increase in illicit tobacco sales (Scollo et al. 2014; Scollo et al. 2015).

Much of their work was produced at a gallop. Their influential telephone survey which concluded that plain packs increased thoughts of quitting was submitted to *BMJ Open* on 8 May 2013, revised on 4 June, accepted on 12 June and published on 22 July (Wakefield et al. 2013). Another of their studies, again based on a telephone survey of smokers, which concluded that there was 'no evidence' of 'major unintended consequences' with regards to illicit tobacco, was submitted to the same journal on 6 June 2014, accepted on 20 June and published on 29 August (Scollo et al. 2014). This is lightning quick by the standards of academic publishing.

Timing was as important as speed. A week before the Chantler Review was published, academics at the UK Centre for Alcohol and Tobacco Studies published a study based on submissions to the first consultation from the tobacco industry. They concluded that industry arguments were 'largely without foundation' and complained that 'stakeholder consultation' provided 'an opportunity for highly resourced corporations to slow, weaken, or prevent public health policies' (Ulucanlar et al. 2014: 12). This did not go unnoticed by Chantler, who quoted several lines from it, seemingly in agreement (Chantler 2014: 28).

In a similar vein, Rowell et al. (2014) published a study titled 'Tobacco industry manipulation of data on and press coverage of the illicit tobacco trade in the UK' shortly before the Chantler Review was published. It accused the tobacco industry of exaggerating the scale of the illicit tobacco trade in the UK, and the *Guardian* quoted one of its authors saying: 'Their misleading claims about illicit should be seen for what they are – a desperate bid to prevent plain packaging from being implemented' (Doward 2014a).

Switching between attack and defence, the network of public health activist-academics were highly effective in aiding the plain packs campaign. In many respects, it was a model of research dissemination. They understood the questions policymakers were asking and conducted original social science research to answer them promptly and in ways that could be easily understood by non-academics. In several cases, they also achieved substantial media coverage. As researchers, they ticked all the boxes.

Thirdly, it is notable that MPs referred to relatively little evidence when speaking in the HoC debates. Over the course of seven debates lasting more than six hours, only the Chantler Review, the Stirling Reviews and Wakefield et al (2013) were cited by more than two MPs. Only four peer-reviewed studies were cited by MPs at all. Although 75 MPs made a contribution from the floor in debates in which relevant evidence was cited, only 22 of them made reference to such evidence, and several of these did no more than briefly mention the Chantler Review on the day it was published. Only eight MPs referenced a specific study, usually Wakefield et al. (2013), and only seven MPs mentioned either of the Stirling Reviews.

Instead, there was an emphasis on anecdotal evidence and personal testimony, such as Anna Soubry saying that she started smoking because of the attractive green pack of her preferred brand. There was much in the way of bald assertions and supposition and much talk about addiction and underage smoking. There was a sense that 'something must be done' and many MPs viewed plain packaging as a natural extension of the tobacco advertising ban, but only a few of them – particularly those associated with the APPG on Smoking and Health – cited specific empirical evidence.

Finally, the media took considerable interest in the issue. As Figure 5 shows, some media outlets were more interested in the evidence than others. Although the *Mirror* and *Daily Telegraph* made few references to evidence in their coverage, the BBC, *Daily Mail* and *Guardian/Observer* often devoted articles to specific studies. The *Guardian*

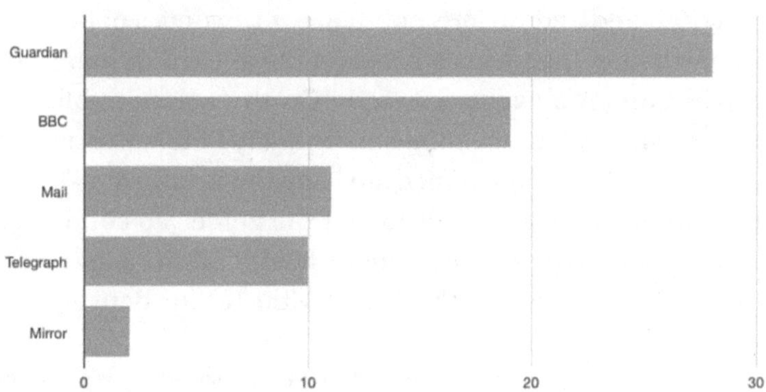

Figure 5. References to evidence by media outlet

published two articles reviewing the scientific literature as it stood at the time and whilst the coverage from the BBC and the *Guardian/Observer* was broadly, and sometimes explicitly, supportive of plain packaging, they occasionally published articles that were more helpful to opponents.

Coverage of academic research was only one aspect of plain packaging as a news story. For example, the *Telegraph/Sunday Telegraph* only published ten articles mentioning relevant evidence, but it published many other stories looking at the issue from a political, legal or economic angle, such as 'MP opponents of plain-packaging for cigarettes accepted hospitality from tobacco giant'; 'Plain packaging on cigarettes: Where does it all end?'; 'Cuba accuses UK of being anti-capitalist over plain packaging plans' and 'Silk Cut maker fights plain packaging'. Moreover, the media published a few articles based on unverifiable claims which may or may not have been true, such as unpublished industry sales data.[8]

Other related stories covered by the media between 2011 and 2015 included the introduction of plain packaging in Australia, the vote to introduce the same policy in New Zealand and various political controversies in Britain. In particular, there was a focus on the alleged influence of David Cameron's adviser Lynton Crosby whose public affairs company had the tobacco company Philip Morris as a client. Crosby always denied advising the Prime Minister to drop plain packaging in 2013, but the perceived conflict of interest was exploited by Labour leader Ed Miliband who described Cameron as the 'Prime Minister for Benson and

[8] For example: https://www.telegraph.co.uk/finance/newsbysector/retailandconsumer/leisure/10718975/Plain-packaging-in-Australia-has-failed-tobacco-giants-claim.html.

Hedge Funds'.[9] The news that several MPs who were opposed to plain packaging had accepted tickets to the Chelsea Flower Show from Japan Tobacco International was also widely reported. This created political pressure that may have been more influential in the government's final decision than any amount of academic research.

Box 1. Typical headlines

'Plain cigarette packaging reduces the allure of smoking for the young' (*Daily Mail*, 2012)

'Plain cigarette packs "encourage smokers to quit"' (BBC, 2013)

'Delay on plain cigarette pack decision "sad day for child health"' (*Guardian*, 2013)

'It's official: less appealing cigarettes come in plain packages' (*Guardian*, 2013)

'"Plain" packaging not a boost to illegal tobacco use, study suggests' (BBC, 2014)

'A step closer to plain cigarette packaging: Review finds evidence that selling products in drab boxes WOULD discourage smoking' (*Daily Mail*, 2014)

'If MPs vote for cigarette plain packaging it will be a disaster for small businesses' (*Telegraph*, 2015)

'If "plain" packaging does not deter smokers, why was industry against it?' (*Guardian*, 2015)

---

[9] https://www.express.co.uk/news/uk/415466/Prime-Minster-for-Benson-and-Hedge-Funds-Miliband-accuses-Cameron-of-lobbying-disgrace

Box 2. Excerpts from the House of Commons

'In Australia, there is already research on what the effects of plain packaging have been. It is very clear that plain packaging increases smokers' urgency to quit and lowers the appeal of smoking.' - Julian Huppert (Lib Dem)

'Stirling University's systematic review of plain packaging concluded that it made cigarettes less attractive and health warnings more effective.' Gavin Shuker (Lab)

'70% of those interviewed in a study in Australia who smoked from plain packets said that they thought the cigarettes were "less satisfying". That is an important finding. They rated quitting as a higher priority than those who continued to smoke from a branded pack did.' Paul Burstow (Lab)

'At the end of the day, however, we have noted the importance of policy being evidence-based. I do not hold a candle for the manufacturers of cigarettes, but I understand that KPMG published a report in October showing that the emerging evidence from Australia was that the introduction of standardised packaging has seen an increase in the levels of illicit tobacco and no reduction in consumption.' Alok Sharma (Con)

'Sir Cyril's report concludes that, if standardised packaging were introduced, it would very likely have a positive impact on public health and that the health benefits would include health benefits for children.' Jane Ellison (Con)

4 SECOND CASE STUDY: THE SOFT DRINKS INDUSTRY LEVY

Background

Food policy has historically been focused on safety, nutrition and on ensuring that people have enough to eat. In the twenty-first century, the issue increasingly came to be seen in terms of its relationship with obesity. Although obesity is a far more complex issue than smoking, tobacco-style regulation of the food supply was proposed as part of the remedy. Food and soft drinks – particularly mass-produced processed food – lend themselves to regulation more easily than physical activity or other possible contributing factors to rising levels of obesity, such as genetics and central heating,

Food differs from tobacco in several important ways. Firstly, since it is essential to life, total abstinence can obviously not be presented as the ideal. Secondly, there is no clear connection between specific food products and specific diseases comparable to the links between smoking and lung cancer or alcohol and liver cirrhosis. Thirdly, there are no obvious negative externalities associated with excessive food consumption that are equivalent to second-hand smoke, drunk driving or alcohol-fuelled violence.

This deprives campaigners of three arguments used to advocate for policies against tobacco and alcohol: that the products are unnecessary, inherently dangerous and harmful to others. Some of these arguments have, however, been applied in a modified form. For example, it can be argued that certain types of food and soft drink are inessential (e.g. sugary drinks) and there is some evidence that certain products are more closely associated with obesity than others (e.g. some ultra-processed food). The absence of negative externalities can be partially overcome by pointing to healthcare costs associated with obesity which often fall on taxpayers.

A further difference is that the evidence on diet and disease is less compelling and more contestable than the main health findings that condemn smoking and alcohol. The academic literature on nutrition and disease is a mass of contradictions (Schoenfeld and Ioannidis 2013) and allows room for those who legitimately question the prevailing narrative on both science and policy. For example, Archer and Arjmandi (2021: 3,725) have complained that 'anti-sugar rhetoric is divorced from established scientific facts and has led to politically expedient but ill-informed policies' while Campos et al. (2006: 59) argued in a leading epidemiology journal that 'the so-called "obesity epidemic" is largely an illusion'. It is difficult to imagine such dissent appearing in medical journals in relation to smoking or, increasingly, alcohol.

Notwithstanding the food adulteration scandals of the nineteenth century and the modern disquiet about factory farming, the food industry does not have the toxic legacy of the tobacco industry. It is a natural employer of nutritional scientists and, traditionally, nothing untoward has been seen in this. That began to change in the 2010s. The stigmatisation of 'Big Food' and 'Big Sugar' has a long way to go before it competes with Big Tobacco, but it is moving in that direction. A 2017 survey of 335 'health researchers, advocates and policymakers' in 40 countries found that 93% of them believed there was a 'fundamental and irreconcilable conflict' between public health objectives and the objectives of the tobacco industry, and 85% felt similarly about the alcohol industry. The figure for the food industry was lower at 67%, but is nevertheless a large proportion (Collin et al. 2017). The survey also found that 73% of respondents felt that public health researchers, advocates and practitioners should not accept funding from the food industry.

Most academics in the field of nutrition are not directly involved with policy and the literature on food policymaking is much smaller than that on alcohol and tobacco. In contrast to the 'smoking controversy' of the twentieth century, the public debate about food and food policy tends to be led by passionate amateurs. Notable figures include journalists, such as Gary Taubes and Nina Teicholz, and medics such as Chris van Tulleken, Aseem Malhotra and the late Michael Mosley, as well as an assortment of bloggers, authors and YouTubers. In Britain, the most influential figure in the obesity debate in the last two decades has not been a scientist, dietitian or academic but a celebrity chef, Jamie Oliver. Perhaps unsurprisingly, restaurateurs have been particularly prominent in the debate about food policy, including Henry Dimbleby, Hugh Fearnley-Whittingstall and Prue Leith.

Organised lobbying for 'anti-obesity' policies is a relatively recent development. The National Obesity Forum, a charity partly funded by pharmaceutical companies, was the leading voice on the issue until 2013 when the small but effective pressure group Action on Sugar was set up as an adjunct to Consensus Action on Salt and Health. It later formally merged to become Consensus Action on Salt, Sugar and Health. The charity Sustain was founded in 1999 to campaign on food and agricultural policy. It later created the Children's Food Campaign which became a major player in the sugar tax campaign, working with Jamie Oliver. The Obesity Health Alliance, an umbrella group of likeminded organisations, was formed in 2015. An All-Party Parliamentary Group on Obesity was founded in 2016.

Despite some differences in views, these interest groups were able to coalesce around the issue of sugar-sweetened beverages in the 2010s. There was a general consensus in the public health literature and in government that obesity was a growing health problem, that the average Briton consumed too many calories and that the government should do something about it (HM Government 2011). Sugary drinks represented low-hanging fruit insofar as they are 'non-essential', high in sugar and contain 'empty calories' (i.e. do not satisfy hunger). There was seen to be no downside to people regarding sugary drinks as unhealthy and reducing their consumption. To that end, sugary drink taxes – usually called sugar taxes or soda taxes – were proposed in a number of countries as a way to both highlight the issue and to deter consumption through the price effect.

The policy

The Soft Drinks Industry Levy (hereafter 'the sugar tax') is a two-tier tax on soft drinks which contain added sugar.

Drinks containing more than 8 grams of sugar per 100 millilitres are taxed at 24p per litre. Drinks containing between 5 and 8 grams of sugar per 100 millilitres are taxed at 18p per litre. The explicit aim of the policy is to reduce rates of obesity and tooth decay by encouraging the soft drinks industry to reduce the amount of sugar in its products. It was announced by the Chancellor George Osborne in the Budget of 2016 and came into effect on 6 April 2018.

Timeline

January 2013: The pressure group Action on Sugar is formed and makes headlines by claiming that 'sugar is the new tobacco'.

January 2014: Mexico introduces a tax on sugary drinks of one peso (3p) per litre which increases the retail price by approximately 10%.

5 March 2014: England's Chief Medical Officer, Sally Davies, says 'we may need to introduce a sugar tax.'

June 2014: A draft report by the Scientific Advisory Committee on Nutrition (SACN) is published. It recommends lowering the guidelines on sugar consumption. The current advice from government is to limit calories consumed from added sugar to 10% of overall calorie consumption. SACN recommends this be lowered to 5%.

July 2015: Publication of the final SACN report which recommends lowering guidelines on added sugar consumption to 5% of daily calorie intake.

July 2015: The British Medical Association publishes a report calling for a tax on sugary drinks that would raise their price by at least 20%.

3 September 2015: *Jamie's Sugar Rush* is broadcast on Channel 4. Presented by the chef and food campaigner Jamie Oliver, it argues strongly for the introduction of a sugar tax.

October 2015: The House of Commons Health Select Committee holds oral sessions discussing government policy on childhood obesity. The committee pays particular attention to the idea of a sugar tax.

11 October 2015: Sarah Wollaston, the chair of the Health Select Committee, accuses the government of 'suppressing' Public Health England's evidence review on sugar. The review was due to be published alongside the government's Childhood Obesity Plan, which also remains unpublished.

22 October 2015: Public Health England's evidence review – *Sugar Reduction: the Evidence for Action* – is published ahead of the Childhood Obesity Plan. It includes a recommendation to tax sugary drinks. A spokesperson for David Cameron says that he 'doesn't see a need for a tax on sugar'.[10]

30 November 2015: The Health Select Committee's report *Childhood Obesity – Brave and Bold Action* is published. Among its key recommendations is a tax on sugary drinks. A debate is held in the House of Commons.

6 January 2016: A study is published in the *British Medical Journal* showing a decline in sugary drink sales in Mexico following the introduction of a sugar tax.

7 January 2016: Prime Minister David Cameron says, 'I don't really want to put new taxes on anything but we do have to recognise that we face something of an obesity crisis'. The

[10] https://www.theguardian.com/society/2015/oct/22/sugar-report-delayed-jeremy-hunt-tax-radical-action-obesity

Department of Health insists that the 'government position has not changed and we have no plans for a sugar tax.'[11]

7 February 2016: Health Secretary Jeremy Hunt says that David Cameron 'has not taken a sugar tax off the table'.

16 March 2016: George Osborne, the Chancellor the Exchequer, announces a two-tier Soft Drinks Industry Levy to begin in 2018. It is expected to raise £520 million per annum in revenue.

The evidence

There were 79 references to relevant, identifiable evidence in the media and 12 in the HoC debates. As Figure 6 shows, 18 pieces of evidence were mentioned in total, half of which were cited once (and only by the media). There were also oblique references in both the media and parliamentary debates to evidence which could not be clearly identified, such as when advocates of the policy asserted that there was evidence that sugar taxes had worked in other countries. Some opponents appealed to evidence-based policy by claiming that there was 'no evidence' that a sugar tax would work or that 'all the evidence' showed that they did not work, but such claims were not referenced and therefore cannot be included.

As with plain packaging, three pieces of evidence were referenced far more than any other: a study of Mexico's sugar tax (Colchero et al. 2016a), Public Health England's evidence review, and a modelling study (Briggs et al. 2012).

---

[11] https://www.dailymail.co.uk/news/article-3388094/Is-sugar-tax-agenda-Ministers-consider-U-turn-growing-public-support-seeing-quick-win-5p-plastic-bag-charge-changing-people-s-habits.html

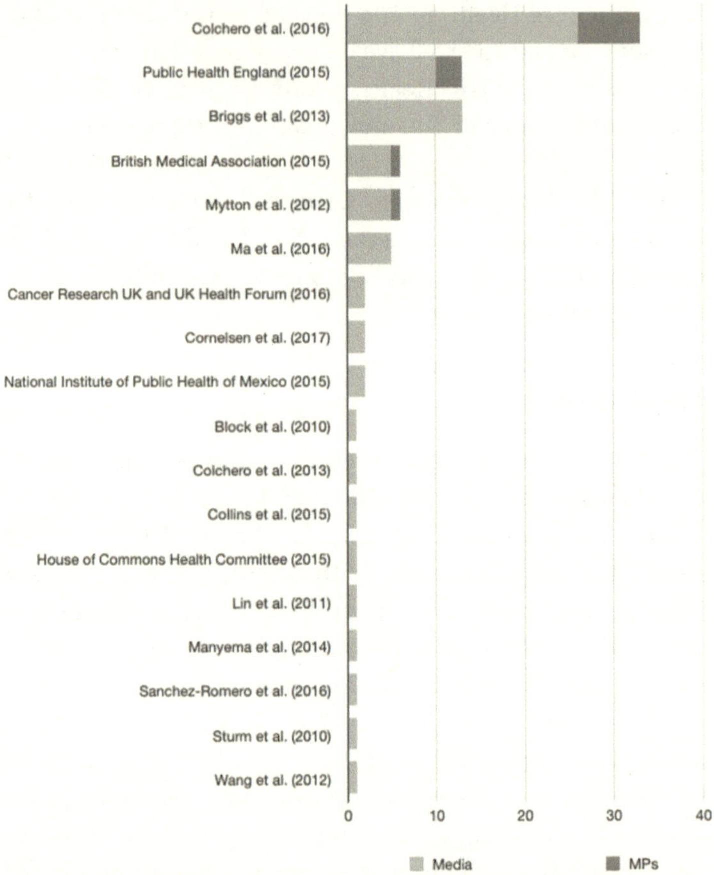

Figure 6. Number of references to evidence in the media and House of Commons

Colchero et al. (2016a)

The Colchero study was written by four academics, two from Mexico's National Institute of Public Health and two from the University of North Carolina. They used soft drink sales data from Nielsen between 2012 and 2014 and compared the post-tax sales figures to a modelled counterfactual in which the tax had not been implemented. The difference between actual and counterfactual sales was 6.1% in 2014, the first year of the sugar tax:

> In total, during 2014 the average urban Mexican purchased 4241 mL (seven 600 mL or 20 oz bottles) fewer taxed beverages than expected (based on pretax trends). (Colchero et al. 2016a: 4)

This decline was estimated to be larger for consumers 'of low socioeconomic status', whose implied consumption fell by 9.1% on average in 2014, and fell more steeply over time, reaching 12% by December 2014 (ibid.: 5). For consumers of low socioeconomic status, the decline was estimated to have reached 17.4% by December 2014 (ibid.).

Public Health England's evidence review (October 2015)

This report (*Sugar Reduction: The evidence for action*) was published by Public Health England on 22 October 2015, two days after the Health Select Committee finished taking oral evidence for its inquiry. The PHE report was subsequently described in the committee's own report as 'the most comprehensive analysis of measures to reduce sugar consumption to date' (House of Commons Health Select Committee 2015: 10).

The report concluded that the government should introduce a range of interventions to address obesity, including a tax on sugary drinks. PHE expected the tax to reduce consumption via the price effect.

> Evidence from both stakeholders and current research studies suggest that increasing the price of high sugar foods and non-alcoholic drinks, whether through taxation or other means, is likely to reduce purchases of these products at least in the short term. There is reasonably consistent evidence from both experimental studies and data from countries that have introduced taxes that consumers can respond to changes in food and drink prices with the effect being larger at higher levels of taxation or price change. These findings align with the evidence from modelling studies which indicate that a tax would lead to a reduction in purchases proportionate to the level of tax applied, suggesting a tax of 10% to 20% would be necessary to have a significant impact on purchases, consumption and ultimately population health. (Public Health England 2015a: 23)

The evidence from 'experimental studies and data from countries' was set out in more detail in Annexe 2 of the report which was compiled by a team at Teesside University. It included references to studies in the peer-reviewed and grey literature, fifteen stakeholder interviews and two pieces of written evidence, but it explicitly excluded sales data from countries where there had not been a published evaluation.

> A number of countries and US states have introduced taxes on high sugar products. Sales data from Norway, Finland, Hungary, France and Mexico broadly suggests decreases in purchases of

> soft drinks/sugar sweetened drinks (SSDs) of up to 12%, following the implementation of taxes. However, data in the public domain did not meet the criteria for inclusion in the review of the literature, therefore it is simply described as background to the review. (Public Health England 2015b: 5)

The figure of 12% comes from a study of Mexico's sugar tax that was not published until January 2016 (Colchero et al. 2016a). There had been no published evaluations of sugar taxes in Norway, Finland, Hungary or France. Nevertheless, the second sentence of the above passage would later be cited in the HoC several times.

Modelling studies were given a low priority in the PHE report and, like the sales data from abroad, was only included as background information (Public Health England 2015a: 23). The authors of the evidence review in Annexe 2 said that results from mathematical modelling 'should be interpreted as tentative projections' (Public Health England 2015b: 10). They also said that there was an 'overall lack of peer-reviewed experimental evidence' (Public Health England 2015b: 7) and that 'the interviews [with fifteen stakeholders] revealed very little unpublished intelligence' (ibid.: 6).

The sidelining of computer modelling and other countries' experiences is interesting because, as we shall see, both sources of evidence featured heavily in the advocacy of sugar tax campaigners. Instead, the PHE evidence review focused on eleven controlled experiments. Most of them involved food rather than drinks, none of them was from the UK and only one of them involved children.

> The 11 primary studies were conducted in France (n = 1), The Netherlands (n = 3) and the US (n = 7) and were largely experimental in either a laboratory (n = 4) virtual setting (n = 4) or controlled field experiments in supermarkets (n = 2) or a cafeteria (n = 1). (ibid.: 23)

The eleven studies all examined the impact of higher prices on food and soft drinks using volunteers in various quasi-natural experiments. The three studies that specifically focused on soft drinks can be summarised as follows:

- A controlled experiment in which the price of sugary drinks was increased in a hospital cafeteria (Block et al. 2010).
- A field study in which 56 households were faced with a 10% 'tax' on 'unhealthy' food and soft drinks. Their purchasing habits were compared with a control group of 57 households who paid the usual market price (Wansink et al. 2012).
- A randomised controlled trial in which participants shopped in a virtual supermarket. The control group faced normal prices while the other group faced a 19% 'tax' on sugary drinks (Waterlander et al. 2014).

These studies tended to support the law of demand and the authors of the evidence review concluded that increasing prices through taxation was likely to reduce sales of the taxed products in the short term. This did not prove that a tax would reduce calorie consumption or obesity, but the studies were mostly RCTs of good quality and partially provided proof of concept.

Briggs et al. (2013)

This modelling study concluded that a 20% tax on sugary drinks in the UK would reduce the number of obese adults by 1.3% (180,000 people) and raise £276 million in revenue. This was widely covered by the media at the time of publication, and its findings were often mentioned in articles throughout the campaign. Headlines included 'Put 20% tax on soft drinks to cut obesity: Price levy will help 285,000 lose weight, says study' (*Daily Mail*) and 'Sugary drinks tax "effective public health measure"' (BBC).

Discussion

Figure 7 shows the number of references to evidence by media outlet. As with plain packaging, the *Guardian/Observer* showed the most interest (n = 34), followed by the BBC (n = 15).

Figure 8 shows the type of evidence that was cited by the media and in the HoC. There were ten modelling studies,

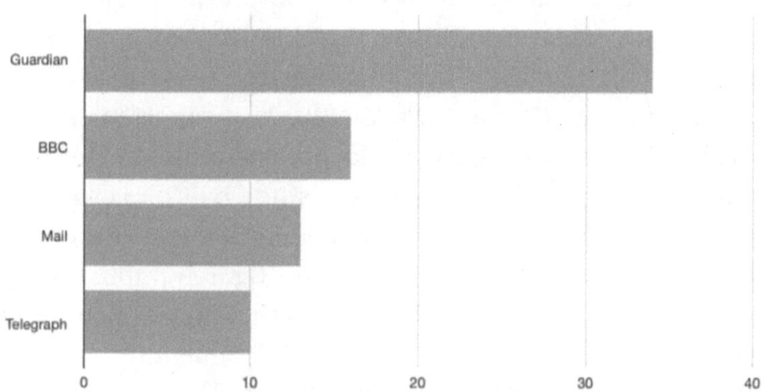

Figure 7. References to evidence by media outlet

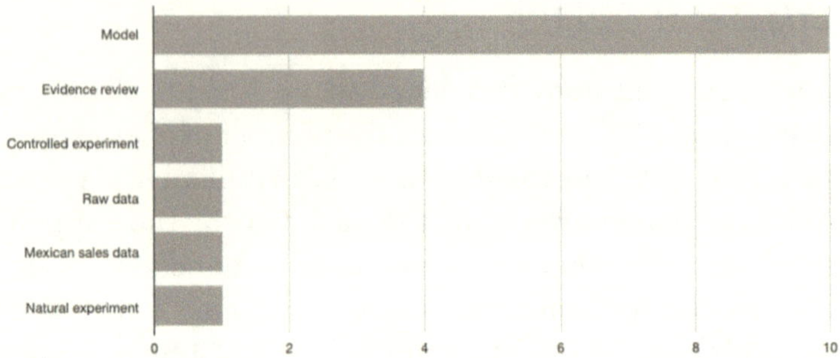

Figure 8. Type of evidence cited (by number of publications)

most of which were only cited once but which included the more influential study by Briggs et al. (2013). There were two academic evidence reviews (Public Health England 2015a and Mytton et al. 2012) and two non-academic (i.e. not peer-reviewed) evidence reviews (British Medical Association and the Health Select Committee). There was one study based on a controlled experiment in a canteen (Block et al. 2010) and one study based on a natural experiment. The 'natural experiment' involved Jamie Oliver introducing a surcharge for sugary drinks in his restaurants. Oliver told the Health Select Committee that his 10p 'tax' had led to a 6–7% fall in sales. When this research was subsequently published as Cornelsen et al. (2017), it reported an 11% decline in sales of sugary drinks per customer. In Figure 8, 'Mexican sales data' refers to the study by Colchero et al. (2016a) and the press release that came before it. 'Raw data' refers to sugary drink consumption figures published by the Mexican Institute of Public Health which appeared to show a smaller reduction in soft drink consumption after the Mexican sugar tax was introduced than suggested by Colchero et al. (2016).

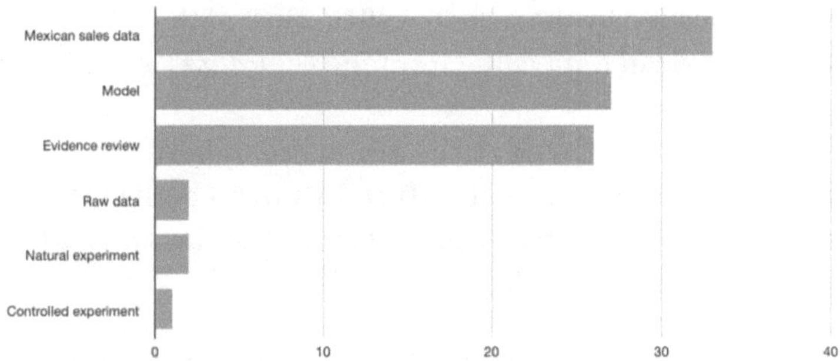

Figure 9. Type of evidence cited (by number of references)

Figure 9 shows the same data but divides it according to the number of mentions each document received. It shows quite an even split between the 'real world' Mexican data (36%), computer modelling (30%) and evidence reviews (29%). Briggs et al. (2013) was the most heavily referenced modelling study (n = 13), Public Health England (2015a) was the most heavily referenced evidence review (n = 13), and the Mexican study was the most heavily referenced piece of evidence overall (n = 33).

Only four peer-reviewed studies were mentioned more than once by the media or by MPs. These were Colchero et al. (2016a), Briggs et al. (2013), Mytton et al. (2012) and a modelling study by Ma et al. (2016). By far the most referenced study, with 26 mentions in the media and seven in Parliament, was Colchero et al. (2016a) which is here used as shorthand for claims about Mexico that were written up in the study of that name, but also includes the same claims made in a press release and blog post from the Mexican National Institute of Public Health which was widely covered by the media in 2015. Most of the references to the Mexican data came from the *Guardian* (n = 14) and the BBC (n = 6).

The only other study to be referenced by both the media and MPs was Mytton et al. (2012). This was a brief evidence review and commentary published in the *British Medical Journal* which concluded:

> Health related food taxes could improve health. Existing evidence suggests that taxes are likely to shift consumption in the desired direction, although policy makers need to be wary of changes in other important nutrients. However, the tax would need to be at least 20% to have a significant effect on population health. (ibid.: 3)

Mytton et al.'s claim that a sugary drinks tax would have to be at least 20% to have a measurable impact on obesity was often repeated during the campaign, but it was not based on experience. The authors acknowledged that there had been no decline in obesity resulting from soda taxes in US states but that the tax rates (of between 1% and 8%) may have been 'too low to observe an effect on population health' (ibid.: 2). The threshold of 20% was derived from modelling studies.

Although not mentioned in the HoC, four out of five media outlets referred to Briggs et al. (2013) more than once and it was the third most referenced piece of evidence overall. Ma et al. (2016) was mentioned five times but only by the media. It was also a modelling study. It concluded that a 40% reduction in the sugar content of soft drinks would lead to a 2.1 percentage point reduction in obesity among adults (one million people) which would lead to the prevention of between 274,000 and 309,000 cases of Type 2 diabetes over a period of 20 years. The authors did not model the impact of a sugar tax *per se* but they mentioned several times in the text that a sugar tax would be one way of achieving such a reduction. Four other modelling studies received one mention in the media each (Wang et al. 2012; Manyema et al. 2014; Collins et al. 2015; Sanchez-Romero et al. 2016).

The evidence review by Mytton et al. (2012) and the modelling study by Briggs et al. (2013) shared two co-authors, Oliver Mytton and Mike Rayner, who had also co-authored a study titled 'Could targeted food taxes improve health?' in 2007. Based on modelling, that study concluded that a 'carefully targeted fat tax could produce modest but meaningful changes in food consumption and a reduction in cardiovascular disease' (Mytton et al. 2007).

Mike Rayner was the chair of the campaigning charity Sustain ('the alliance for better food and farming'). Sustain created and funded the Children's Food Campaign, which became a prominent player in sugar tax advocacy. Rayner had been advocating for taxes on food and soft drinks for several years. He had an unusual conflict of interest in that he was an ordained priest in the Church of England and had written a blog post in 2012 in which he explained that he saw bringing about a sugar tax as a divine mission.

> In all of this I see a sacred dimension. You may not believe that I have heard God right but I think God is calling me to work towards the introduction of soft-drink taxes in this country. (Rayner 2012)

Rayner was not the only academic to be emotionally invested in the issue. Two of the five authors of Ma et al. (2016) were heavily involved with the campaign group Action on Sugar. One of them, Kawther Hashem, was its Campaign Lead. The other, Graham MacGregor, was its chair.

One of the American authors of Colchero et al. (2016a) was Barry Popkin, a longstanding advocate of sugar taxes who had been promoting them in the media for over a decade and whose previous journal articles included (in 2009) 'The Public Health and Economic Benefits of Taxing Sugar-Sweetened Beverages'. The Colchero study was part-funded by Bloomberg Philanthropies, an organisation funded by the billionaire and former New York City mayor Michael Bloomberg which spent $10 million lobbying for the Mexican sugar tax (James et al. 2020) and which, in its own words, 'helped Mexico pass a one-peso per liter tax on sugary drinks'.[12]

All four of the most heavily referenced peer-reviewed studies therefore involved authors who had been prominent advocates of the policy for some time.

The only other sources of evidence that received significant mentions from the media and MPs during the sugar tax campaign were the reports from PHE and the BMA. Both were published in 2015 and summarised the evidence in favour of taxing sugary drinks. The section of the BMA report covering 'fiscal measures that favour healthy diets' was only a page and a half long, but it was heavily referenced. The BMA recommended not only taxing 'unhealthy' food and drink but subsidising 'healthy' food.

The only other piece of evidence to receive more than one mention in the media was a five-page report from

[12] https://web.archive.org/web/20210416153347/https://www.bloomberg.org/public-health/promoting-healthy-food-choices/

Cancer Research UK and the UK Health Forum (2016) which claimed that a 20% sugar tax would prevent 3.7 million cases of obesity over ten years and reduce health spending by £10 million per annum. The report claimed that such a tax would lead to 29% of adults being obese by 2025, as opposed to 34% in a counterfactual. The modelling upon which this was based was conducted by the UK Health Forum, which closed in 2019, and is no longer available online. Published in February 2016, it was the last significant piece of evidence published before the sugar tax was announced.

In the two HoC debates, which lasted a total of five hours, only four documents were referenced, including two peer-reviewed studies. It is notable that no modelling studies were mentioned in the debates, despite being frequently mentioned in the media. The MPs seem to have been more impressed by the data from Mexico and the alleged experience of other countries. A policy that had been tried in another country and was seen to work may have been more compelling to politicians than an academic experiment or a computer model. Such 'real world' evidence not only appeals to the availability heuristic, but, as we shall discuss in later chapters, may be more credible to policymakers who are sceptical of 'some study that's been carried out in an ivory tower' (Katikireddi et al. 2013: 493–4). This may explain why France, Norway, Hungary and Finland were mentioned by some MPs despite there being no published evidence about these countries' experience with sugar taxes. For example, Helen Jones MP said:

> A tax on sugary drinks would probably have to be at the level of 10% to 20% to make a change in

> behaviour, apparently – Public Health England suggests that range. There is evidence from Mexico and France that at that level, people's behaviour starts to change and they start to choose sugar-free alternatives. (Hansard 2015)

The reference to France is puzzling as it had a very small sugar tax of €0.0716 per litre, roughly equivalent to adding 2p to the price of a can of *Coca-Cola*, and there was no evidence of an impact on consumption or obesity. A study subsequently found 'at most a very small reduction in soft drink purchases' (Capacci et al. 2019: 1). It is very likely that France was mentioned because it was referenced, somewhat misleadingly, in the PHE report.

Over the course of more than five hours of debate, only eight MPs cited evidence that can be traced to a published document. Neither debate was purely about sugar taxes. Other policies, such as food reformulation and labelling were also discussed. Nevertheless, the scarcity of references to evidence is striking. Aside from the PHE report and Colchero et al. (2016a), only two pieces of evidence were mentioned by MPs at all, neither of them more than once.

Both debates focused on framing the problem rather than demonstrating that a sugar tax was necessarily the solution (indeed, several proponents made it clear that a sugar tax alone would *not* be the solution). Various statistics were repeatedly cited to show the need for upstream regulation. These included the claim that a quarter of children were leaving primary school obese, that obesity cost the NHS £5.1 billion a year, that children consumed three times as much sugar as was recommended, that there were nine teaspoons of sugar in a fizzy drink and that the UK consumed more than 5,727 million litres of sugary soft drinks a year. This framing was often combined with personal anecdotes about how few sugary drinks MPs said they consumed when they were children and predictions about how much money the sugar tax would raise in revenue.

This framing was broadly accepted by opponents of the sugar tax who instead argued that it would be regressive ('hit the poor hardest' –Andrea Jenkyns) and offered alternative solutions, such as better labelling and more education. Some opponents, such as Will Quince, used pejorative language to describe the tax ('illiberal', 'patronising', 'nanny statism at its worst') but offered very little in the way of published evidence showing that the tax would not work or would have negative consequences, although some MPs did refer to empirical data as part of their arguments, such as the claim that sugar consumption was in decline.

George Osborne's speech announcing the new tax in the 2016 Budget was typical of how MPs made their case. He did not cite any evidence of efficacy or make any predictions about the impact it would have on childhood obesity. Instead, he gave an estimate of how much revenue it would bring in (£520 million) and cited various statistics to frame the problem.

> Here are the facts that we know: five-year-old children are consuming their body weight in sugar every year. Experts predict that within a generation more than half of all boys and 70% of girls could be overweight or obese. Here is another fact that we all know: obesity drives disease. It increases the risk of cancer, diabetes and heart disease,

> and it costs our economy £27 billion a year. That is more than half the entire NHS pay-bill.
>
> Here is another truth we all know: one of the biggest contributors to childhood obesity is sugary drinks. A can of cola typically has nine teaspoons of sugar in it. Some popular drinks have as many as 13 teaspoons. That can be more than double a child's recommended added sugar intake.[13]

Similarly, when the childhood obesity strategy was finally published in August 2015, it framed the problem but did not cite any evidence that the sugar tax was a solution except insofar as the money raised would be spent on 'programmes to reduce obesity and encourage physical activity and balanced diets for school-aged children' (Department of Health 2016: 4). The Health Select Committee report was only marginally more research-oriented, referencing (though not explicitly), just two relevant pieces of evidence, the modelling study by Briggs et al. (2013) and the unpublished data from Mexico.

In summary, three pieces of evidence appear to have had the most influence in the sugar tax debate between 2013 and 2016. By far the most heavily cited study combined actual sales data from Mexico with a modelled counterfactual (Colchero et al. 2016a). Another was a modelling study using UK data (Briggs et al. 2013). The other was an evidence review from PHE which focused on RCTs but had

[13] https://hansard.parliament.uk/Commons/2016-03-16/debates/16031632000001/FinancialStatement

more impact from briefly mentioning sugar taxes in other countries where evidence of efficacy was very scarce.

Why were these pieces of evidence so influential? The PHE report benefited from the authority of the organisation publishing it and the publicity surrounding its supposed 'suppression' by the government. Briggs et al. (2013) put a specific figure on the potential benefits of a sugar tax and was published at a time when the idea of taxing soft drinks was gathering momentum. Colchero et al. (2016a) had the benefit of being 'real world' evidence rather than experimental or theoretical. It also had the benefit of getting two bites of the media cherry, being press-released in 2015 and published the following year. The Colchero study was published on 6 January 2016 and Ma et al. (2016) was published the following day. January 7 also saw a press release from Cancer Research UK projecting a 45% increase in obesity-related cancer by 2035. All three studies were widely covered in the news and their back-to-back publication helped create the 'swarm effect' mentioned in relation to anti-smoking activism in Chapter 3 and drew a response from the Prime Minister (see timeline above).

None of the studies directly showed that a sugar tax would reduce obesity or even necessarily reduce calorie consumption. Instead, the data from Mexico was taken as evidence that higher prices would reduce sales and the modelling studies were taken as evidence that reducing sales would reduce obesity. As with plain packaging, the most cited pieces of evidence appeared in stages, with early work providing a theoretical framework by which the policy could be understood, followed by evidence from another country and an expert review endorsing the policy.

As with plain packaging, there were many news articles about the policy which did not mention evidence, data or statistics, but which focused on politics and personalities. These included interviews with Jamie Oliver, reports on the amount of sugar in various products, estimates of the costs to the NHS associated with obesity, the accusation that the government had suppressed the PHE report, the NHS introducing a sugar tax in its own buildings, claims about how much revenue the tax would raise, and reports about David Cameron and/or Jeremy Hunt rejecting the idea or later approving it.

Box 1. Typical headlines

'Put 20% tax on soft drinks to cut obesity: Price levy will help 285,000 lose weight, says study' (*Daily Mail*, 2013)

'Sugar is as dangerous as alcohol and tobacco, warn health experts' (*Telegraph*, 2014)

'Tax sugary drinks by 20%, say doctors' (BBC, 2015)

'The drinks with up TWENTY teaspoons of sugar: Doctors urge ministers to slap a 20% tax on sugary drinks to fight obesity crisis' (*Daily Mail*, 2015)

'Mexican soda tax cuts sales of sugary soft drinks by 6% in first year' (*Guardian*, 2015)

'Jamie Oliver's tax on sugar won't work and will leave the poor even worse off' (*Mirror*, 2015)

'The science is in: the case for a sugar tax is overwhelming' (*Guardian*, 2015).

'Sugar tax in Mexico cuts sales of sugary drinks by 12%' (*Telegraph*, 2016)

'Why a sugar tax could slash 3.7million obesity sufferers by 2025' (*Mirror*, 2016)

Box 2. Excerpts from the House of Commons

We have discussed evidence from Mexico, which we heard in the Committee, but other countries such as Norway, Hungary and Finland have taken the same approach. Although not all the evidence has been peer-reviewed, published and assessed, all the details of the national experiments point in the same direction. – Philippa Whitford (SNP)

A tax on sugary drinks would probably have to be at the level of 10% to 20% to make a change in behaviour, apparently—Public Health England suggests that range. There is evidence from Mexico and France that at that level, people's behaviour starts to change and they start to choose sugar-free alternatives. – Helen Jones (Lab)

We know from the experience in Mexico that a 10% levy on sugary drinks has led to a 6% reduction in consumption. Perhaps more importantly, it has led to a 9% reduction in consumption among the heaviest users.– Sarah Wollaston (Con)

Sugar tax advocates have pointed out the introduction of a sugar tax in Mexico and the corresponding 6% decline in soft drink sales since the tax was introduced. However, research in *The BMJ* does not show evidence of a link between the introduction of the tax and the small decline in soft drinks consumption. – Will Quince (Con)

5 THIRD CASE STUDY: MINIMUM UNIT PRICING

Background

For most of the twentieth century, alcohol researchers in Britain and much of Europe tended to think that 'the drinking of the general population and the problematic drinkers was inherently different' (Raninen and Livingston 2020: 1,773). Alcohol policy focused on alcoholism and drunkenness, with alcoholism seen as a disease and drunkenness seen principally as a public order issue. This implied targeted interventions for a minority of troubled or troublesome individuals. In contrast to the Nordic countries, which had experienced or flirted with prohibition in the 1920s, the UK favoured education and treatment, albeit with alcohol taxes and licensing laws that were restrictive by the standards of most European countries.

This began to change in the 1970s when a belief in 'the collectivity of drinking cultures' became more prominent. Borrowing from the theoretical work of the French statistician Sully Ledermann (1956), some alcohol researchers and sociologists argued that heavy drinking and alcohol-related harm were directly linked to per capita alcohol consumption and that this was not because heavy drinkers consumed a large quantity of alcohol (thereby having a disproportionate effect on the mean average), but because the entire distribution of consumption was *determined* by average consumption. According to Skog (1985: 97), 'the population will tend to behave as a collective' and will 'move in concert up and down the consumption scale, thereby creating a close connection between the general level of consumption in the population and the prevalence of heavy use.' This became known as the single distribution theory.

This movement led to *Alcohol Control Policies in Public Health Perspective*, a short book published in 1975 that came to be known as the Purple Book. Few books earn a nickname without having been influential and the Purple Book quickly became the standard text in a new public health movement. Most of its eleven authors were Scandinavian, including Kettil Bruun, a Finnish sociologist who was dismayed by the relaxation of alcohol control laws in his homeland in the late 1960s. After prohibition ended in Finland in 1935, the government introduced strict control measures and used coercion against those whom it branded alcoholics. Bruun disapproved of singling out individuals for 'correction, treatment, or rehabilitation' (Bruun et al. 1975: 67) and so, in one sense, his prescription was liberal, but the flip side to absolving individuals of blame was condemning the drinks industry for selling the product and blaming the government for allowing it to be easily bought. Seeing alcohol as a societal problem, the authors of the Purple Book saw supply-side, society-wide policies as the solution, including bans on marketing, heavy licensing restrictions and high taxes. The explicit aim was to reduce per capita alcohol consumption, thereby (so it was assumed) reducing consumption among the heaviest drinkers.

With funding from Scandinavian alcohol retail monopolies that were keen to emphasise the value of heavy state regulation, this new breed of alcohol researchers helped turn the population-based approach into the dominant model of alcohol control (Moskalewicz et al. 2022). Although the single distribution theory and the policies derived from it have been criticised by some public health researchers (Roche 1997; Uhl 2015; Raninen and Livingston 2020), they have been embraced by the World Health Organisation (WHO), most neo-temperance groups and many public health bodies including the National Institute of Clinical Excellence (2010: 28) which gives a textbook summary of the theory when it states that:

> the number of people who drink a heavy or excessive amount in a given population is related to how much the whole population drinks on average. Thus, reducing the average drinking level, via population interventions, is likely to reduce the number of people with severe problems due to alcohol.

The key texts of the movement today are the book *Alcohol: No Ordinary Commodity* by Babor et al. (2010) and the WHO's *Global Status Report on Alcohol and Health*. The former has been described by Britain's leading anti-alcohol campaigner, Ian Gilmore, as the 'Bible' (Health Committee 2012: Ev 2) and is regularly cited by activist-academics when they need to show that their policy agenda is 'evidence-based'. Three of its authors had helped write the

Purple Book in the 1970s and all of them 'uncompromisingly support a radical alcohol control approach and devalue health promotion-oriented prevention as well as professional alcoholism treatment', according to Uhl (2015: 5). Both *Alcohol: No Ordinary Commodity* and the WHO promote strict Scandinavian-style supply-side policy interventions targeting 'the Three As': affordability, availability and attractiveness (advertising is sometimes substituted for attractiveness). The WHO calls these the 'best buys' to underline their ostensible cost-effectiveness.

It has been a remarkable coup for an agenda drawn up fifty years ago by 'a motley bunch of sociologists dressing ourselves up as public health experts' (as one of the Purple Book's authors, Robin Room (2014: 45), self-deprecatingly described his faction). Today, the whole population approach is explicitly central to the Scottish government's approach to alcohol policy although the same cannot be said of the British government which continues to put the Home Office in charge of its alcohol strategy, a sign that it still sees alcohol as primarily a public order issue.

Strategically, the UK's anti-alcohol movement has much in common with the anti-smoking movement and there has been some conscious emulation. The All-Party Parliamentary Group on Alcohol Misuse was formed in 2006 with the state-funded charity Alcohol Concern as its secretariat, mirroring the All-Party Parliamentary Group on Smoking and Health which ASH established in the 1970s. In November 2007, in the wake of the smoking ban, the Alcohol Health Alliance was formed. Modelled on the Smoke-Free Action Coalition 'with individuals who had been involved with ASH since its inception providing guidance and support' (Thom et al. 2016: 7), it brought together

24 organisations to lobby for policies related to the affordability, availability and advertising of alcohol. Led by Ian Gilmore, its members include the Institute of Alcohol Studies, a group set up in the 1980s by the Alliance House Foundation after the UK Temperance Alliance was disbanded. The Alliance House Foundation is the direct descendant of the United Kingdom Alliance for the Suppression of the Traffic in all Intoxicating Liquors, a nineteenth century prohibitionist outfit. Although it no longer demands legal suppression and says that 'an alcohol-free society can be reached by agreement',[14] it is a reminder that gospel temperance remains a force in the alcohol policy debate.

By 2010, affordability had become the main focus of the anti-alcohol coalition and minimum unit pricing was its primary policy objective. Setting a floor price for alcohol appealed to different elements of the coalition and even drew in parts of the alcohol industry. It was predicted to reduce per capita alcohol consumption, but belief in the single distribution theory was not a prerequisite for support. It equally appealed to those who thought the focus should be on the heaviest drinkers, since heavy drinkers often buy the cheapest alcohol. It also appealed to those, such as the police, who were concerned about public order and believed that problems in the nighttime economy were caused by revellers 'pre-loading' with cheap alcohol at home. This led to some confusion in the messaging as the campaign proceeded, with some claiming minimum pricing was aimed at the whole population while others insisted that it was a targeted measure, but it created a unity of purpose in the short term.

[14] https://www.alliancehousefoundation.org.uk/ (retrieved 01.07.21)

The policy

Minimum unit pricing (MUP) imposes a floor price on a unit of alcohol. The intention is to eliminate the sale of 'cheap' alcohol which is associated with heavy and harmful drinking. In May 2018, Scotland became the first country to introduce such a system, with a floor price of 50p per unit.

Timeline

June 2008: The Scottish government publishes a discussion paper on alcohol which supports the introduction of minimum unit pricing (MUP).

2008: Mathematical modellers at Sheffield University, later known as the Sheffield Alcohol Research Group (SARG), publish their first estimates of the impact of MUP in England.

March 2009: The Scottish National Party (SNP), which is running a minority government, announces plans to introduce MUP.

September 2009: SARG publish their first model looking at the potential impact of MUP in Scotland.

8 January 2010: The House of Commons Health Committee publishes its report on alcohol and recommends the introduction of MUP.

November 2010: MSPs reject MUP in the Scottish Parliament by 76 votes to 49. The policy is removed from the Alcohol etc. (Scotland) Bill.

October 2011: After winning a majority in the Scottish Parliament, the SNP tables the Alcohol (Minimum Pricing) (Scotland) Bill. The legislation does not specify what the floor price will be.

March 2012: The UK government announces plans to introduce MUP in England and Wales.

May 2012: The Alcohol (Minimum Pricing) (Scotland) Bill is passed by 86 votes to 1. The legislation includes a six-year sunset clause and a requirement for ministers to evaluate the policy after five years.

July 2012: The Scotch Whisky Association (SWA) files a petition for judicial review with the Scottish Court of Session and makes an official complaint to the European Commission citing EU competition law.

November 2012: UK government announces its intention to introduce MUP at 45p per unit in England and Wales. It launches a public consultation.

March 2013: It is reported that the UK government plans to drop minimum pricing in England and Wales due to opposition from various cabinet ministers.

May 2013: The SWA's legal challenge fails in the Outer House of the Court of Session. The SWA appeals the decision.

July 2013: The British government abandons MUP, citing 'legal uncertainty' and 'question marks about the evidence behind it'. In the foreword to the Home Office report 'Next steps following the consultation on delivering the Government's alcohol strategy', Home Secretary Theresa May explains that the consultation had 'not provided evidence that conclusively demonstrates that Minimum Unit Pricing (MUP) will actually do what it is meant to: reduce problem drinking without penalising all those who drink responsibly' (Home Office 2013: 3). Instead, the government bans the sale of alcohol below the price of duty plus VAT.

December 2015: The European Court of Justice rules that MUP would only breach EU competition law if measures that were less restrictive on trade, such as an increase in alcohol duty, would be more effective in achieving the public health goal. The case is referred to the Court of Session.

April 2016: The Sheffield Alcohol Research Group publishes a new model which concludes that MUP would be more effective in reducing alcohol-related harm than alcohol duty increases.

October 2016: The Court of Session rules that MUP is legal, but later grants permission to the SWA to take its case to the UK's Supreme Court.

November 2017: Citing the Sheffield research, the Supreme Court rejects the SWA's legal arguments and rules that MUP is 'a proportionate means of achieving a legitimate aim'.

1 May 2018: MUP is introduced in Scotland at 50p per unit under the Alcohol (Minimum Pricing) (Scotland) Act and the Alcohol (Minimum Pricing per unit) Order.

The evidence

The period between MUP being proposed and implemented in Scotland lasted ten years and led to considerable debate in both media and political circles. In total, relevant evidence was referenced 147 times in the five media outlets and 18 times in the HoC debates (plus numerous mentions in the Scottish Parliament). By far the most heavily cited evidence was computer modelling from the Sheffield Alcohol Research Group (n = 103) which was later buttressed by 'real world' evidence from Canada produced by a team at the Centre for Addictions Research in British Columbia led by the psychologist and former president of the Kettil Bruun Society, Tim Stockwell (n = 26).

The Sheffield Alcohol Research Group (2008–16)

As Figure 10 shows, the Sheffield team was responsible for five of the six most cited pieces of evidence, including four modelling studies published on their own website (Brennan et al. 2008; Purshouse et al. 2009b; Meng et al. 2010; Meng et al. 2012) and one study published in the *Lancet* (Purshouse et al. 2010). Perhaps benefiting from first-mover advantage, the most heavily cited Sheffield study was the first: Brennan et al. (2008) with 30 references in total.

The media picked up on two of the Sheffield team's other peer-reviewed studies (Holmes et al. 2014; Brennan et al. 2014) as well as two other self-published reports (Purshouse et al. 2009a; Angus and Ally 2015), and a report published in association with Cancer Research UK (Angus et al. 2016b). In addition, the Sheffield team was commissioned by the BBC to produce an estimate of how many deaths among over-65-year-olds could be prevented by MUP (BBC 2012). Their model was also used by the Home Office to produce the 2012 Impact Assessment (Home Office 2012b). All this research supported the case for MUP by projecting reductions in deaths, hospitalisations, crime and unemployment.

Zhao et al. (2013) and Stockwell et al. (2012a, 2012b)

Starting in 2011, Tim Stockwell's team was busy with a series of peer-reviewed studies looking at the experience of Canadian provinces where a form of minimum pricing

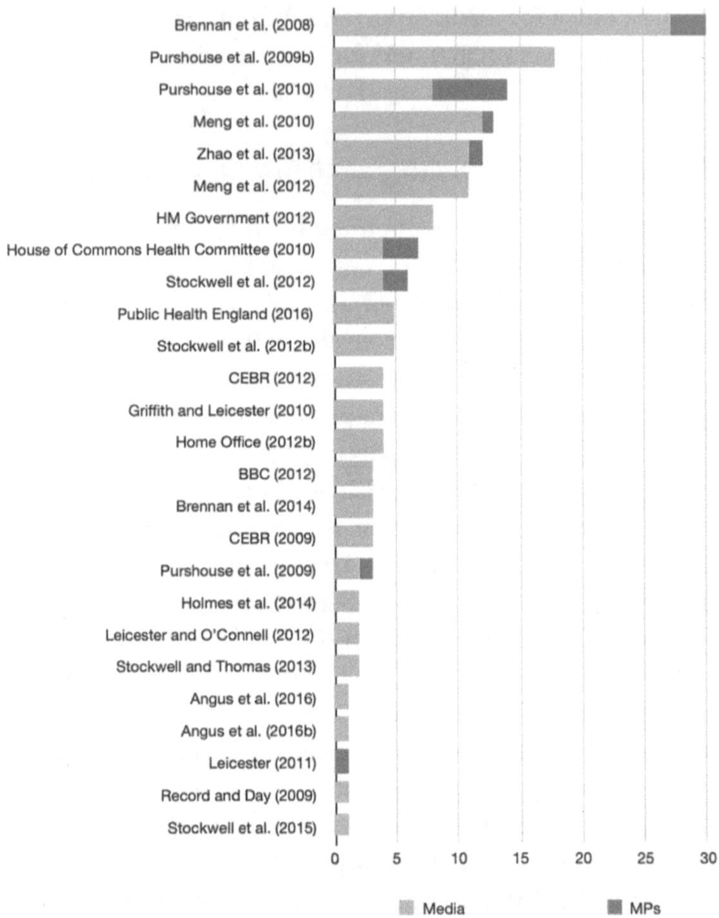

Figure 10. Number of references to evidence in the media and House of Commons

known as social referencing pricing existed. The first of these looked at the impact of an increase in minimum alcohol prices on consumption (Stockwell et al. 2012a and Stockwell et al. 2012b). Their most heavily cited study claimed to have found a 32% reduction in alcohol-related mortality from a 10% increase in the minimum price in British Columbia (Zhao et al. 2013). A subsequent study reported a significant fall in alcohol-related crime when minimum prices were raised in the same province (Stockwell et al. 2015). Stockwell also co-authored an evidence review for the anti-alcohol charity the Institute of Alcohol Studies (Stockwell and Thomas 2013), which was supportive of MUP. Although not reported by the five media outlets included here, he also published a study responding to 'alcohol industry criticism of Canadian research on minimum pricing' (Stockwell et al. 2013) and wrote an editorial for the *British Medical Journal* in which he urged the British government to introduce MUP (Stockwell 2015).

Discussion

There are strong echoes of the two previous case studies in which the argument was made first with theoretical evidence and later bolstered by 'real world' evidence which appeared to show early signs of success in another country. Again, the bulk of the most influential evidence came from a small group of researchers. With MUP, the Sheffield and Stockwell teams were behind the great majority of the evidence cited in favour of the policy. Figure 11 illustrates this by combining the publications from each institution. Of the 164 references to evidence in the media and HoC debates, 103 (63%) were based on the Sheffield model with a further 26 coming from Stockwell's team (16%).

Two economic think tanks – the CEBR and the IFS – attracted 14 references between them and were usually cited by opponents of MUP. The IFS published three papers

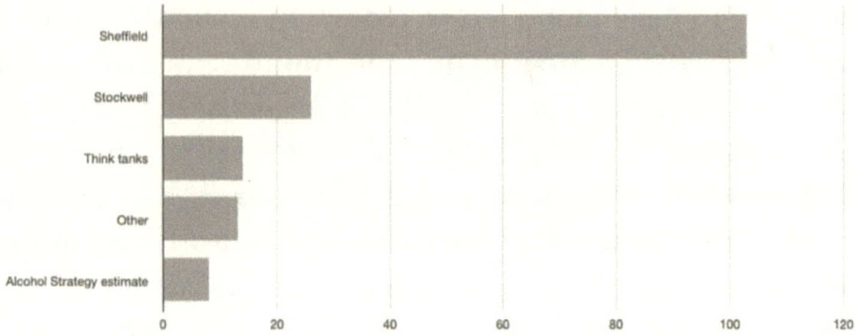

Figure 11. Type of evidence cited (by number of references)

related to MUP: Griffith and Leicester (2010) estimated that MUP would increase retailer revenues by £700 million per annum, Leicester (2011) estimated that 71% of all off-licence alcohol units would be affected by MUP, and Leicester and O'Connell (2012) updated the earlier work. This research appeared to undermine the claims of some pro-MUP campaigners that only a small number of drinkers would be affected by the policy.

In 2009, the *Guardian* published a rare op-ed opposing MUP which cited the report from the CEBR (2009) and claimed that 'the average cost to a household would be £68 a year; the total cost to consumers would be £1.8bn; and the total benefit to wider society, including the reduced costs of the NHS, policing and victims of crime, would amount to only £200m.' The newspaper made two other (disparaging) references to this report in the years that followed.

The early evidence review from the HoC Health Committee earned seven mentions and a Public Health England review which supported MUP attracted five mentions. Both leant heavily on the Sheffield research. David Cameron's claim in the Alcohol Strategy that a 40p MUP 'could mean 50,000 fewer crimes each year and 900 fewer alcohol-related deaths per year by the end of the decade' (HM Government 2012: 2) is an unattributed government estimate that seems to have never been published in full although it bears an obvious resemblance to findings from published models and originated in an iteration of the Sheffield model.[15] His figures were cited eight times. The only peer-reviewed, academic study cited by the media or politicians that did not emerge from the Sheffield or Stockwell groups was an obscure piece of research mentioned in the *Telegraph* which claimed that a 50p MUP would make food prices fall by 2.8%, based on the assumption that supermarkets lower the price of food if they make more profit from alcohol (Record and Day 2009).

As can be seen in Figure 12, the *Guardian* (and *Observer*) covered the MUP campaign extensively and often mentioned evidence. Both newspapers were openly supportive of the policy. The *Mirror* and the *Daily Mail/Mail on Sunday* were less enthusiastic while the *Sunday People* explicitly opposed it. Several BBC articles referencing evidence were tied to *Panorama* documentaries which promoted MUP, including one in which the BBC commissioned new modelling from the Sheffield team (BBC 2012). Regardless of whether they mentioned specific evidential claims, every media outlet dedicated many dozens of articles to the minimum pricing issue and the various political and legal disputes it provoked, but the *Guardian/Observer* was more inclined to include a reference to the Sheffield projections when it did so. The *Telegraph* and the *Daily Mail* tended

[15] As SARG later acknowledged. See Chapter 8.

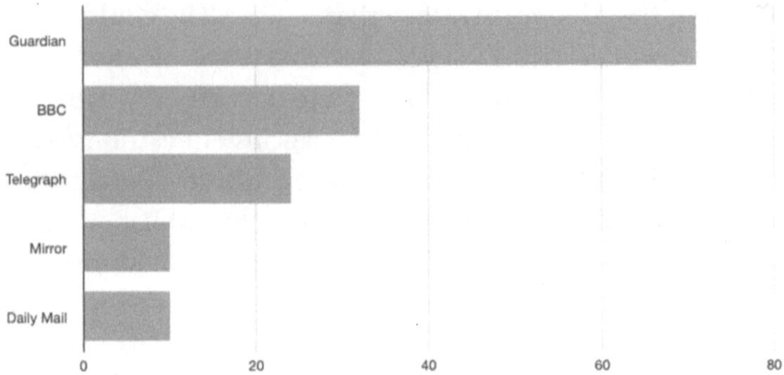

Figure 12. References to evidence by media outlet

to focus more on the economics of the policy and how it would affect businesses and consumers.

There were no fewer than seven HoC debates between 2010 and 2012 in which MUP featured prominently but as can be seen in Figure 10, references to relevant evidence were rare. Only nine MPs cited claims from the Sheffield studies, one of them disparagingly. Stockwell's research was mentioned just twice while the recommendations of the Select Committee were mentioned three times. Aside from a reference to an IFS report by an opponent of MUP, no other evidence pertaining to what effect the policy would have on health, social or economic outcomes was mentioned, even in vague terms.

Instead, MPs used various framing devices to signal that alcohol abuse was a problem that demanded action. In the second debate, for example, Nick Smith said:

> A recent Alcohol Concern report showed that more than 92,000 children and young people under the

> age of 18 were admitted to hospital as a result of alcohol misuse between 2002 and 2009. Girls are more likely to need hospital treatment than boys. Furthermore, a university of Manchester study found that some young women were consuming more than a week's allowance of alcohol units in a single night. Excessive drinking leads them to take more risks, such as walking home alone when drunk, particularly after they have sampled a ladies 'drink for free' promotion. Since 1970, we have seen a threefold increase in cirrhosis, but it is ninefold for those under the age of 45. The age at which people develop cirrhosis has been falling, and even teenagers are now developing liver failure. (Hansard 2011)

In the fourth debate, Sarah Wollaston used a dramatic analogy before appealing to the interests of taxpayers:

> If a jumbo jet fully laden with passengers crashed over Britain every fortnight, drastic action would be taken, and that is what we are talking about—22,000 people die every year in Britain as a result of alcohol.

> ... What about taxpayers? The cost of the epidemic is out of control. It is at least £20 billion, but if we look at the finer details of the impact on productivity, we will see that the evidence given to the Health Committee when it looked at this issue showed that the cost could be as high as £55 billion. At a time when the NHS has to make efficiency savings

> of £20 billion over the next four years, is it right that we are flushing down the drain at least £20 billion a year on alcohol? (Hansard 2012)

It is possible that MPs considered it to be no more than common sense that raising the price of cheap alcohol would have a beneficial effect and therefore focused on showing *why* the policy was urgently needed, rather than on *how* it would work. They may also have felt little need to cite the Sheffield modelling since it was already so well known, having received ample coverage in the media and in government documents on both sides of the Scottish border since 2008.

Scotland's Health and Sport Committee was deferential to the modelling in 2012 and the Scottish government delayed making a decision on what the minimum price would be until the latest iteration of the model had been published. In Westminster, the Sheffield model seems to have been highly regarded by the Home Office, even forming the basis of its Impact Assessment, until the Home Secretary, Theresa May, suddenly decided that the evidence was inconclusive. Whatever the merits of the Sheffield model, governments risked putting all their eggs in one basket by giving a near-monopoly on MUP research to a small group of academics for whom it was their first major commission. Although some of the group's conclusions and assumptions were challenged by the IFS and CEBR, no government department seems to have looked beyond Sheffield when commissioning research into the policy.

The sense that MUP research was something of a closed shop is heightened by Tim Stockwell's team being the only other major supplier of evidence. Stockwell was one of the earliest advocates of minimum pricing and was one of the authors of the first Sheffield study (Brennan et al. 2008). By the 2010s, he had become synonymous with efforts to dispute the benefits of moderate alcohol consumption for cardiovascular health and overall mortality,[16] but Petra Meier, the director of the Sheffield group, had met him earlier in his career, as she later recalled:

> My foray into the alcohol world started with taking up a lectureship at the University of Sheffield. Not that anyone there was doing alcohol research at the time, but I was suddenly in a very research-active environment, and there was an expectation that we would identify a niche and quickly bring in grants. My previous research had focused on illicit drug use, but it seemed there were far more opportunities in alcohol research.
>
> My new department was full of systematic reviewers and health economists, so we tried our luck and got funding for a project reviewing and modelling alcohol pricing and promotion policies.
>
> Having literally no clue whatsoever about alcohol policy in the United Kingdom, or elsewhere, I remember how a colleague and I, desperate for some expert input, trawled the web and kept finding the names 'Robin Room'and 'Tim Stockwell'. We fired off a couple of emails and a day later both Robin and Tim had agreed to help, sent copious amounts of relevant reading material,

[16] See, for example, Roerecke and Rehm (2013).

> and invited me to come to the next Kettil Bruun Society conference due to start a few weeks later. Once there, Robin and Tim made a real effort to introduce me to all the lovely folk in the field, and with it being such a friendly and supportive scientific community I decided to make it my 'home' and build up alcohol research at Sheffield. (Room 2014: 135)

By her own account, Meier was introduced to a particular view of alcohol research soon after entering the field. Robin Room was a co-author of both the Purple Book and *Alcohol: No Ordinary Commodity* and was one of Britain's earliest exponents of Scandinavian-style supply-side policy interventions that were derived from the whole-population approach to alcohol control. The Kettil Bruun Society is the spiritual home of this approach and Robin Room had been its first president between 1987 and 1989. Petra Meier went on to become president in between 2021 and 2023.

As providers of research, the Sheffield team was proficient in giving policymakers what they often say they want: timely and clear answers to policy-relevant questions. Several of their studies seemed designed to overcome specific political obstacles. In 2013, Theresa May rejected the policy because, she said, the evidence did not 'conclusively' demonstrate that it would 'reduce problem drinking without penalising all those who drink responsibly' (Home Office 2013: 3). Seemingly in response to concerns that MUP would unfairly punish moderate drinkers and be regressive, the Sheffield team published a study in the *Lancet* which concluded that 'moderate drinkers were little affected by a minimum unit price of £0·45 in our model' and that

MUP would cost moderate drinkers in the lowest income quintile a mere 4p per annum (Holmes et al. 2014: 1,655).

When the British government announced a ban on the sale of below-cost alcohol rather than introduce MUP, the Sheffield team published a study titled 'Potential benefits of minimum unit pricing for alcohol versus a ban on below cost selling in England 2014: modelling study' in the *British Medical Journal* which concluded that MUP would have 'an approximately 40–50 times greater effect' (Brennan et al. 2014: 1).

When the European Court of Justice ruled that MUP would only be legal under EU law if the same public health objectives could not be met by other means (specifically, by alcohol duty increases), the Scottish government commissioned the Sheffield team to produce new modelling which was then used as evidence in court. This resulted in a report titled 'Model-based appraisal of the comparative impact of Minimum Unit Pricing and taxation policies in Scotland' which concluded that alcohol duty increases were 'a less well-targeted and robust approach than MUP and, in particular, impose greater costs on drinkers whose alcohol consumption is low risk' (Angus et al. 2016a: 89).

Of our four case studies, MUP is unique in that the Westminster government decided against enacting it while the Scottish government, which had access to the same evidence, keenly supported it. The SNP was already convinced of its merits by 2008 when there was no evidence for the policy beyond the economically banal observation that price affects consumption. For several years, the Scottish Labour Party and the Scottish Liberal Democrats opposed minimum pricing while the Labour Party and Liberal Democrats in Westminster supported it. The Conservatives, for their part, declared themselves fully committed to the policy before suddenly rejecting it, citing a lack of evidence. None of this seems consistent with politicians following the classic model of evidence-based policymaking.

Box 1. Typical headlines

'Alcohol pricing could save £950m' (BBC, 2009).

'Binge drinkers should be priced out' (*Guardian*, 2010)

'Alcohol minimum pricing measures would bring retailers £700m' (*Guardian*, 2010)

'Sheffield University study adjusts booze price impact' (BBC, 2012)

'Minimum alcohol price would cost moderate drinkers £1.8billion a year' (*Mirror*, 2012)

'Minimum alcohol price could save lives of 50,000 binge-drinking pensioners' (*Daily Mail*, 2012)

'Canada is proof that state-controlled drinking is good for health' (*Guardian*, 2013)

'Minimum alcohol pricing would save 860 lives a year, study finds' (*Guardian*, 2014)

'The alcohol pricing U-turn shows the power of the business lobby' (*Guardian*, 2014)

Box 2. Excerpts from the House of Commons

It is estimated that a minimum price of 50p per unit of alcohol would save about 3,000 lives a year, and that a minimum price of 40p per unit of alcohol would save 1,100 lives a year. – Kevin Barron (Lab)

Will the policy work? Yes, there is very clear evidence that it will. Several meta-analyses were studied in the university of Sheffield report that was commissioned by the previous Government. Those show that it is clear that pricing is a very good mechanism not only for controlling overall consumption, but for targeting those who are most at risk: young people and heavy drinkers' – Sarah Wollaston (Con)

The Centre for Economics and Business Research conducted research on minimum pricing and concluded that the heaviest drinkers are the least responsive to higher prices. For example, at a minimum unit price of 40p, the CEBR found that harmful drinkers, which the policy is supposed to be targeting, would reduce their weekly consumption by only 1.7 units per week, which at the end of the day is less than one pint of weak beer. – Philip Davies (Con)

The effect of a minimum price on moderate drinkers will be low, as they consume less alcohol. If a 50p minimum price were introduced, it would mean an increase in spending on alcohol of less than 23p a week for a moderate drinker; but a heavy drinker could pay slightly more than £3 a week. – Nick Smith (Lab)

6 FOURTH CASE STUDY: FIXED ODDS BETTING TERMINALS

Background

Unlike tobacco, alcohol and sugary drinks, gambling has a long history of being banned in Britain. Casinos and off-course bookmakers were not legalised until the Betting and Gaming Act of 1960. Liberalisation led to something of a free-for-all which was addressed by the 1968 Gaming Act, limiting casino numbers and establishing the Gaming Board. The National Lottery was introduced in 1994, and the Gambling Act (2005) came into force in 2007, legalising gambling advertising and removing a number of rules that were considered archaic, such as the prohibition on entering a casino within 24 hours of becoming a member. It also replaced the Gaming Board with the Gambling Commission.

The 2005 Act introduced less liberalisation than the government originally intended. Plans to build 'super-casinos' were scaled down in the final legislation before being abandoned altogether after Gordon Brown became Prime Minister in 2007. When the economist Alan Budd carried out a review for the government in 2001, he argued that gambling regulation since 1960 reflected 'an attitude that gambling is, at best, something to be grudgingly tolerated and contained, rather than allowed to be encouraged' (Budd et al. 2001: 69). The Blair government believed that attitudes had changed, but the backlash from the media and many backbench MPs suggested that the public were only prepared to tolerate gambling so long as they did not have to see it or think about it too often. Although a majority of British adults consistently reported having gambled in the last year, they seemed to draw a distinction between 'soft' gambling, such as playing the lottery or bingo, and 'hard' gambling such as casino games. In 2007, British attitudes towards gambling were more negative than positive, with most believing that there were too many opportunities to gamble and that gambling should be legal but discouraged (Wardle et al. 2007).

In recent years, gambling has been repositioned as a public health issue for reasons explained by Wardle et al. (2019: 2):

> Harms related to gambling reflect social and health inequalities, with negative effects unequally distributed among economically and socially disadvantaged groups and are commonly associated with a range of mental and physical health comorbidities. At its most severe, gambling can contribute to loss of life.
>
> ... Harms affect a much larger proportion of the population than just those who might be defined as problem gamblers: for every one person with problems, an estimated five to ten people are adversely affected.

> ... Harms from gambling affect health and wellbeing and, even at low risk levels, contribute to a loss of quality of life similar to the long-term consequences of a moderate stroke, moderate alcohol use disorder, and urinary incontinence.

Similar to the whole population approach to alcohol, the public health approach to gambling focuses on discouraging gambling across the whole population whereas the harm reduction approach seeks to identify risk factors for problem gambling and find interventions that will target them (Allami et al. 2021). Harm reduction does not preclude regulation or a degree of coercion (it might limit stakes or ban the use of cash machines in casinos, for example), but it puts more focus on giving individuals the tools to self-regulate. Although it is questionable whether targeting a large number of gamblers at low risk is more effective than targeting a small number of gamblers at high risk (Delfabbro and King 2017), advocates of the public health approach explicitly seek to emulate policies that have been used to tackle the consumption of tobacco, alcohol and sugary drinks (Goyder et al. 2020). As Atherton and Beynon (2019: 5) put it:

> Public health action to reduce harm from gambling should not focus solely on individuals but should include a wide range of population-based measures including advocacy, information, regulation and appropriate prohibition in a co-ordinated way.

The academic literature on gambling *as a public health issue* is small and relatively immature. An umbrella review published in 2019 found that most of the evidence on gambling harm reduction focused on voluntary schemes and educational programmes, including 'pre-commitment and limit setting (24%), self-exclusion (20%), youth prevention programmes (20%), and machine messages/feedback (20%)' (McMahon et al. 2019: 380). Such nudges fall short of the kind of mandatory restrictions, advertising bans and 'fiscal measures' that some public health academics would prefer (Goyder et al. 2020) but the absence of evidence did not deter the authors from concluding that more coercive policies were needed. On the contrary, it was seen as an indication that a public health approach would be more effective.

> The 'inverse evidence law' highlights the tendency for there to exist the least evidence and research about interventions that are most likely to be effective (McMahon et al. 2019: 386).

Similarly, the authors of a *Lancet Public Health* mapping study – all public health academics who had not published research on gambling before – concluded that it was 'imperative to ensure that a scarcity of evidence is not used as a justification for inaction in addressing the growing burden of gambling-related harms' (Blank et al. 2021: e62).

Gambling's transition from a private habit to a public health issue was underway in the early 2010s but was not fully complete. It was symbolically important that official statistics on gambling and problem gambling were gathered and published by the NHS after 2012, but calls for gambling to be regulated by the Department of Health rather than the Department for Culture, Media and Sport fell on deaf ears (there are echoes here of the complaints about alcohol policy still being controlled by the Home Office).

Health groups have not traditionally had a strong or consistent line on gambling regulation. Certain individuals have spoken out against specific gambling issues, such as when the National Lottery was introduced (McKee and Sassi 1995), but public health organisations have tended not to have a corporate view and have not actively campaigned in the way they have for anti-smoking policies. That began to change in 2019 when the Royal Society for Public Health formed the Gambling Health Alliance, but that took place after the campaign against fixed odds betting terminals had been won.

Fixed odds betting terminals (FOBTs), technically known as B2 machines, were introduced to betting shops in 2001. Under the 2005 Gambling Act, they were limited to four per shop with a maximum stake of £100 per spin. They allowed players to play casino games, of which roulette was the most popular, at speeds as fast as 20 seconds per spin. The main concerns about FOBTs were that they caused gambling disorder, led gamblers to lose excessive sums of money, and were used to launder money. There were also concerns that the four-per-shop limit had led bookmakers to open more shops than were needed for retail betting, thereby saturating high streets and 'clustering' in low-income neighbourhoods.

Concerns about FOBTs were aired as early as 2003. In 2005, a *Guardian* article headlined 'Roulette machines blamed for rise in gambling addiction' reported that the problem gambling charity GamCare had claimed that 'one in four calls to its helpline now concern the new craze' of FOBTs.[17] Wider public concern did not emerge until a coalition of interest groups coalesced around the issue and the former professional poker player Derek Webb founded two campaign groups – the Campaign for Fairer Gambling (CFFG) and Stop the FOBTs – after finding three card poker, which he had invented, on a FOBT in 2007. He considered legal action but, as he said in 2013, 'rather than sue I backed a campaign to make my point' (Ramesh 2013). Over the next four years he spent £3 million on the campaign before moving on to lobbying against online gambling (Ahmed 2017).

The 'anti-gambling' movement at the time of the campaign against FOBTs (2012–18) was not dominated by public health activists or academics. Instead, it was a coalition of sometimes unlikely bedfellows including religious groups (such as the Salvation Army, Quaker Action on Alcohol and Drugs, the Methodist Church and the Evangelical Alliance), think tanks at both ends of the political spectrum (ResPublica, the IPPR and the Centre for Social Justice), several newspapers (notably the *Times* and the *Guardian*), and elements of the rival arcade, casino and pub industries. Other organisations involved in the campaign included the Local Government Association and the Royal British Legion. The term 'anti-gambling' is used to describe this coalition for the sake of brevity and in the broadest sense since it includes organisations that are implacably opposed to all forms of gambling as well as those who have specific, limited concerns and those who are themselves part of the

[17] https://www.theguardian.com/business/2005/may/09/gambling.uknews

gambling industry. What was largely absent, in contrast to the three interest groups discussed above, was leadership from public health organisations.

As with the interest groups discussed in the other case studies, the anti-gambling coalition was instrumental in setting up an All-Party Parliamentary Group. Formed in 2016, it was initially called the APPG on Fixed Odds Betting Terminals but changed its name to the APPG on Gambling-Related Harm when the FOBT battle was won.

The policy

Anti-FOBT campaigners lobbied the government to reduce the maximum stake on the machines from £100 per spin to £2 per spin. This would make the machines unplayable for most gamblers and amount to *de facto* prohibition.

Timeline

July 2012: A DCMS committee recommends that Adult Gaming Centres be allowed FOBTs and that casinos be allowed more FOBTs. It also recommends that local authorities be granted permission to allow betting shops to have more than four FOBTs (DCMS 2012). The latter recommendation was made to alleviate concerns about 'clustering' of betting shops.

6 August 2012: Channel 4 broadcasts *Dispatches: Britain's High Street Gamble*, a documentary which provided evidence of the 'clustering' of betting shops in poorer areas.

5 November 2012: The BBC broadcasts an episode of *Panorama* showing footage of angry FOBT players physically attacking the machines. It said that FOBTs had 'been

branded "the crack cocaine of gambling" by industry insiders.'

March 2014: The Chancellor George Osborne announces an increase in gaming duty on FOBTs from 20% to 25% to take effect from 2015.

April 2014: The government announces restrictions on those who play FOBTs at £50 or more per spin. From April 2015, these players have to play on account or pay betting shop staff in cash.

16 September 2014: The BBC dedicates another episode of *Panorama* to the issue. Titled 'Why are gambling machines addictive?', it is presented by Wendy Bendel whose partner was a problem gambler and FOBT player who took his own life.

24 October 2016: The government launches a call for evidence on gaming machines.

31 October 2017: The government launches a 12-week public consultation on cutting the stake limit.

March 2018: The Gambling Commission recommends the maximum stake be reduced to £30 or less.

17 May 2018: Culture Secretary Matt Hancock announces that the stake limit on FOBTs will be cut to £2. An Impact Assessment is published on the same day.

29 October 2018: In his Budget statement, the Chancellor Philip Hammond announces that the reduced stake limit will come into force in October 2019, with remote gaming duty rising to 21% to make up for the expected tax revenue shortfall.

1 November 2018: Sports minister Tracey Crouch resigns in protest at what she claims is a delay in implementation of the new limit and calls for it to be introduced in April 2019.

14 November 2018: The government announces that the implementation of the new limit will be brought forward to April 2019.

1 April 2019: The £2 stake limit comes into force under the Gaming Machine (Miscellaneous Amendments and Revocation) Regulations 2018.

The evidence

The campaign to reduce FOBT stakes to £2 was supported by far less research evidence than we have seen in the other case studies. Very few peer-reviewed studies had looked at this form of gambling and the small body of relevant academic evidence was largely ignored. Instead, both sides relied on research they had commissioned themselves. The Association of British Bookmakers (ABB) commissioned research from KPMG and RS Business Solutions. The British Amusement Catering Trades Association (Bacta) was opposed to FOBTs and commissioned research from the CEBR and NERA.[18] The CFFG commissioned a large body of research and polling from Landman Economics, NERA, YouGov, ResPublica, 2CV and others.

Most of this research was removed from the internet after 2018. The Stop the FOBTs and CFFG websites were closed down. The Gambling Commission website was revamped and much of its old material taken offline. FOBT research was taken down from the websites of consultancies

[18] As the trade association for amusement arcades, Bacta saw FOBTs as a threat. In 2014, the *Mirror* reported that Bacta was lobbying the government for its members to be permitted to have FOBTs themselves. (https://www.mirror.co.uk/news/uk-news/gambling-lives-fury-amusement-arcades-4023238)

such as Landman Economics and NERA (if it was ever there to begin with). The ABB was closed down and its website taken offline. Several pieces of research were never made public at all, including a KPMG report commissioned by the ABB and possibly some of the later documents from Landman Economics and the CEBR.

MPs cited almost no evidence in the HoC debates, and media references to published evidence were generally brief and superficial. However, unlike in the other case studies, the government explained its rationale for the policy decision in detail and cited various pieces of evidence, most of which came from documents published by two government agencies: the Gambling Commission and the Responsible Gambling Strategy Board. In chronological order, the three most significant documents were the following:

DCMS (January 2016)

In April 2015, the government mandated that players of FOBTs who wished to stake over £50 per spin had to 'load cash via staff interaction or use account-based play', i.e., they could not play anonymously. In practice, account-based play meant playing with a loyalty card which allowed better tracking of play, provided more opportunities for staff to intervene and discouraged high-stake bets. This provided an opportunity to gather some evidence about the behaviour of gamblers when stakes on these machines were reduced. An evaluation of the reform was published by DCMS in January 2016. It found that there had been a 45% decline in the number of bets placed above £50 per spin, but a large increase in the number of bets placed at £40–50. The average duration of sessions rose by 10% and the total amount spent changed very little.

The evaluation was unable to show whether the policy had any effect on problem gambling. A marked increase in the average time spent playing FOBTs per session was noted, but it was unclear whether this was due to players spending the same amount of money at lower stakes or spending more time thinking through their actions. The second of these explanations seems less likely since the average speed of play did not change significantly after the reform and the total amount spent on FOBTs dropped only slightly (by 3.7% in the first quarter after the reform and by 0.7% in the second quarter (year-on-year)) (DCMS 2016: 22).

Responsible Gambling Strategy Board report (January 2017)

Following another call for evidence in October 2016, DCMS sought advice from the Responsible Gambling Strategy Board (RGSB) which was set up in 2008 to advise the Gambling Commission and government on gambling research, education and treatment. The RGSB published a 44-page report in January 2017 which concluded that:

> There is sufficient evidence of harm associated with gaming machines (primarily B2s) in licensed betting offices (LBOs) to apply the precautionary principle. Doing so is not, however, entirely straightforward. It requires judgement about the balance of risks. (RGSB 2017: 2)

Taking their evidence from routine data such as the British Gambling Prevalence Survey and analyses based on it, such as Orford et al. (2012), the RGSB found that a high proportion of problem gamblers played FOBTs and that FOBTs 'possess several characteristics known to be associated with greater risk of harm' (RGSB 2017: 2). However, it also found 'some other forms of gambling to have a greater association with problem gamblers' and that mere association did not prove that FOBTs (or any other gambling product) *caused* problem gambling, rather it could be that problem gamblers engaged in various gambling activities and found FOBTs appealing.

> Many commentators appear to take it for granted that reducing maximum stakes on B2 gaming machines would necessarily make a material contribution to reducing gambling-related harm. The evidence suggests that a reduction in harm is far from certain. (ibid.)

The RGSB concluded that machine gambling in betting shops was not uniquely associated with problem gambling (ibid.: 19–20). The claim that such a unique relationship existed was based on one study analysing data from the 2007 British Gambling Prevalence Survey (LaPlante et al. 2011). Subsequent analysis of data from 2010 and 2012 did not find such an association after adjusting for the number of other gambling activities in which players participated (RGSB 2017: 20).

The report referenced two studies of loyalty card holders which found that people who played machines in betting shops on a weekly basis were more likely to become problem gamblers (Wardle et al. 2014a, Wardle et al. 2017). However, the report noted that these individuals were 'highly engaged gamblers' who were 'not representative of all machine players' (RGSB 2017: 20). Moreover, Wardle et al. (2014a) found that a large number of players went from being problem gamblers to non-problem gamblers during the two-year study period, with no change in the overall problem gambling rate.

While the RGSB report concluded that a 'reduction in maximum stake might have some effect on harm' (RGSB 2017: 3), it cautioned that players could respond by playing at lower stakes for longer, thereby spending the same amount of money, or by switching to alternative gambling activities. And, therefore: 'The effect on the volume of harm is, to say the least, highly uncertain.' (ibid.: 30)

The RGSB report quoted the following from a review of the international literature:

> Electronic gaming machines are associated with harms and this is an undeniable claim. Whether or not it is the most virulent form that requires special public health attention over and above other gambling products is debatable. (Blaszczynski 2013: 70)

The RGSB said that its view was 'more nuanced' than this and that:

> it could be a mistake not to act on B2 machines simply because there is insufficient evidence to conclude that they are the *most* harmful form of gambling. If other forms of machine play, or other

> forms of gambling, are harmful to a similar but unacceptable extent, then action should be taken on them as well' (emphasis in the original) (RGSB 2017: 25).

This was also their response to those who warned that a clamp-down on FOBTs could lead to players switching to remote (i.e. online) gambling where the stakes were even higher.

> We do not think that the anomalous position of remote play is a convincing argument for relaxing the controls on machine play in LBOs. It is more a reason for considering the imposition of controls on equivalent games on remote platforms. (ibid.: 27)

The RGSB also mentioned public opinion which, by this time, was firmly against FOBTs.

> It is also important to take account of public opinion in considering the balance between the protection of the vulnerable and enabling the enjoyment of those who gamble. There is some evidence of a shift in public views about gambling towards a more negative stance.' (ibid.: 4)

Although the RGSB concluded that 'changing a single characteristic of one gambling product' (i.e. stake limits on FOBTs) was unlikely to 'make a significant impact on levels of gambling-related harm', it concluded that the maximum stake should be reduced from £100 to £50 or less (ibid.: 4). They made no specific recommendation of what the limit should be, noting that there was 'no evidenced-based way of determining any uniquely correct new level' (ibid.). They did, however, caution against reducing the stake limit to £2, saying that this 'would effectively abolish B2 gaming machines altogether' and that 'we would find it difficult to regard so strong an action as being proportionate on the basis of the existing evidence' (ibid.: 38–39).

Gambling Commission (March 2018)

DCMS sought advice from the Gambling Commission, which published a 97-page report in March 2018. The report concluded that there was a 'precautionary case' for a stake limit that was 'materially lower than £50' (Gambling Commission 2018a: 2).

> In our view, a precautionary approach should involve a stake limit at or below £30 if it is to have a significant effect on the potential for players to lose large amounts of money in a short space of time. (ibid.)

The Commission said that a stake reduction was 'unlikely on its own to have more than a limited impact on gambling-related harm' (ibid.: 4) and recommended a package of other measures, including mandatory tracked play to provide more information to consumers and regulators and to allow 'operators no excuse if they fail to identify players that are starting to show signs of problematic gambling' (ibid.: 2).

In addition to reviewing the existing evidence, the Commission carried out or commissioned several new pieces of research. The first used the same methodology as LaPlante (2011) which had found no association between specific gambling activities and problem gambling after adjusting for the level of gambling involvement *with the exception of FOBTs*. The new research found no independent association with any form of gambling, *including* FOBTs (Gambling Commission 2018a: 6). The Commission also acquired detailed data from betting shops covering 20 billion FOBT spins which showed session duration, stakes and expenditure. It had made this data available on its website the previous year (Gambling Commission 2017). It showed that in the twelve months from July 2015 and June 2016, there were 170,760 sessions in which players lost over £1,000, all of them involving stakes higher than £2.

The Commission mentioned the 2015 reforms which required extra effort from players wishing to stake over £50, and found that players adapted to the 'soft limit' in ways that undermined its intention:

> Experience from the £50 staking regulation – which prompted far fewer stakes above £50 but led to longer sessions – suggests that players will seek other opportunities to satisfy their appetite for risk. In particular, consumers might choose to play for longer, alter their staking strategies or switch to other gambling products. (Gambling Commission 2018a: 8)

From this, the Commission inferred that some players would respond to a lower stake limit by switching to other gambling machines, such as B3 jackpot machines which had a £2 stake limit but a much faster speed of play[19], or by shifting online (ibid.: 9).

Taking B3 (jackpot) machines as a comparison, the Commission calculated how much a player might be expected to lose in a nine-minute session. On a B3 machine, the average loss was £35 whereas on a B2 (FOBT) machine, average losses ranged from £1.46 with a £2 stake to £72.90 with a £100 stake. Staking at £50, the loss would be £36.45 – similar to a B3 machine – but this was only the *average* loss. The potential *maximum* loss was much larger on a FOBT. To achieve parity with B3 machines in terms of maximum losses, the Commission found that players of FOBTs should stake no more than £16.

> A maximum stake somewhere between £16 and £50 would make B2 and B3 broadly equivalent (ibid.: 10).

The Commission's recommended figure of £30 (or less) may have been derived from splitting the difference between £16 and £50, in addition to observing that most players did not bet more than £30 per spin in any case.

> Our analysis of data from billions of plays on B2 machines reveals that most sessions involve an average stake no higher than £30. So, we think that a precautionary approach should involve a stake limit no higher than £30. (ibid.: 11)

[19] While B2 machines (FOBTs) had a minimum spin time of 20 seconds, B3 machines played at 2.5 seconds per spin.

This recommendation was based on two implicit assumptions. Firstly, that the aim was to reduce the potential for large losses (rather than, for example, reducing the rate of problem gambling), and secondly, that the losses that could be incurred on B3 machines were acceptable.

The Commission stressed that it was for the government to decide what the limit should be and that this would 'depend on the weight that Ministers attach to risk of harm, implications for the way different products are regulated, consumer choice, and public and stakeholder opinion' (ibid.: 2). There was nothing in the report to suggest that the Commission favoured a £2 stake, which it acknowledged would result in a *de facto* ban on the most popular FOBT game (roulette).

> A very low stake limit is likely to mean that roulette would no longer be a commercially viable product. Consumers would still have a wide choice of other activities, but removing a popular product from the high street would be a significant change, and any restriction on freedom of choice requires careful consideration. (ibid.: 9)

In the media coverage that followed publication, it was often implied that the Commission had recommended a stake limit of exactly £30. This was untrue, but the markets seem to have assumed that the Commission was recommending a limit closer to £30 than to £2 since shares in gambling firms climbed when the report was released.[20]

[20] https://www.bbc.co.uk/news/business-43455480

Discussion

The evidence cited for and against the FOBT reform differed from the evidence in the other case studies in several important respects. It is notable that the research that was commissioned by anti-FOBT groups overwhelmingly focused on *framing* the problem, rather than on providing evidence of what would happen if the stake was cut to £2. FOBTs were still relatively obscure products at the start of 2012. The challenge for the anti-gambling coalition was to persuade the public that the machines were a social evil and were unusually 'addictive'. The narrative had several elements: (a) Britain was suffering from a problem gambling epidemic, (b) FOBTs were more addictive than other gambling products, (c) betting shops were proliferating, especially in deprived neighbourhoods, (d) some FOBT players were losing very large sums of money, and (e) the regulatory anomaly of high stakes on high-street casino games facilitated unacceptably high losses. Convincing politicians that FOBTs were uniquely problematic may have been enough to secure the policy change. In January 2013, Hugh Robertson MP, then the sports minister, said there was a 'lack of evidence' that FOBTs were a 'major problem' but that 'once the problem is proved to exist, the Government will act' (Peev 2013).

Aside from the Gambling Commission (2018a) report, the two most cited pieces of evidence were the report from the APPG on FOBTs (2017) and a claim from Gambling With Lives (2020) about how many suicides were linked to problem gambling. These sources are included because they gave *some* suggestion as to what would happen if FOBTs were regulated as campaigners hoped, but they were primarily focused on framing the problem.

The APPG on FOBTs report was not an official government document; indeed, the group was admonished for breaching parliamentary standards by presenting it as an official document. Nevertheless, it is useful to study its contents as it represents the views of some of the most engaged MPs and was widely reported in the press. The APPG held a series of hearings which the Association of British Bookmakers (ABB) refused to attend, describing the group as a 'kangaroo court ... financed by those with interests in the casino, arcade and pub industries'.[21] The APPG was indeed partly funded by rival elements of the gambling industry, including Bacta, the Hippodrome Casino, Novomatic UK (a slot machine manufacturer), as well as the CFFG. It was no surprise when the APPG report concluded that the maximum stake on FOBTs should be lowered to £2.

Like most of the material from the anti-FOBT coalition, the report focused on framing the problem and presenting FOBTs as unusually dangerous gambling products, but there was some evidence cited about the likely economic impact of a stake reduction. Reports by NERA Economic Consulting (2014) and Landman Economics (Reed 2015) were referenced. Both were commissioned the CFFG and suggested that the ABB's claims about job losses and shop closures were exaggerated.

> The submissions quote from the NERA report in 2014 noting that the impact of stake reduction on "the number of shop closures could be between

[21] https://news.sky.com/story/betting-against-gambling-may-be-a-losing-game-10749992

> 700 and 1200 which would leave the industry with just 5 to 10% fewer shops than there were in 2000, before the introduction of B2 machines. The likely impact on the betting industry is therefore very substantially smaller than had been previously suggested by the ABB (APPG on FOBTs 2017: 16)

There was little direct evidence about what impact a lower stake would have on problem gamblers and there was scant evidence about FOBTs in general. Indeed, Dr Simon Cowlishaw of the University of Bristol told the APPG that 'he was puzzled that in the UK there is an incredibly small level of independent research' (ibid.: 49). Nevertheless, the APPG concluded that:

> The wealth of evidence now accumulated and the many anecdotal and personal stories of harm mean that it is now time for the Government to act decisively to properly regulate FOBTs. (ibid.: 51).

The pressure group Gambling With Lives (2020) produced a statistic that arrived late in the campaign claiming that there were between 250 and 650 gambling-related suicides in the UK per annum. Gambling With Lives later described their workings in a submission to a House of Lords Select Committee (which is the reference given here). Based on estimates from three studies from the UK, Hong Kong and Sweden, it seems to have been the source for Tracey Crouch's claim, in her resignation letter on 1 November 2018, that two people killed themselves every day as a result of problem gambling. Crouch seems to have attributed a large proportion of these suicides to FOBTs, saying: 'There was never any excuse for delay. Bringing forward by six months the day maximum stakes are capped will save an estimated 120 lives.'[22]

Unlike in the other case studies, there was no evidence from another country to indicate that the policy would (or would not) work. The nearest thing to 'real world' evidence was the DCMS (2016) analysis of the 2015 reform which introduced a soft limit of £50. This offered some limited evidence of how players respond to stake reductions, but that reform affected relatively few gamblers whereas a £2 stake limit would make the machines commercially unviable. In any case, the DCMS evaluation provided scant evidence that the £50 stake limit had significantly reduced session losses. A study commissioned by the (industry funded) Responsible Gambling Trust received some coverage in the *Daily Mail* upon publication. Based on a controlled experiment, its authors concluded that 'gambling at higher stakes impairs decision-making, which in turn may reduce self-control' (Parke et al. 2014: 14). But they did not recommend a cut to FOBT stake limits and instead called for research to be conducted in betting shops with players who were spending their own money (ibid.: 88).

Figure 13 shows the 52 references to relevant evidence in the media and HoC debates between January 2012 and 14 November 2018, and Figure 14 breaks the citations down by category. The 2018 Gambling Commission report was mentioned far more than any other document (n = 24), although it should be noted that many references were negative, with the Commission criticised for not recommending

[22] https://www.mirror.co.uk/news/politics/fixed-odds-betting-terminals-limit-13605504

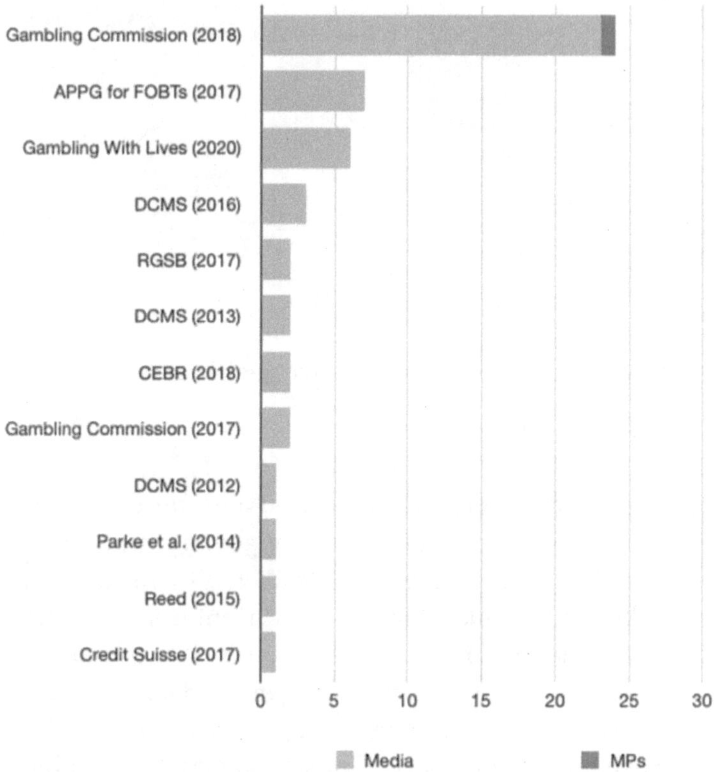

Figure 13. Number of references to evidence in the media and House of Commons

a £2 stake, and many mentions were brief or in passing. The report itself was rarely discussed in detail.

The Gambling Commission report set out a framework for what the aim of the policy should be and what the criteria should be to formulate it. It was the first time these basic questions had been seriously addressed. The anti-FOBT

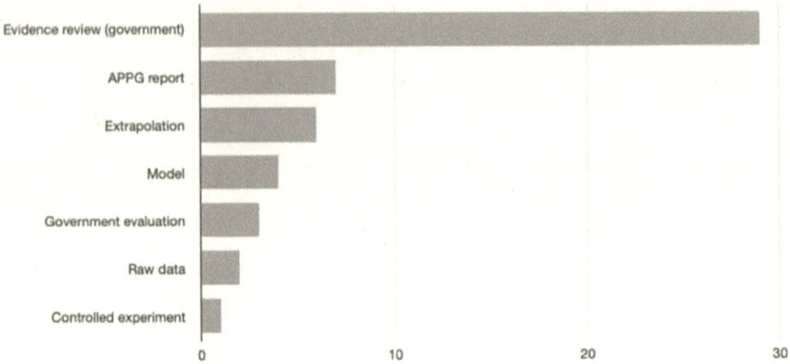

Figure 14. Type of evidence cited (by number of references)

coalition and the media had created a narrative of spiralling gambling 'addiction' driven by gaming machines in betting shops, but this was contradicted by Britain's rate of problem gambling which was low by international standards and had not risen in twenty years. Using regulation to control the number of problem gamblers was a less realistic goal than reducing the harm problem gamblers do to themselves, i.e. losing large sums of money. The Gambling Commission focused on the latter.

Acknowledging public concern about the machines and knowing that the government was going to act, the Commission sought a coherent and logical solution to the problem of heavy losses. Using B3 jackpot machines as a benchmark for acceptable gambling losses, the Commission calculated that the maximum stake of FOBT (B2) machines should be between £16 and £50. Presumably aware that the government was under political pressure to take the maximum stake well below £50, it delivered a final recommendation of £30 or less.

The logic of the Commission's methodology did not come out of nowhere. The claim that 233,071 FOBT sessions had ended with losses of over £1,000 in 2015/16 had been circulating in the media since May 2017. This figure was quoted in the *Lancet* in September 2017 and in a report from the ResPublica think tank in October 2017. The Association of Directors of Public Health quoted it in their response to the 2017 DCMS consultation and it was frequently mentioned in the media (sometimes rounded down to 230,000). Although the Gambling Commission was cited as the source of this number, it is higher than the figure of 170,760 published online and subsequently cited by the government (Gambling Commission 2017). Regardless of whether the true figure was 233,071 or 170,760, it was clearly seen as unacceptably high by many people. The Gambling Commission sought to make losses more acceptable by reducing the stake on B2 (FOBT) machines to a level that would make potential losses similar to those associated with the less controversial B3 (jackpot) machines.

But when the government made its decision, it set itself a different goal. It decided to set the stake level so low that it would be practically impossible for a player to lose more than £1,000 in a session and extremely difficult to lose more than £500. Data from the Gambling Commission (2017) showed that no one playing at £2 or less had lost more than a £1,000 in a session in 2015/16 whereas there had been 373 sessions ending in a loss of over £1,000 when people played at a stake between £2.01 and £10.

This amounted to a zero-tolerance policy from the government for this particular form of gambling. Preventing people from losing £1,000 on gambling had never been a principle of UK regulation. The same data from the Gambling Commission showed that there were 1,733 sessions ending in losses over £1,000 on B3 machines (for which the maximum stake was £2) in 2015/16, but this elicited no concern from the government, the public or anti-gambling campaigners. Nor was there any significant public concern about those who placed a bet of £1,000 or more on a single event, as often happened, or who regularly lost more than a £1,000 in a casino.

Nevertheless, the £2 stake could be said to be evidence-based insofar as the evidence on FOBT expenditure in 2015/16 suggested that it would achieve the government's new goal of eliminating session losses of more than £1,000 on this particular gambling product. By the same token, a maximum stake of £16 or, more realistically, £30 would have been evidence-based if the goal of policy had been to achieve parity with B3 machines.

One of the criticisms of evidence-based policy is that evidence can be helpful in achieving a policy objective, but it cannot tell us what the objective should be. The FOBT campaign highlights that problem. Policy objectives can be dictated by political pressures which may have little relationship to evidence. The RGSB and Gambling Commission both mentioned public opinion in their reports, as did Tracey Crouch. And so, while a range of stake limits could have been justified by various policy objectives, it seems unlikely to be a coincidence that the government ultimately settled for the limit that had been the focus of a strong political and media campaign, despite the RGSB explicitly cautioning the government against doing so.

Since the government had never previously argued for regulation preventing gamblers losing more than £1,000 in a session, there was an element of the 'Texas sharpshooter' about its justification for the £2 stake in May 2018.[23] The agitation against FOBTs had been successful in rousing public concern, but there was little in the published literature to guide politicians to an evidence-based solution. In the absence of a coherent plan for setting the 'correct' stake limit, the government commissioned its arms-length agencies to come up with a plausible rationale. In effect, it was left to the Gambling Commission to identify the problem and find the evidence for a solution. The government accepted the logic of the Commission's proposals but tightened the criteria in such a way to allow the toughest – and most popular – course of action to be 'evidence-based'.

In contrast to the sugar tax and plain packaging campaigns, there was very little use of experiments. The exceptions were Parke et al. (2014) and Collins et al. (2016), the first of which was only cited once by the media while the latter was not cited at all.[24] There was no possibility of a natural experiment along the lines of the Mexican sugar tax because FOBTs were relatively new and were not widely used around the world. The kind of modelling used in the sugar tax and minimum pricing debates was possible but was only done in relation to FOBTs with regards to the economic impact of a stake reduction. On this issue, commissioned research from KPMG for the ABB went toe to toe with research commissioned from Landman Economics for the

[23] The mythical Texas sharpshooter fires a gun at a barn and then draws a target around the bullet holes.

[24] Commissioned by Bacta, Collins et al. (2016: 57) used a computer simulation and concluded that the FOBT stake limit should be cut to 'something closer to £10'. The RGSB report mentioned this study in its 2017 report, but unflatteringly. It found that it had 'serious methodological weakness' and said: 'We do not believe that any weight should be placed on its conclusions' (RGSB 2017: 30).

CFFG, and later with research commissioned from NERA and the CEBR by Bacta. The KPMG report predicted 21,000 job losses and the closure of half of Britain's betting shops whereas the research commissioned by the anti-FOBT coalition predicted a far milder impact on the industry and forecast benefits to the economy and the Treasury overall. The KPMG claims were widely quoted in the media despite the report on which it was based never being published (it was later leaked to the *Times*).

Figure 15 shows that evidence mentions in the media were more evenly spread than in the other case studies and that there were fewer of them, but although evidence was cited rarely in the news coverage and in the two parliamentary debates, there was no lack of media attention. On the contrary, the *Guardian*, *Mirror* and *Mail* groups published more than 100 FOBT-related articles each, but they focused on personal testimony, surveys and routine statistics. A *Guardian* editorial from May 2018 provides a typical example:

> The government's evidence is damning: in England, 13.6% of players of such machines are problem gamblers – the highest rate for any major gambling activity. Players are disproportionately likely to live in areas of high deprivation. And those who are unemployed are more likely to most often stake £100 than any other socioeconomic group. The buzz of gambling depends on uncertainty, but these machines have ensured two things: huge profits for the high street bookmakers that house them, and misery for a significant number of their users – and those gamblers' families. In a single

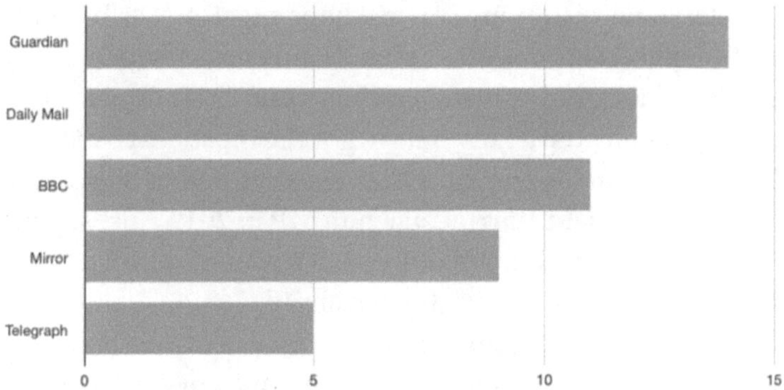

Figure 15. References to evidence by media outlet

> year, there were more than 233,000 cases of individual gamblers losing more than £1,000.[25]

The phrase 'crack cocaine of gambling' had been used about other forms of gambling in the past and was applied to FOBTs early in the campaign. It was almost invariably used in media reports thereafter. The amount of money players could theoretically lose also played a big part in the campaign. If a gambler played every 20 seconds at £100 a spin and lost every time, they would lose £18,000 in an hour. The ABB (2013: 21) argued that it would be impossible to load so much money into the machine in such a short space of time and that the odds of losing 180 times in a row were 11 million trillion to one, but the claim nevertheless underlined the possibility of large losses in a session.

[25] https://www.theguardian.com/commentisfree/2018/may/17/the-guardian-view-on-fixed-odds-betting-terminals-the-bookies-lose-at-last

Personal testimony was perhaps most powerful of all. Although sometimes dismissed as anecdotal evidence, the stories of former problem gamblers and their families had an impact on politicians. 'I have got the most heart-rending letters and emails and calls that I've ever had in 30 years of being an MP,' said Harriet Harman MP in 2012, 'just saying, "Please, do something about this. It's ruined my life, it's ruined my family, it's really dangerous."'[26]

The CFFG spokesman Matt Zarb-Cousin was himself a former problem gambler and he told his story to the press many times during the campaign. Journalists who reached out to problem gambling charities could mine a rich seam of human interest stories. All the newspapers in our analysis apart from the *Telegraph* were broadly supportive of the stake reduction, with the *Sunday People* and *Daily Mail* actively campaigning for it. They published numerous articles in which journalists visited betting shops, speaking to gamblers and 'gambling addicts'. Even on the more neutral BBC News website, headlines included 'I lost £40,000 on fixed odds machines' (2015); 'I lost £400k using high street betting machines' (2015); 'I've been turned into a hardened gambler' (2015); 'FOBT addict: "I spent month's wages in 30 mins"' (2016); 'Fixed-odds betting machines "ruined my life"' (2017); 'I lost £5,000 in 48 hours on fixed-odds betting machines' (2017) and 'I lost £250,000 on betting machines' (2018).

None of this proved that FOBTs were uniquely 'addictive'. Defenders of the status quo argued that it was possible to find problem gamblers losing large sums of money on any gambling product and yet no one in the FOBT debate

[26] https://www.dailymail.co.uk/news/article-2183830/Gambling-The-46bn-cost-Britains-roulette-machine-addiction.html

was proposing a ban on gambling *per se*. The question was whether there was something about FOBTs that made them exceptionally addictive and unusually harmful. It was this question, rather than the merits of the £2 stake policy specifically, that the campaign was fought over.

Various figures were cited to claim that rates of problem gambling among FOBT players were (or were not) higher than among players of other products. Analysis of data from the English and Scottish Health Surveys of 2012 found that 7.2% of those who played machines in bookmakers (the nearest proxy to a FOBT player) were problem gamblers. This was not the highest rate, however. Rates were higher among those who played on betting exchanges (10.6%), spread betting (20.9%), poker in pubs or clubs (13.2%), 'other events (not online)' (12.9%) and 'any other gambling' (9.8%) (Wardle et al. 2014b: 116). Analysis of the 2015 Health Surveys for England, Scotland and Wales told a similar story. Among FOBT players, the rate of problem gambling was 11.5%. This was the fifth highest, below poker in pubs and clubs, betting exchanges, spread betting and 'other events (not online)' Conolly et al. 2017: 45).

The surveys which produced these numbers were not designed to find causation between problem gambling and certain gambling products. A major confounding variable was the number of gambling activities engaged in by the individual. Problem gamblers tend to participate in multiple gambling activities. This explains why there is a high rate of problem gambling among people who play obscure games covered by the categories of 'other events (not online)' and 'any other gambling'. Casual gamblers do not typically seek out such games. It was possible that the same was true of FOBTs, but this important nuance tended to be ignored by politicians and the media during the campaign, while both sides marshalled evidence to show that FOBTs were or were not independent risk factors for problem gambling.

In the early stages of the campaign, the ABB relied on the findings of the 2013 triennial review which noted 'the lack of evidence on whether B2 gaming machines in themselves have had any significant effect on the level of problem gambling in Britain' (DCMS 2013: 22). They also cited a study by Williams et al. (2008) which found no clear link between FOBTs and problem gambling once frequency of play was taken into account. Later, they cited analysis from the Gambling Commission (2018a: 6) which found no independent association between problem gambling and any specific gambling product, including FOBTs. This was in contrast to the findings of the study by LaPlante (2011) which the CFFG often cited.

None of this was directly relevant to the question of whether a £2 stake limit was evidence-based. Even if it could be shown that FOBTs were more problematic than other forms of gambling, it would not necessarily require government action, let alone the £2 stake policy. The anti-FOBT coalition was certainly able to show that 'addiction' to FOBTs was damaging to some individuals, but very little evidence was produced to show that a £2 stake limit was the most appropriate policy response. Almost no evidence was cited in the two HoC debates, as Figure 13 shows. The claims of the anti-FOBT interest group were overwhelmingly focused on demonstrating that a problem existed. From this it was assumed – correctly, as it turned out – that policymakers would respond with the toughest measures on the table.

Box 1. Typical headlines

'Roulette machines: the crack cocaine of gambling' (*Guardian*, 2013)

'Gamblers spending nearly £1billion a week on "crack cocaine" gaming machines' (*Mirror*, 2016).

'Gambling watchdog calls for £30 upper limit on machines' (*Telegraph*, 2018)

'Gambling watchdog fails to curb fixed-odds betting stakes to £2' (*Guardian*, 2018)

'Punters would lose £500 a session under Gambling Commission's recommendation for fixed bet terminals' (*Mirror*, 2018)

'Fixed-odds betting terminal limit U-turn to save 120 lives' (*Mirror*, 2018)

'Campaigners blast Gambling Commission for allowing players to wager £30 a spin on "crack cocaine" fixed odds terminals instead of setting maximum stake at £2' (*Daily Mail*, 2018)

'Bookies brace for more than £200 m profit hit as Government caps "crack cocaine" betting machine stakes at £2' (*Telegraph* 2018)

Box 2. Excerpts from the House of Commons

According to the latest available data, across Great Britain 11.5% of players of gaming machines in bookmakers are found to be problem gamblers, and a further 32% are considered at risk of harm. In England, 13.6% of players of FOBTs are problem gamblers—the highest rate for any gambling activity. – Tracey Crouch (Con)

Last year, according to the NHS, record numbers of people were hospitalised through gambling addiction – Janet Daby (Lab)

FOBTs are not the most dangerous form of gambling; they are the fifth most dangerous. – Laurence Robertson (Con)

In particular, we note from gaming machine data that, of the 170,000 sessions on B2 roulette machines that ended with losses to the player of over £1,000, none involved average stakes of £2 or below, but losses of that scale still persist at stakes of £5 and £10. – Tracey Crouch (Con)

It has come to something when Members of this House, particularly those on the Labour benches, cheer when a decision is made that will put up to 20,000 decent working-class people out of their jobs when there is no evidence to do so. - Philip Davies (Con)

7 PACKAGES OF EVIDENCE

The quantitative analysis of evidence utilisation in the four case studies reveals a number of similarities. With the exception of the FOBT campaign, which was an outlier in several respects, they all relied on a body of evidence showing how the policy could work in theory, which was then followed by one or more studies suggesting that the policy had recently worked in another country. In the case of MUP and the sugar tax, the theoretical evidence was provided by modelling. In the case of plain packaging, it came from surveys asking individuals how they felt about images of plain packs. These studies illustrated how the policies could work and were subsequently reinforced by 'real world' evidence from Canada (MUP), Mexico (sugar tax) and Australia (plain packaging). The FOBT campaign relied on a weaker set of evidence, but the Gambling Commission used betting shop data to show how various stake limits might work in practice and there was an element of 'real world' evidence in the evaluation of the £50 soft limit reform of 2015.

Moreover, all four campaigns were supported by external reviews commissioned by the government and independent experts (the Chantler Review) or by quasi-independent, government agencies (Public Health England, the Gambling Commission). The Public Health

England alcohol review of 2016 came too late to make a difference to the campaign in England, but all the others were hugely influential.

Taken together, these amounted to *packages of evidence* consisting of a theoretical framework, real-world proof of concept and approval by independent experts, as shown in Table 1.

These packages of evidence were not necessarily presented as such to policymakers. They simply happen to be the most cited pieces of research in our analysis, suggesting that the media and politicians were most interested in them. The answer to the question of what type of evidence is most influential in this kind of policymaking is, in broad terms, a combination of theoretical research laying out the concept followed by 'real world' evidence and the endorsement of experts in a summary review. Apparent success in another country appeals to the *availability heuristic* while the official blessing of august institutions, peer-reviewed journals and respected academics appeals to *authority*. These can be useful heuristics for policymakers. It is

Table 1. Packages of evidence

	Theoretical	Real world	Expert opinion
Plain packaging	Stirling Review	Australia	Chantler Review
Sugar tax	Oxford Modelling	Mexico	Public Health England
Minimum pricing	Sheffield Modelling	Canada	Public Health England
FOBTs	Gambling Commission	£50 soft limit	Gambling Commission

reasonable for a politician to trust the advice of experts, and it is natural for them to ask what happened when the policy in question was introduced elsewhere. The packages of evidence help politicians answer three important questions:

How does this work in theory?
How has it worked in practice?
What do other people think?

Each of the four policy disputes produced 'superstar' studies which were cited far more than any other piece of research. All of them appeared to support the policy change, although less strongly in the case of FOBTs. In this chapter, we will review each of them.

Plain packaging

In theory: The Stirling Reviews

The Stirling Reviews covered a total of 54 studies, most of which involved surveys or focus groups in which people were asked how they felt about plain packs after being shown photos of them. Although there were some exceptions, these studies were largely consistent in finding that plain packs made people feel that the cigarettes were less attractive/appealing and made health warnings more noticeable/salient. Typical examples are White et al. (2012) which used an online survey of young Brazilian women and found that branded packs were rated as 'more appealing, better tasting, and smoother on the throat than plain packs' and Ford et al. (2013) in which academics, mostly from Stirling University, interviewed 11 to 16 year olds in their home and showed them photos of various cigarette packs and a mock-up of a plain pack. The plain pack was rated more negatively than the others and participants who were deemed susceptible to smoking tended to rate the novelty and brightly coloured packs more highly than the other packs.

The authors of the Stirling Review acknowledged the main shortcoming of this type of study:

> Many of the studies use hypothetical scenarios, and are therefore not truly able to test how individuals would react or behave if plain packaging was to be introduced. (Moodie et al. 2012: 89)

Given this limitation, the authors' conclusion that there was 'strong evidence to support the propositions set out in the Framework Convention on Tobacco Control relating to the role of plain packaging in helping to reduce smoking rates' seems overconfident (ibid.: v).

The Stirling Reviews were methodologically sound insofar as they accurately summarised the relevant evidence base, but they only addressed one question among many that faced policymakers. With the exception of a study which looked at retail transaction times, they all focused on consumer perceptions of plain packaging and public acceptability of the policy. None of them looked at potential unintended consequences, economic impacts or consumer surplus, and there was no cost-benefit analysis.

The Stirling Review was neither peer-reviewed nor published in a journal. Nor was it truly independent. Commissioned by the government, its lead author, Crawford Moodie, had been the co-author of five of the 37 documents cited and three other authors of the review had been involved with a further four studies. In 2009, Moodie had co-written an editorial for the *European Journal of Public Health* titled 'Plain packaging: a time for action' in which he said '[p]lain cigarette packaging then cannot come too soon' (Moodie and Hastings 2010: 10). It concluded as follows:

> A Philip Morris document, concerning issues of importance for the Worldwide Regulatory Affairs Group, emphasised that 'we don't want to see plain packaging introduced anywhere regardless of the size or importance of the market'. As [anti-smoking campaigner] Simon Chapman says, it is the industry's Armageddon. Bring it on.'

The co-author of that article was his Stirling University colleague Gerard Hastings, who also co-authored the Stirling Review. The article indicates that they were already committed to the policy in 2009 despite the limited evidence available at the time.

In practice: Wakefield et al. (2013)

Introduction effects of the Australian plain packaging policy on adult smokers: a cross-sectional study' by Melanie Wakefield et al. (2013) was cited in the media and HoC debates many more times than any other study. Based on a telephone survey of 536 smokers in Australia during the roll out of plain packaging in November 2012,[27] participants were asked if

[27] Plain packaged cigarettes began appearing on the shelves in October and it became illegal to sell conventional packs from 1 December.

they were currently buying cigarettes in plain or conventional packaging and were asked seven questions about their perceptions of smoking and smoking cessation. For example:

"'I'd like you to tell me if you think that now, your cigarettes are higher, lower or about the same in terms of a)'Quality' b) Satisfaction?'

"'On a scale of 1 to 10, where 1 is lowest and 10 is highest, how would you rate quitting as a priority in your life?'

Participants were also asked how much they smoked, which brand they smoked, how often they had tried to quit in the past and whether they had seen any of the three anti-smoking advertisements that were being 'broadcast on television as part of a national antismoking mass media campaign' (ibid.: 3).

The main findings from the study were that smokers who used plain packs perceived their cigarettes to be of lower quality than they were a year earlier, found them less satisfying than a year earlier, and were more likely to have thought about quitting in the past week. However, the second of these associations was not statistically significant after adjustment for confounders, and only the last association was statistically significant in the fully adjusted model (ibid.: 9).

The authors were inconsistent in describing the findings, sometimes incorrectly stating that an adjusted figure was an unadjusted figure (ibid.: 4). One statistically non-significant association was incorrectly described as significant (ibid.) and the authors implied that several other non-significant associations were meaningful, as follows:

> Compared with those who smoked fewer than five cigarettes/day, smokers of between 5 and 10 cigarettes a day (OR = 1.57, p = 0.098) *tended to*

> *be more likely* to be smoking from a plain pack.' (emphasis added) (ibid.: 4).
>
> '... plain pack smokers ... *trended towards* perceiving their cigarettes to be less satisfying than a year ago (OR = 1.70, p = 0.052).' (emphasis added) (ibid.)
>
> ... the effect sizes diminished further (lower quality OR = 1.32, p = .318; lower satisfaction OR = 1.36, p = 0.307) but remained *in the same direction*. (emphasis added) (ibid.: 7)
>
> Compared with branded pack smokers, smokers who were smoking from plain packs rated their cigarettes as being lower in quality and as *tending to be* less satisfying than 1 year ago.' (emphasis added) (ibid.)

This misleading language was also used in the abstract where the authors claimed that plain pack smokers 'tended to perceive their cigarettes as less satisfying than a year ago' (ibid.: 1). This association was not statistically significant in either of the adjusted models.

For reasons that were not explained, the authors only referred to the first adjusted model in the text and ignored the second model which adjusted for 'covariates, and proportion of sample smoking from a plain pack each week of the interview' (ibid.: 9). This allowed the authors to claim in the abstract that 'those smoking from plain packs perceived their cigarettes to be lower in quality (adjusted OR (AdjOR) = 1.66, p = 0.045)' (ibid.). In the fully adjusted model, this association was not statistically significant (OR = 1.41 (0.85 to 2.35), p = 0.187).

Adjusting for confounding variables was important because there were significant differences between the two groups of smokers at baseline. Respondents smoking from a plain pack, who made up 72.3% of the total, were more than twice as likely to have made a quit attempt in the past (OR = 2.61 (1.62–4.21), $p < 0.001$) and were less likely to smoke cheaper cigarettes. It is not clear why this should be, but it suggested that the smokers with the plain packs may have been less resistant to anti-smoking policies from the outset. The authors acknowledge that 'there may have been residual confounding, so that those less interested in quitting may have been more likely to avoid the plain packs' (ibid.: 8). If so, this was a significant limitation.

A further confounding variable (that could not be adjusted for) was the introduction of new, larger graphic warnings alongside plain packaging. Previous research had shown that the salience of health warnings 'wears out' over time and that 'there may be health promoting advantages in changing the health warnings from time to time' (Borland et al. 2009a: 362). If so, it was possible that the increased tendency to think about quitting was due to the change in the warnings rather than the abolition of branding. The authors acknowledge this, saying:

> Our study is not able to tease apart the independent contributions of plain packaging and the new larger health warnings, since they co-occurred. (Wakefield et al. 2013: 8)

The most obvious limitation of the study is that it was not clear whether cessation ideation would translate into cessation. Since it only involved smokers, anyone who had quit smoking as a direct result of plain packaging was absent from the cohort. The authors did not address this limitation directly, but they did point to two other studies suggesting that such a causal pathway could be assumed:

> The finding that smokers smoking from a plain pack evidenced more frequent thoughts about and priority for quitting than branded pack smokers is important, since frequency of thoughts about quitting has strong predictive validity in prospective studies for actually making a quit attempt. (ibid.)

The citations were Borland et al. (2009a) and Borland et al. (2009b). The first of these studies does not include any data on quit attempts and therefore does not support the authors' statement. The second study does not look at cessation ideation *per se*, although it gives some support to the authors' claim. It found that 'some reactions to warning labels have consistent and independent predictive power for the making of subsequent quit attempts, *but this does not appear to extend to predicting success of those attempts*' (emphasis added).

Overall, Wakefield et al. (2013) suffered from a number of weaknesses and there was substantial scope for residual confounding. Its only statistically significant finding, after full adjustment, was an increase in cessation ideation among plain pack smokers, but this may have been caused by the new warnings rather than the removal of branding, and the study was unable to show whether thoughts of quitting led to quit attempts, let alone to cessation. Although portrayed as 'real world' evidence of the efficacy of plain packaging, it did not measure the primary outcome (smoking cessation).

In practice: Australian smoking rates and tobacco sales

Although not among the 'superstar' studies, Australian data on tobacco consumption and smoking prevalence was cited relatively often after it was published in mid-2014 and is worth examining, especially given the UK government's stated interest in seeing how the policy had fared in Australia. The figures were open to interpretation. Proponents of plain packaging argued that in relative terms, the decline in overall smoking between 2010 and 2013 – shown in Figure 16 and taken from the Australian Institute of Health and Welfare (2014) – was 12.7%, the largest in the time series. Opponents argued that in absolute terms, the decline was an unexceptional 2.3 percentage points. Moreover, there seemed to be no decline among the target cohort of 12–17-year-olds. The survey found a statistically non-significant rise among this age group, from 2.5% to 3.4% between 2010 and 2013.

A major limitation was that the survey was carried out every three years and plain packaging had only been in place for the last 13 months of the 2010–13 period, making it impossible to know whether the long-term decline had accelerated after implementation, or even whether it had declined at all in 2013.

Tobacco sales data came from the Australian Bureau of Statistics (2014) and is shown in Figure 17. The decline in sales in the year starting December 2012 was 2.3%, smaller than the 4.4% decline the previous year. At the time, the

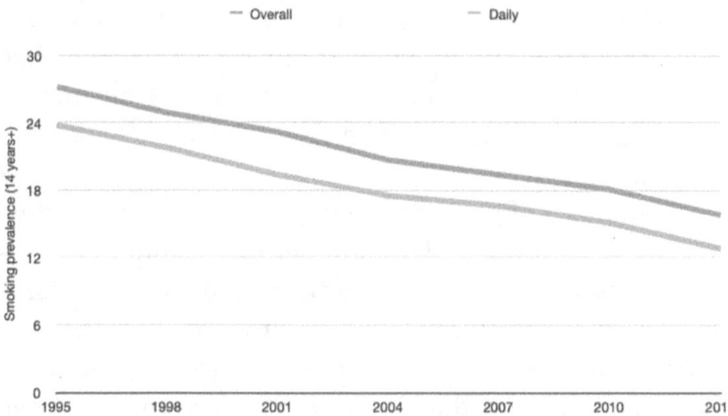

Figure 16. Daily and overall smoking prevalence in Australia 1995–2013

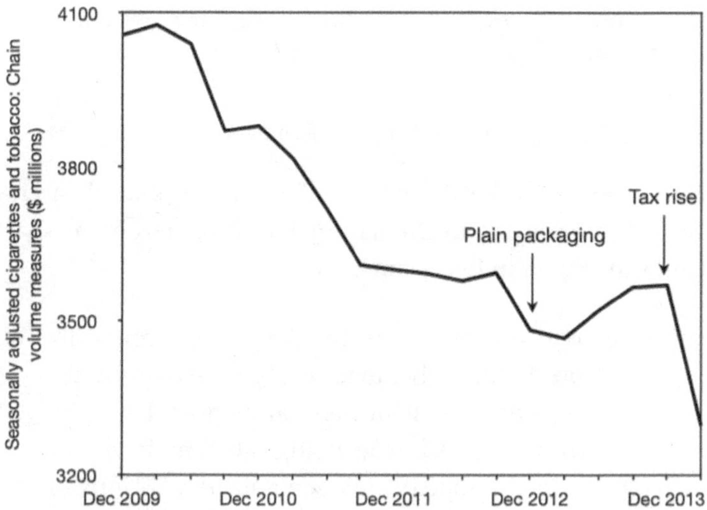

Figure 17. Seasonally adjusted tobacco sales in Australia: December 2009-March 2014 ($ millions)

Australian government said that sales had fallen by 3.4% in 2013, which was still in line with the secular trend, while Philip Morris International claimed – based on unpublished figures – that sales had risen by 0.3% (Daube and Chapman 2014).

Opponents of plain packaging argued that the decline in sales had slowed under plain packaging and that sales rose for three quarters before being reduced by a large (12.5%) tax rise in December 2013. Proponents of the policy argued that overall sales were lower in the year following implementation and that they were at record lows by March 2014. None of this evidence was remotely conclusive. Nothing in the data came close to proving that the decline in smoking prevalence accelerated after plain packaging was introduced and there was some evidence that cigarette sales rose in the immediate post-implementation period. However, policymakers may have found it reassuring that neither measure had risen by 2014.

Expert opinion: The Chantler Review

Conscious of the key limitation of conflating stated and revealed preferences in the survey-based research, Sir Cyril Chantler wrote in his review:

> I recognise that stated intentions are generally weak predictors of behaviour (regardless of whether the situation is hypothetical or not). I see the importance of Stirling as being the consistency of its results on appeal, salience and perceptions of harm, most notably that standardised packaging is less appealing than branded packaging. This

> evidence is direct and not reliant on stated intentions. Evidence from other spheres shows a strong non-conscious link between appeal and subsequent behaviour regardless of stated intentions. (Chantler 2014: 5)

He gives one citation for this: a meta-analysis by two psychologists, Webb and Sheeran (2006), titled 'Does Changing Behavioural Intentions Engender Behaviour Change? A Meta-Analysis of the Experimental Evidence.' The reference is puzzling because, as its title suggests, the study is about intentions, not appeal. The article does not mention the word 'appeal' at all. However, the citation cannot be a mistake because he uses it in a footnote when making the same point later in the text (Chantler 2014: 29).

The meta-analysis concluded that 'a medium-to-large change in intention (d = 0.66) leads to a small-to-medium change in behaviour (d = 0.36)' (Webb and Sheeran 2006: 249). However, this was not generally true in the case of the three studies pertaining to smoking in the meta-analysis. The first found that a smoking prevention programme 'had neither a significant effect ($p > 0.01$) on intention to smoke nor on smoking behaviour' (Chatrou et al. 1999). The second, which also looked at a smoking prevention programme, found evidence of 'changes in knowledge, attitudes, and behavioural intention, but not in social influence variables or behaviours' (D'Onofrio et al. 2002). The third used RCTs in which groups of smokers were shown videos highlighting the dangers of smoking, with the control group watching a film unrelated to smoking. In one experiment, those who watched the anti-smoking video were more likely to try to stop smoking and more likely to succeed. In the other experiment, neither effect was seen (Sutton and Hallett 1988).

Webb and Sheeran's discussion of the evidence further suggests that the relationship between intentions and behaviour is likely to be weak in the case of risky and habitual behaviour such as smoking. Referencing other studies, they note that 'when behaviour is practiced repeatedly and the context of performance is stable, past behaviour is a better predictor of future behaviour than is intention'. Moreover, 'intentions were only significantly related to behaviour when habit strength was weak. When participants possessed moderate or strong habits, their intentions had little influence on their subsequent behaviour' (Webb and Sheeran 2006: 252).

In any case, very few of the studies in the Stirling Reviews looked at intentions. Of the 17 studies in the second version of the review, none asked nonsmokers if plain packaging made them less likely to start smoking. Only one (Wakefield et al. 2013) asked smokers if they were planning to quit but there was no statistically significant difference between users of plain packs and users of branded packs on this measure.[28] Most of the studies focused on perceptions, attitudes and opinions. Chantler argued that these studies showed that plain packaging was less appealing, and this was obviously true, but they did not show that this led to behaviour change, and the meta-analysis Chantler cited does not support his claim that there is 'a strong

[28] Those smoking from plain packs were more likely to say that they had thought about quitting in the last week but were not significantly more likely to be planning to quit in the next 30 days or the next six months (in the adjusted models).

non-conscious link between appeal and subsequent behaviour' (Chantler 2014: 5).

Chantler argues that there is 'a causal pathway between concepts such as appeal and behaviour' (Chantler 2014: 30), citing two studies about food and alcohol advertising which are only tenuously related to packaging, and two studies about behavioural cues. The first of these is a meta-analysis about attitudinal bias (defined as 'the observation that substance-related cues tend to grab the attention of experienced substance users' (Field et al. 2009: 1)). It found that the correlation between substance-related cues and substance craving was statistically significant but 'very small (r = .19)' and was 'significantly larger for craving for illicit substances and caffeine than for craving for alcohol and tobacco' (ibid.: 20). The second study was a meta-analysis looking specifically at smoking cue reactivity which found that smoking cues activate certain areas of the brain. These studies were relevant to Chantler insofar as he seems to have assumed that conventional packs, but not plain packs, provided a behavioural cue to smoke. However, since none of the studies looked at packaging, and conventional cigarette packs in the UK already had large graphic warnings designed to deter smoking, this was debatable.

Finally, he mentions that 'emerging evidence from Australian studies show outcomes that support likelihood of behaviour change, including increased calls to quitting helplines, hiding packs in social situations, smoking less around others, and smoking fewer cigarettes overall' (Chantler 2014: 30). The findings related to the Quitline and hiding packs came from Young et al. (2014) and

Zacher et al. (2014)[29] respectively. While these findings might imply that plain packs are less appealing, Chantler does not give a reference for the more important claim that plain packaging was associated with smokers consuming fewer cigarettes. None of the studies in the Stirling Review looked for evidence of this and a subsequent study found no such association (Maynard et al. 2015).

Chantler claimed in his review that criticism of the survey-based and Australian studies from the industry rarely went beyond limitations mentioned by the researchers. While this was sometimes true, those limitations were often important. In the case of the Quitline study, the authors acknowledged their 'inability to differentiate the impact of the increased size of graphic health warnings that happened simultaneously with tobacco plain packaging from the impact of plain packaging itself' (Young et al. 2014: 32). The same study showed that the introduction of graphic warnings several years earlier had coincided with far more calls to the Quitline. On the other hand, the authors argue plausibly that the abolition of branding may have made the Quitline number more prominent on the pack and they attempted to control for exogenous variables, such as anti-smoking advertising campaigns.

The evidence that plain packs were less appealing was clearly strong and Chantler seems to have been impressed by the 'real world' evidence from Australia, such as the Quitline study and Wakefield et al (2013). Aside from some inconclusive and contradictory figures pertaining to tobacco sales in Australia, Chantler had no hard data to work with. He chose to ignore the only study that had looked

[29] Chantler mistakenly names Wakefield as the lead author of the Zacher study (Chantler 2014: 24).

at the impact of plain packaging on smoking prevalence (Kaul and Wolf 2014). Chantler's team met with Kaul and Wolf, but he did not mention their research in his report.[30]

Although not required to look at the illicit trade issue, Chantler dismissed the KPMG report which claimed that Australia had a large and growing black market in tobacco as 'flawed' (Chantler 2014: 33) and said that he was 'not convinced by the tobacco industry's argument that standardised packaging would increase the illicit market' (ibid.: 37). Chantler cited data from the Australian Customs and Border Protection Service which he said 'shows no significant effect on illicit tobacco following the introduction of plain packaging' (ibid.: 33), but that data shows a rise in the number of detections from 45 to 76 between 2011/12 and 2012/13 and a rise in the number of cigarettes seized, from 141 million to 200 million (Australian Customs and Border Protection Service 2013: 91). While causality cannot be proven and increased detection may have been due to better enforcement, these figures are at least consistent with the claim of plain pack opponents that the policy could fuel the black market.

Sugar tax

In theory: Briggs et al. (2013)

The much-cited modelling study by Briggs et al. looked at the potential impact of a 20 % sales tax on sugary drinks. The authors, who included an economist and several known

[30] Kaul and Wolf put a 27 page transcription of this meeting online: https://web.archive.org/web/20150321052425/http://www.ipe-saarland.de/english/news/

advocates of sugar taxes, were frank about the strengths and weaknesses of their study and put their work in the context of the existing literature. The crucial variables were the own-price and cross-price elasticities for beverages and the effect of changes in calorie intake on body weight. Although it is not clear which studies were used to provide the price elasticity estimates, the own-price elasticities for sugary drinks were in line with estimates from the economics literature (at around –0.8 to –0.9). The authors assumed some substitution towards other beverages but no substitution towards food.

The impact on body weight was relatively simple to calculate, as the authors noted, using an established model 'based on the second law of thermodynamics' (Briggs et al. 2013: 3). Estimates were produced for three adult age groups and three income groups. The model projected that the youngest age group (16–29-year-olds) would experience the largest decline in calorie consumption. Declines in sugary drink consumption were similar across all income groups and were relatively large (15% overall). This was projected to result in a 1.3% decline in obesity among UK adults, with the largest declines among the youngest age group (7.6%) and the highest income group (2.1%). No statistically significant impact was projected for people aged 50 or over and no timeframe was given for any of the projections.

Sugar tax revenue was projected to be £276 million per annum. The authors carried out a sensitivity analysis looking at the impact of a 10% tax and found that the impacts would be roughly halved, with a 0.6% reduction in obesity and revenues of £139 million per annum.

Modelling is inherently uncertain and some assumptions in this study turned out to be wrong, such as the expectation that there would be a pass-through rate of the tax of 100% (Scarborough et al. (2020) later found that it was much lower). A universal flaw in sugar tax modelling at this time was an under-appreciation of the extent to which consumers choose lower quality over lower quantity when faced with price rises. Subsequent research has concluded that the own-price quantity demand for sugary drinks in Mexico is four times more elastic than assumed in sugar tax models (Andalón and Gibson 2017; Gibson and Kim 2019).

Briggs et al. did not model health effects or healthcare savings, but the dynamic model of weight loss used in the study was the best available, accounting for physiological adaptation and changes in energy expenditure. It was even possible that the model may have underestimated both the impact on obesity and the cost to consumers since it used self-reported sugary drink consumption figures which were nearly four times lower than those derived from sales data (Briggs et al. 2013: 5).

One limitation of the study is that it did not model the effects on light, moderate and heavy consumers. The authors acknowledge that '[s]ome evidence suggests that high consumers are less price sensitive than low consumers' (ibid.: 5) but did not elaborate on the implications of this. If heavy consumers are less price sensitive, the model would overestimate the impact on obesity, particularly if obesity rates were highest among heavy consumers. The model also did not adjust for the heterogeneity of consumer behaviour. Subsequent research has found that taxes on food and soft drinks have less effect on consumers who have low self-control (Schmacker and Smed 2023). In the context of the childhood obesity strategy, a further limitation of the study is that it did not model the impact on children.

In practice: Colchero et al. (2016a)

By far the most heavily cited piece of evidence in the sugar tax debate was the data from Mexico which first appeared in a press release in 2015[31] and then in the *British Medical Journal* in January 2016. Its main finding was:

> Relative to the counterfactual in 2014, purchases of taxed beverages decreased by an average of 6% (−12 ml/capita/day) and decreased at an increasing rate up to a 12% decline by December 2014. (Colchero et al. 2016a: 1)

Although described as an observational study, the use of a counterfactual required some modelling and therefore some assumptions. The authors say that 'it was not possible to construct a true experimental design' (ibid.: 3) and do not seem to have considered using a neighbouring country as a control. Instead, they extrapolated daily per capita consumption from Nielsen sales data between 2012 and 2014. Trends in 2014 were compared to a counterfactual based on pre-existing sales trends which adjusted for seasonality and socioeconomic factors such as unemployment. Shown on a graph, sales of taxed beverages can be seen gradually falling before the tax was introduced and falling more steeply than the counterfactual in 2014, with the gap widening as the year went on.

[31] An earlier press release in 2014 claimed there had been a 10% decline in the taxed drinks in the first three months of the tax, but this was not picked up by the media. https://web.archive.org/web/20141101202249/https://www.insp.mx/epppo/blog/preliminares-bebidas-azucaradas.html

The authors acknowledge that causation could not be proven and note that the sugar tax coincided with 'health campaigns about sugar-sweetened beverages' and 'anti-obesity programs' which may have affected sales (ibid.: 6). And while they had figures for milk sales, they do not seem to have had figures for milkshakes, which were not taxed and may have been a substitute for carbonated drinks. Alcohol sales were also not included.

The study did not look at overall calorie consumption or obesity and therefore was limited in what it could conclude about the sugar tax as an anti-obesity measure. The authors estimated that over the course of 2014, the average Mexican's sugary drink consumption was 12ml/day less than it would have been in the absence of the tax and consumption of untaxed beverages was 37ml/day higher. The authors say that most of the rise in untaxed beverages came from bottled water, but even if there was no substitution to any caloric drinks and no other behavioural change, it would imply a drop in daily energy consumption of around five calories, arguably a trivial decline.

Expert opinion: Public Health England review

Annexe 2 of the PHE report *Sugar Reduction: the Evidence for Action* used a proscriptive methodology, focusing on experimental studies which mostly involved food rather than soft drinks. These studies were generally of a high calibre and showed the expected inverse relationship between price and sales, but they did not look at substitution effects, which were known to be an issue (e.g. Fletcher et al. 2014), nor did they look at the impact on overall calorie consumption and body weight.

Important evidence was overlooked in the PHE review. Several studies had looked at the impact of sugary drink taxes on body weight, mostly in the USA, and found little or no effect. A common finding was that consumers substituted taxed beverages for untaxed sugary beverages such as fruit juice and milkshakes. A systematic review by Maniadakis et al. (2013: 519) concluded:

> Price increase may lead to a reduction in consumption of the targeted products, but the subsequent effect on caloric intake may be much smaller. Only a limited number of the identified studies reported weight outcomes, most of which are either insignificant or very small in magnitude to make any improvement in public health... The effectiveness of a taxation policy to curb obesity is doubtful...

This evidence was directly relevant to the question at hand, but it was only briefly mentioned in Annexe 2 of the PHE report, where it was effectively dismissed with the vague, generic criticism that 'analyses of this kind are subject to a range of potential confounders and biases' (Public Health England 2015b: 18). The Maniadakis review only appears as an endnote in the Annexe and was ignored altogether in the main report. This body of research was not mentioned in any of the other major documents and was never referenced by the media or in the HoC debates.

In the PHE literature review, 'real world' case studies were not included because of a lack of robust evaluation and modelling studies were only used as 'background material'. Despite these self-imposed restrictions, the Annexe includes a strong claim based on 'real world' evidence near the start of the executive summary:

> Sales data from Norway, Finland, Hungary, France and Mexico broadly suggests decreases in purchases of soft drinks/sugar sweetened drinks (SSDs) of up to 12%, following the implementation of taxes. (ibid.: 5)

The report itself argued for a sugar tax 'based on the emerging evidence of the impact of such measures in other countries' (Public Health England 2015a: 8), adding that it was 'supported by a number of economic modelling studies' (ibid.: 17). In words that would be echoed several times in the HoC, PHE stated:

> Data on the effectiveness of these measures, while not always robustly evaluated, suggests that reductions in sales have been seen as a result of the imposition of taxes in Norway, Finland, Hungary, France and Mexico. (ibid.: 23)

Similar claims were made several times in the HoC debates, but a close reading of Annexe 2 shows how little robust evaluation was behind them. The evidence for a reduction in sales in Mexico came from a press release, the evidence from France came from an unreferenced simulation and the evidence from Finland came from 'unofficial reports'. For Norway, the Annexe cites a WHO report which in turn cites a study that observed a shift from sugary drinks to diet drinks among Norwegian children and attributed it to a package of measures which included a sugar tax (Public Health England 2015b: 16–17).

The Annexe cites a report from the pressure group Sustain as evidence for the striking claim that 'sales of products subject to the [Hungarian food and drink] tax have fallen by 27% with an observed reduction in consumption of 20% to 35%' (Public Health England 2015b: 16). The Sustain report cites a report from the Hungarian National Institute for Health Promotion (2013) which PHE (or Sustain) had fundamentally misunderstood. It showed that 26–35% of people who consumed products subject to the tax said they had 'changed their consumption habits in a favourable direction' (ibid.: 9). This is very different to a decline in *consumption* of 20–35%, which would be implausibly large.

In contrast to the exhaustive Stirling Reviews, the PHE sugar review took a narrow view of the evidence, focusing on experimental studies while ignoring and dismissing the only studies that looked at the relationship between sugary drink taxation, calorie consumption and body weight. Although the evidence review in Annexe 2 claimed that there was very little robust, peer-reviewed evidence from other countries, such evidence did exist (notably from the USA), and it made a sweeping claim about sugar taxes in a number of countries which was based on weak evidence, secondhand sources and misinterpretations.

Minimum pricing

In theory: The Sheffield studies

The Sheffield model was overwhelmingly the most cited evidence in the media and in the HoC during the campaign for minimum pricing. The Scottish Impact Assessment published in March 2018 cited the Sheffield model dozens of times (Scottish Government 2018). The model underpinned almost every aspect of the Impact Assessment, not just in relation to health but also to crime, employment, tax revenue and consumer expenditure. To a large extent, the Sheffield model *was* the Impact Assessment, just as it had been in Westminster a few years earlier. The only other academics to be heavily referenced in the document were Tim Stockwell's team in Canada, whose studies were cited ten times (ibid.: 10, 42).

The model itself was complex and highly detailed. The first Sheffield report (Brennan 2008) ran to 217 pages and including dozens of tables covering a broad range of outcomes, including hospitalisations, mortality, crime, unemployment and workplace absences. Some of these outcomes were dropped in subsequent reports but every report looked at the impact of a range of minimum prices on hospitalisations and deaths, with the putative benefits monetised.

Like Briggs et al.'s sugar tax model, the MUP model combined econometrics with epidemiology. Its cornerstone was an estimate of own-price and cross-price elasticities for a range of drinks. Unlike Briggs, the Sheffield team used different price elasticities for moderate and heavy consumers. Cross-price elasticities were particularly important since MUP was expected to drive consumers away from the most heavily affected drinks, such as strong cider, towards substitutes. But although the impact on the rest of the market resulting from a price rise on one product could be observed from historic sales data, there was no precedent for a floor price affecting every product simultaneously. Under MUP, the price of all drinks at the bottom of the market would become the same (on a per unit basis) while prices in the upper and mid-market would not rise at all. The Sheffield model was therefore inherently more speculative than a model projecting the substitution effects of a price rise on a single product or – as with the sugar tax model – on a single category.

Even if the process had been simpler in theory, all price elasticity estimates derived from sales data are specific to a certain time and place and are not necessarily transferrable to other countries in a different year. A literature review by Manning et al. (1995: 125) found that own-price elasticity estimates ranged from –0.80 to –2.0 for spirits, from –0.64 to –1.0 for wine and from –0.25 to +0.24 for beer. This is an extremely wide spread and models based on such data will produce very different results depending on whether they use estimates from the top, bottom or middle of these ranges.

Manning et al. (1995: 141) found that heavy drinkers were less price sensitive than moderate drinkers and that for the heaviest 5% of drinkers 'estimated price elasticity is not statistically different from zero.' This finding, which has been reported elsewhere and might strike the reader as being no more than common sense, was highly relevant to the issue of MUP since the policy was promoted as an intervention that targeted heavy drinkers. If price rises had little effect on these consumers, MUP would largely fail to achieve its objective. This was underlined in a 2018 study which, using quantile regression methods, found that 'heavy drinkers are much less responsive to price in terms of quantity' and noted that:

> If harmful drinkers were less price responsive than moderate drinkers, then the effects predicted in

> the [Sheffield] modelling work will be incorrect. Since the marginal health and social harms are assumed to be increasing with consumption, the modelling work will thus overstate the health and social harm reduction of minimum unit pricing. (Pryce et al. 2018: 439–40)

The Sheffield model was based on the assumption that heavy drinkers were *more* price responsive than average. While acknowledging Manning et al.'s findings and accepting that a large meta-analysis had found heavy drinkers to be less price sensitive, they noted that their own estimates showed 'own-price elasticity magnitudes increasing with mean quantity of alcohol consumed' (Brennan et al. 2008: 51). And so, for example, a moderate drinker had an own-price elasticity for off-trade spirits of around −0.52 in their model while the equivalent figure for a 'harmful' drinker was around −0.67. Although the authors suggested that this was partly due to heavy drinkers 'showing the greatest level of substitution behaviour', it was a significant departure from the literature and, if incorrect, would exaggerate the benefits of MUP.

A similar issue related to high-strength cider, which was often mentioned in the context of MUP because it tended to be the cheapest form of alcohol on a per-unit basis and was associated in the public's mind with alcoholism and street drinking. As advocates of MUP often noted, the price of strong 'white' cider would increase enormously at 45p or 50p per unit. However, the Sheffield research did not specifically model the impact of MUP on drinkers of strong cider. In its elasticity estimates, all cider was put in the same category as beer. In effect, consumers of strong white cider were assumed to have the same price elasticity as consumers of cask beer or mid-strength cider. In the model, a heavy consumer of off-trade white cider was assumed to have an own-price elasticity of around −0.62 while the equivalent figure for a moderate consumer of off-trade mid-strength cider was around −0.42. In a separate analysis published in 2014, the Sheffield academics concluded that demand for off-trade cider was more elastic than for any other drink (−1.268) (Meng et al. 2014). There was nothing to directly contradict this in the economics literature since the price elasticity of cider had hitherto been virtually ignored, but it seemed counterintuitive that the alcoholic beverage most associated with harmful and dependent drinking had the least inelastic demand, especially since the authors' estimates also suggested that drinkers of cider were unlikely to switch to other alcohol products if the price rose.[32] At the least, traditional cider and white cider should have been grouped separately.

Other flaws in the model were identified by the statistician John Duffy (2013) who, writing in *Significance,* argued that economic data and risk functions from other countries were inappropriately applied to Scotland and that since the model's estimates included no confidence intervals or standard errors, it was difficult to know whether the putative benefits of MUP were statistically significant. He also claimed that despite the extensive data shown in the Sheffield reports, 'there is in general not enough information to rerun parts of the model' (ibid.: 26).

Many of the problems with the model were not the fault of the modellers. The data required to make reliable

[32] An estimate from HMRC subsequently indicated that demand for off-trade cider was inelastic (−0.74) (Sousa 2014: 19).

projections about an untested policy simply did not exist. However, it is notable that the more questionable assumptions fed into the model, particularly with regards to price elasticity, were more likely to exaggerate the benefits than understate them.

It was unrealistic to expect politicians to assess the pros and cons of a complex computer model and since nobody attempted (or was able) to independently rerun the model and no alternative modelling was commissioned, much depended on the credibility of the Sheffield researchers. One reason why Scotland's Health and Sport Committee had faith in the Sheffield team was their track record, specifically their apparently accurate prediction of how Scotland's 2011 ban on multi-buy discounts on alcohol would affect sales. Giving evidence to the committee, SARG's Alan Brennan said:

> There was an 8% reduction in beer sales, a 5% reduction in wine sales and a 3% reduction in spirit sales ... I am not claiming that such a level of accuracy of the model will happen on every parameter, but I was interested to find that our report on the effects of a total discount ban talked about an 8% reduction in beer sales ... a 6.1% reduction in wine sales ... and a 2.7% reduction in spirit sales. (Scottish Parliament 2012: 10, paragraph 47).

Evidently impressed, the committee concluded:

> In its prevailing view, on balance, given the detailed evidence provided by those involved in preparing the modelling and, in particular, the

> reliability demonstrated by the analysis of the discount ban (as highlighted in paragraph 47 above), the Committee is persuaded of the value and reliability of the Sheffield work. (ibid.: 11)

However, evidence subsequently emerged to suggest that the discount sales ban had no such impact on alcohol sales. A study published in 2013 concluded that 'the ban on multi-buys in Scotland has failed to impact upon the volume of alcohol purchased' because 'retailers appear to have responded by simply replacing multi-buys with simple price reduction' (Nakamura et al. 2013: 562, 565). This echoed the findings of the official evaluation of the policy by NHS Scotland which concluded that:

> During the 52-week period before the introduction of the ban, the volume of pure alcohol sold off-trade per adult in Scotland was similar to the previous 52-week period. (Curnock et al. 2012: 1)

Both of these studies used England and Wales as control groups and found little or no contrast with the Scottish experience post-implementation.

In a further projection that went unnoticed by both sides of the MUP debate, one iteration of the Sheffield model claimed that reducing the drink-driving limit from 80mg/100ml to 50mg/100ml 'would reduce fatalities by 6.4% and injuries by 1.4% in the first year after its implementation' (Rafia and Brennan 2010: 5). Although this projection was specific to England and Wales, it was reasonable to assume a similar effect in Scotland (the model itself was based on data from Australia), but after Scotland reduced the drink-driving limit to 50mg/100ml in 2014, a study in the *Lancet* found no reduction in road traffic accidents over the next two years and an increase in such accidents compared to a counterfactual (Haghpanahan et al. 2019). Similarly, a study in the *Journal of Health Economics* concluded that the change 'had no effect on drink driving and road collisions' (Francesconi and James 2021).

Further questions about the Sheffield model emerged in September 2012 when BBC *Panorama* commissioned the team to project how many deaths among pensioners would be prevented by the introduction of a 50p minimum price. Their answer, based on modelling, was 5,000 per annum or 'nearly 50,000' over ten years. This statistic formed the basis of a *Panorama* episode titled *Old, Drunk and Disorderly?* but was implausible from the outset since the most recent Sheffield model for England had estimated that a 50p floor price would only prevent 2,930 deaths per annum across the entire population (Purshouse et al. 2010: 1,357).

After a complaint from a viewer, the BBC withdrew the 50,000 figure and re-edited the programme for the iPlayer with a new figure of 11,500, offering the following explanation:

> The School of Health and Related Research at the University of Sheffield has confirmed to Panorama that unfortunately, due to human error, figures they produced specifically for the programme *Old, Drunk and Disorderly?* broadcast on 10th September 2012 were incorrect. The figures are in fact 4–5 times lower than those originally given to Panorama. The University emphasised the human error was wholly on their part and

> has apologised unreservedly to the BBC. The programme was temporarily removed from iPlayer and re-edited to reflect the correct figures.[33]

While there was no suggestion of deliberate wrongdoing by the Sheffield researchers, their failure to spot an error of this magnitude, despite working with the model for several years, was surprising. Since faith in the model depended on the statistical prowess and good judgement of the modellers, it underlined the risks of relying so heavily on one team of researchers.

In practice: The Canadian experience – Zhao et al (2013)

Tim Stockwell and colleagues at the Centre for Addictions Research of British Columbia produced four studies about minimum pricing during the campaign, of which Zhao et al (2013) was the most heavily cited in the media and HoC.

The main claim of Zhao et al. (2013: 1,059) was that a 10% increase in the average minimum price for alcohol in British Columbia was associated with a 31.72% reduction in alcohol-specific deaths. This claim was made explicitly in the abstract and the media understandably inferred that (a) minimum prices had risen by 10% in the province, and (b) the number of alcohol-specific deaths fell by 31.72%.

This is not what happened, however. Aside from the fact that British Columbia had a system of 'social referencing pricing' which required a floor price for various alcoholic beverages but did not set a minimum price for a unit of alcohol, the authors use a complex model to estimate

[33] https://www.bbc.co.uk/programmes/b01mrmfd

the impact of a 1% increase in the floor price after adjusting for a large number of variables. They assume that the health benefits rise in a linear fashion and, therefore, that a 10% increase will produce ten times as many benefits as a 1% increase. By logical, though implausible, extension of their findings, a 40% increase would eliminate all alcohol-specific deaths.

Between 2004 and 2009, there was a series of increases in the floor price of alcoholic beverages. The minimum price of a litre of spirits rose from $25.91 to $30.66, with increases in 2004, 2006, 2008 and 2009. The minimum price of a litre of packaged beer rose from $3.00 to $3.54. And the minimum price of a litre of draft beer rose from $2.05 to $2.22 (ibid.: 1,060). The increases for beer took place in 2006 and 2008.

This resulted in nominal price rises of 18.3% (spirits), 18% (packaged beer) and 8.3% (draft beer). Over the same period, general prices, as measured by inflation, rose by 9.1%. It is not clear whether the authors controlled for inflation, but in real terms the minimum price of spirits and packaged beer rose by around 8–9%.

The main problem with the study was that it was very difficult to reconcile its findings with the mortality data from British Columbia. Figures published by the Centre for Addictions Research of BC (2013) show that there was a generally rising trend in alcohol-related deaths in this period, albeit with a drop in 2009, as Figure 18 shows.

Zhao et al. use data from 2002 and 2009. Since most of the authors worked at the Centre for Addictions Research of BC, it is puzzling that they did not also use the figures from 2010 and 2011 which must have been available to them. Two of the authors – Tim Stockwell and Kate

Figure 18. Wholly alcohol-attributable deaths, British Columbia 2002–2011

Vallance – co-authored a report in 2013 based on data from 2002 to 2011 which noted that 'rates of hospitalizations in BC for conditions related to alcohol have shown a significant increase since 2002, reflecting an overall increase in alcohol consumption in the province' (Thompson et al. 2013: 2).

Although the study makes estimates based on the number of deaths, the mortality *rate* is arguably the more relevant metric, but population growth does not explain the rise in the number of alcohol-specific deaths in BC. Between 2002 and 2009, the population grew by 7% whereas the number of deaths rose by 23%. Moreover, the 2009 figure is unusually low, possibly because the financial crisis made alcohol less affordable to some people (an exogenous factor not mentioned by the authors). At any rate, by 2011 the number of deaths was 41% higher than it had been in 2002.

The authors claim that a '10% increase in minimum price for spirits and liqueurs was estimated to be associated with an immediate 35.25% reduction in rate [sic] of wholly AA [alcohol-attributable] deaths' (Zhao et al. 2013: 1,064). This would be a remarkably large effect if true, but there is no sign of it in the publicly available data. A more precise claim would be that the number of alcohol-specific deaths *would have been* X% higher in the absence of an increase in the minimum price. Whilst this is possible, it is untestable in practice and would require substantial countervailing factors pushing up the mortality rate for it to be plausible in theory.

Full analysis of the model is impossible without the details of the inputs. There are several reasons why its findings may not have been transferrable to the UK (e.g. the pricing system did not put a price on a unit of alcohol, alcohol retail in BC was largely a state monopoly, the minimum pricing system had been in place for years), but the important point is that the key finding was based on a model rather than on direct observation, and what the model purported to show was very different from what those who cited it believed it had shown. The model estimated that a 1% rise in the average minimum price of alcoholic beverages was associated with a 3.172% decline in alcohol-specific mortality. This was multiplied by ten to produce the headline statistic but, as Stockwell's team later said, 'We could equally well have said that a 10% *decrease* in minimum price would be associated with a 32% *increase* in wholly alcohol-related deaths' (emphasis in the original) (Stockwell et al. 2013: 1,172). It was an estimate rather than an observation.

As Mellor and Green (2023: 1,475) said of a similar public health study based on a contentious counterfactual, 'presenting modelled data as actual cases is not only overstating the value of the work, but when explained to the public, it can undermine public confidence in health messages ... when modelled data are presented, it needs to be clear that the data are modelled and not actually measured cases'. In this instance, the distinction was far from clear and many people, quite understandably, inferred that there had been a 31.72% decline in alcohol-related deaths following a 10% increase in the minimum price. For example, Dr Vivienne Nathanson of the British Medical Association, said in 2013:

> Real-life experience of minimum pricing in Canada has shown some tremendous results – with a 10% increase in the price of cheapest drinks leading to a 32% reduction in wholly alcohol-related deaths.[34]

In an op-ed for the *Telegraph*, Alastair Campbell wrote:

> Where minimum unit pricing has been tried in British Columbia, a 10% price increase led to a one-third fall in deaths attributed to alcohol.[35]

This impression was fostered by the study's abstract and a press release titled 'Drop in alcohol-related deaths by nearly a third follows minimum alcohol price increase of 10

[34] https://www.theguardian.com/society/2013/jul/17/minimum-unit-price-alcohol-shelved

[35] https://www.telegraph.co.uk/news/health/10309607/Britain-has-a-drinking-problem-and-it-needs-help.html

percent'. Although it was taken to be 'real world' evidence, closer examination shows that it owed more to assumptive modelling, which is inherently more subjective and less reliable.

Expert opinion: Public Health England

The 2016 PHE report on alcohol was cited much less often than the expert reviews in the other cases. By the time it was published, the Scottish government had long been committed to MUP and the Westminster government had effectively ditched the idea, although officially it was still under review.

The report was about alcohol policy in general, but it spent several pages discussing MUP. It mostly repeated the findings of the Sheffield and Canadian research, which PHE took at face value, and was keen to address one of the objections of the Westminster government by providing evidence that moderate drinkers would be 'minimally affected by a 60 pence MUP' (Public Health England 2016: 91).

FOBTs

In a campaign that lacked much direct evidence about the impact of a stake limit reduction on FOBTs, reports from two of the government's arm's length organisations stood out. Neither of them was peer-reviewed and both arrived late in the day, but they provided a framework for setting policy and a justification for action. When DCMS (2018) announced the new regulations, it referred to both reports but introduced a crucial new rationale of its own.

In theory: Gambling Commission (2018a)

The main contribution of this report was its interpretation of newly released raw data on gambling expenditure on B2 and B3 machines, as described in the previous chapter. The principle was relatively simple. Based on the spin time and odds of the two machines, it was easy to calculate the potential average losses at different stake levels. The Commission looked at a nine-minute session because that was the average time of a session according to industry data. Having implicitly accepted B3 machine losses to be acceptable, the Commission sought to see how high the stakes could go on B2 machines before losses exceeded those from B3 machines. The only question was whether to use average session losses or maximum potential session losses as the test. If it was the former, the appropriate stake limit on FOBTs was around £50. If the latter, it was around £16. The logic behind this calculation was justifiable and the simple mathematics were correct, although a major flaw in the research was that it paid little attention to the possibility that session times would lengthen if stakes were reduced, thereby increasing the scale of potential losses.

In practice: DCMS (2016)

As discussed in Chapter 6, this report looked at the impact of the 'soft limit' of £50 per spin introduced in 2015. It found that the duration of sessions rose by 10% and the total amount spent on FOBTs fell only slightly (a year-on-year decline of 3.7% in the first quarter after the reform and a 0.7% decline in the second quarter). This suggested that nudge-style interventions had little impact on overall spending, but it told policymakers very little about what would happen if a much lower stake limit was set.

Expert opinion: Gambling Commission (2018a)/ Responsible Gambling and Strategy Board (2017)

Although the Gambling Commission and Responsible Gambling and Strategy Board offered a justification for cutting the stake limit, DCMS ultimately created its own evidence for cutting the limit to £2. The Gambling Commission (2018a) report focused on the real-world data on gambling expenditure on B2 and B3 machines but had primarily based its advice on the average and maximum losses that could be expected at different stake levels. This led to an implicit recommended stake limit of between £16 and £30. DCMS relied on the same data, but when it announced the £2 stake limit in May 2018, it set a threshold on acceptable FOBT losses at £1,000, saying:

> ... over 170,000 sessions on B2 roulette ended with losses between £1,000.01 and £5,000. These sessions persist at average stakes of £5 and £10, but by contrast, none involved average stakes of £2 or below. In addition, according to this data, it is very hard for a player to lose more than £500 in a session using average stakes up to £2. (DCMS 2018: 15)

This argument had not been made before, even by anti-FOBT campaigners, and yet it became the central justification for DCMS's decision. The calculations are correct. Of the 128 million FOBT sessions recorded in the period in question (July 2015–June 2016), 170,217 sessions ended with losses between £1,000.01 and £5,000. As Table 2 shows, only 373 of these involved stakes of no more than £10, including 12 sessions involving stakes of no more than £5. When stakes were no more than £2, only 14 sessions ended with losses of over £500 and there were no losses exceeding £1,000. But as this table also shows, 29,376 B3 machine sessions (for which £2 was the maximum stake) ended with losses of over £500, including 1,733 sessions that resulted in losses of over £1,000.

Whether any of these rare losses justified reducing the stake to £2 was a value judgement, but it is notable that DCMS, unlike the Gambling Commission, did not seek to achieve parity with B3 machines. Despite losses of over £1,000 being far more common on B3 machines than on FOBTs played at up to £10 per spin, DCMS (2018: 25) said

Table 2. Gambling machine session losses in UK betting shops (2015–16)

Machine/ stake	Greater than £5000	£1000.01 to £5000	£500.01 to £1000	£200.01 to £500	£100.01 to £200
B2: £40.01–50	84	65,792	235,135	769,225	656,294
B2: £30.01–40	11	20,397	123,698	690,197	915,404
B2: £20.01–30	4	9,902	79,562	658,641	1,243,902
B2: £10.01–20	0	3,469	37,457	461,897	1,369,248
B2: £5.01–10	0	361	5,252	94,240	416,708
B2: £2.01–5	0	12	528	15,840	91,313
B2: Up to £2	0	0	14	882	8,473
B3: Up to £2	0	1,733	27,643	362,210	1,136,169

'the Government has decided to maintain the status quo on B3 gaming machines.' While the Gambling Commission had proposed a stake reduction on the basis of bringing potential losses on B2 machines in line with those of B3 machines, DCMS implicitly judged that session losses over £1,000 were unacceptable on B2 machines but were tolerable on B3 machines.

One curious aspect of the underlying dataset that went unmentioned is that whilst there were 170,217 FOBT sessions ending with a loss of over £1,000, there were 209,464 sessions ending with *wins* of over £1,000. Similarly, there were 543 sessions ending in losses of over £5,000, but 592 sessions ending in wins of over £5,000. And while there were 626,897 sessions ending with losses between £500.01 and £1,000, there were 700,063 sessions ending with wins of between £500.01 and £1,000.

At every point below this, the machines won. For example, there were 3,008,317 sessions ending with losses of between £200.01 and £500, whereas there were only 2,628,258 sessions ended with wins of this amount. But when it came to big wins and losses, the players won more times than the FOBTs. Moreover, big wins required big stakes. None of the people who won more than £5,000 staked less than £20 a spin and none of the people who won more than £1,000 staked as little as £2 (Gambling Commission 2017).

The reasons for this anomaly are not clear, but it was no fluke (the previous year's data show a similar pattern).[36] By banning large stakes, DCMS made big losses practically

[36] Despite the machine's statistical edge over time, players could use their sole advantage over the machine and walk away after a big win. A successful £14 bet on a single roulette number, for example, would immediately yield £500 (the maximum prize per spin).

impossible, but it also made big wins impossible – *and big wins were more common than big losses.* Since winning money is one of the primary benefits of gambling, this surprising and little-known fact should have featured in any cost-benefit analysis.

8 EVALUATION

In the classic model of evidence-based policymaking, post-implementation evaluation is the final stage of the process. In each of our four case studies, the policy had a primary objective and at least one secondary objective, as shown in Table 3.

Table 3. Primary and secondary objectives of each policy

	Plain packaging	Sugar tax	Minimum pricing	FOBT reform
Primary objective	Deter young people from taking up smoking	Reduce/ prevent childhood obesity	Reduce alco-hol-related health harms	Reduce problem gambling losses
Secondary objective	Encourage existing smokers to quit	Reduce/ prevent tooth decay	Reduce other alco-hol-related problems, e.g. crime	Reduce problem gambling rates

Plain packaging

The post-implementation review (PIR) was published by the Department of Health and Social Care (DHSC) in 2022. It concluded that the plain packaging regulations 'had met their original objectives, without producing any significant unintended consequences' (DHSC 2022: 2).

DHSC commissioned a systematic review from the University of Stirling to explore 'the response of consumers, retailers, and tobacco companies to standardised packaging' (ibid.: 9). As with the Stirling Reviews ten years earlier, the lead author was Crawford Moodie (2019). The review assessed eleven studies (seven of which had been co-authored by Moodie) focusing on issues such as compliance, pricing strategies and self-reported consumer responses. Only one of them (Breton et al. 2018) looked at cigarette sales and it found 'no clear deviation in the ongoing downward trend' although the review did not mention this finding. (By contrast, a study published in *Tobacco Control*, which was not mentioned in the PIR, claimed that the decline in tobacco sales accelerated under plain packaging (Hiscock et al. 2020)).

With little academic research related to smoking and cessation available, the PIR noted that there was an unusually large decline in smoking prevalence between 2015 and 2016 which it attributed to the introduction of plain packaging (DHSC 2022: 19) (see Table 4). This is implausible, however, since plain packs were not mandatory in shops until May 2017 and very few tobacco products were sold in plain packaging before January 2017 (Critchlow et al. 2019). A more likely cause, not mentioned in the PIR, was the sharp rise in the number of people vaping in 2016. Data

Table 4. UK adult smoking prevalence, 2011–19 (DHSC 2022: 19)

Year	UK smoking prevalence	Percentage point change	Percentage change
2011	20.2%		
2012	19.6%	–0.6%	–3.0%
2013	18.8%	–0.8%	–4.1%
2014	18.1%	–0.7%	–3.7%
2015	17.2%	–0.9%	–5.0%
2016	15.8%	**–1.4%**	**–8.1%**
2017	15.1%	–0.7%	–4.4%
2018	14.7%	–0.4%	–2.6%
2019	14.1%	–0.6%	–4.1%

from the Office for National Statistics (2022) show the proportion of adults using e-cigarettes rose from 2.8% in 2015 to 5.8% in 2016. This then flattened off at 5.5% in 2017.

The PIR mentioned five studies related to the key objectives of encouraging smokers to quit and discouraging young people from taking up smoking. Four of them used surveys to gauge the reaction of smokers and young people to plain packs, similar to the studies that had been produced during the campaign. The other was the only study to date evaluating the impact of plain packaging on the smoking rate. Using monthly smoking prevalence data, Breton et al. (2021: 197) built a model adjusting for seasonality, price rises and other confounding variables which found 'a statistically significant level decrease in the odds of being a smoker after May 2017 (adjusted OR 0.93; 95% CI: 0.87 to 0.99)'. However, the decrease was even greater when May 2016 was chosen as the start date. Since plain packs were rarely sold until 2017, the authors argued that, if the association was causal, 'the suggestion is that smokers were influenced more by the prospect of standardised packs ... than the actual adoption of standardised packaging' (ibid.: 198). This seems speculative, at best.

The PIR acknowledged that some consumers had downgraded to cheaper brands after plain packaging was introduced, as some opponents of the policy had warned and as the Impact Assessments had predicted, but there was no published research looking at the impact of plain packaging on the illicit tobacco trade.

Sugar tax

A group of public health academics were commissioned to evaluate the sugar tax with a £1.6 million grant from the NIHR Public Health Research programme (NIHR 2017). The team of ten researchers included Adam Briggs, Oliver Mytton and Peter Scarborough, who had done the original modelling in 2013, and prominent advocates of the tax such as Mike Rayner and Harry Rutter.

The SDIL Evaluation Study found that the sugar content of soft drinks declined in the immediate period before and after the introduction of the tax (Scarborough et al. 2020) and estimated that the amount of sugar consumed from soft drinks fell by 9.8% (compared to a counterfactual), amounting to a decline of 29.5 grams per household per week (Pell et al. 2021). Since there was no decline in the overall number of drinks purchased, this implied that it was a reduction in the products' sugar content, rather than a reduction in sales, that made the difference.

A decline in the sugar content of soft drinks did not necessarily mean there had been a decline in overall calorie consumption, let alone in obesity. The National Child Measurement Programme shows a statistically significant rise in the number of children exceeding the government's threshold for obesity in England between 2017/2018 and 2019/20.[37] As shown in Table 5, the following year saw a much larger rise which seems to have been related to COVID-19 restrictions.

Table 5. Child obesity prevalence (England)[38]

	Reception (aged 4/5)	Year 6 (aged 10/11)
2013/14	9.5%	19.1%
2014/15	9.1%	19.1%
2015/16	9.3%	19.8%
2016/17	9.6%	20.0%
2017/18	9.5%	20.1%
2018/19 (first year of sugar tax)	9.7%	20.2%
2019/20	9.9%	21.0%
2020/21	14.4%	25.5%
2021/22	10.4%	23.6%

[37] In Mexico, meanwhile, prevalence of obesity among adults rose from 32% in 2012 to 36% in 2020 and among children from 14.7% in 2006 to 20% in 2021 (Shaman-Levy et al. 2022: 3).

[38] https://digital.nhs.uk/data-and-information/publications/statistical/national-child-measurement-programme/2021-22-school-year

Clearly, rates of childhood obesity did not decline after the sugar tax was introduced. However, in January 2023, as part of the official evaluation, Rogers et al. (2023a) published the results of a model which claimed that the rate was 8% lower than expected among Year 6 girls when compared to a counterfactual based on trends between 2013 and 2016. There was no such effect on girls of reception age nor on boys of any age. The authors attributed the lack of impact on younger children to their relatively low consumption of sugary drinks at baseline and blamed the lack of impact on Year 6 boys on the effects of advertising (ibid.: 12). The claimed impact on Year 6 girls only applied to the period after the *announcement* of the tax in 2016. There was no impact from the introduction of the tax itself in 2018. The authors therefore attributed the slower rate of growth in obesity among this group to reformulation of soft drinks in 2016 and 2017, rather than to the price effect.

In November 2023, a study from the same team claimed that the announcement of the tax in March 2016 was followed by a decline in hospital admissions for tooth extraction, although only among children aged 0–9 years and mostly among children aged 0–4 years (Rogers et al. 2023b). Although the authors acknowledged that the lack of impact on children aged 10 or over was not what earlier modelling had forecast, they attributed it to older children having thicker tooth enamel (ibid.: 8).

There is no doubt that soft drinks were reformulated at an accelerated pace between 2016 and 2018, but the suggestion that the announcement in March 2016 led to an almost immediate (relative) reduction in obesity and tooth decay, albeit among a minority of children, is difficult to reconcile with the evidence showing that '[the] proportion of intervention drinks over the lower levy sugar threshold reduced after the announcement of the SDIL *only slowly at first but with rapid changes just prior to the implementation*' (Scarborough et al. 2020: 9 – emphasis added). Most of the reformulated drinks did not appear on shop shelves until the last six months before the tax took effect in April 2018 (ibid.: 11). Since it takes time for a child to develop obesity and tooth decay, any improvement in these health outcomes in 2016 and 2017 is unlikely to be related to the sugar content of soft drinks.

In December 2023, the study by Pell et al. (2021) which had claimed that sugar consumption from soft drinks had fallen by 9.5% was retracted by *BMJ Open* along with an editorial titled 'UK's sugar tax hits the sweet spot' that had been published in the *British Medical Journal* on the same day. It was replaced by a new version of the study which estimated that the decline had been just 2.7% or eight grams per household per week (Rogers et al. 2023c). As this amounted to less than two calories per person per day, it raised further doubts about the plausibility of the claims about obesity and tooth decay.

Minimum pricing

Minimum pricing was officially evaluated by Public Health Scotland, which published a series of studies commissioned from external academics and internal staff. They found that per capita alcohol consumption declined after MUP was implemented, both in absolute terms and relative to England and Wales. The estimated reduction in consumption was close to the 3.5% projected in the Sheffield model, but the benefits predicted by the model were generally absent.

With regards to crime, Krzemieniewska-Nandwani et al. (2021: 5) found 'no apparent changes in the trend direction or statistically significant changes in the level of alcohol-related crime and disorder' immediately after MUP's introduction, except in one local authority where alcohol-related crime went up.

With regards to health, So et al. (2021) interviewed 23,455 attendees at Accident and Emergency departments in England and Scotland before and after the introduction of MUP. They found no evidence that MUP had improved outcomes:

> The odds ratio for an alcohol-related emergency department attendance following minimum unit pricing was 1.14 (95% confidence interval 0.90 to 1.44; $p = 0.272$). In absolute terms, we estimated that minimum unit pricing was associated with 258 more alcohol-related emergency department visits (95% confidence interval –191 to 707) across Scotland than would have been the case had minimum unit pricing not been implemented. (ibid.: viii)

Contrary to the modelling, which predicted a 7% reduction in alcohol consumption among heavy drinkers in the first year, the Public Health Scotland evaluation of the impact on heavy drinkers found 'no clear evidence' of a benefit and some evidence of harm as a result of higher prices:

> The introduction of a £0.50 MUP in Scotland led to a marked increase in the prices paid for alcohol

> by people with alcohol dependence. There is no clear evidence that this led to reduced alcohol consumption or levels of alcohol dependence among people drinking at harmful levels. There is some evidence it increased financial strain among economically vulnerable groups but no clear evidence that it caused wider negative consequences, such as increased criminality, illicit substance use or acute withdrawal. (Holmes et al. 2022: 194–5)

There was also evidence of substitution effects and harm to third parties:

> There is some evidence that MUP led to people drinking at harmful levels switching from consuming stronger ciders to spirits, and particularly vodka, in response to these price increases. (ibid. 21)

> Some people with alcohol dependence and their family members reported concerns about increased intoxication after they switched to consuming spirits rather than cider. In some of these cases, people also expressed concerns about increased violence. (ibid. 22)

Research conducted independently of the official evaluation tended to echo these themes. Comparing Scotland to England, Rehm et al. (2022) found that MUP was associated with a small decline in average alcohol consumption of less than one unit per week. This was mainly driven by women while the heaviest drinking men increased their consumption.

A 2023 study written by several of the original Sheffield modellers also found no decline in consumption among 'harmful drinkers' although they found a 3.5% decline among people drinking at somewhat lower levels ('hazardous drinkers').

> ... the lack of evidence for a decline in the prevalence of harmful drinking arising from MUP is contrary to model-based evidence that informed the introduction of the policy. (Stevely et al. 2023: 47)

In addition, a study by Kopasker et al. (2022: 1) estimated that MUP resulted in a 1% reduction in food expenditure in Scotland, with 'less spending on fruit and vegetables and increased spending on crisps and snacks'.

The raw health data was inconclusive. Alcohol-related hospital admissions neither rose nor fell significantly after MUP was introduced. Alcohol-specific deaths fell in the first full calendar year of MUP in Scotland (while rising slightly in England and falling in Wales). In 2020, alcohol-specific deaths rose in Scotland to their highest level since 2011, but a similar spike was seen across the UK and seems to have been due to heavy drinking in response to COVID-19. There was another increase across Britain in 2021. The alcohol-specific mortality rate in Wales, which introduced MUP in April 2020, rose more sharply than in England between 2020 and 2023.

As with the sugar tax, a study using a counterfactual was published in 2023 claiming that the policy had a positive impact. Using England as a control, Wyper et al. (2023: 1,366) concluded that the number of deaths wholly attributable to alcohol in Scotland was 13.4% lower in the 32 months after the policy was introduced 'compared with our best estimate of what would have been expected had the legislation not been implemented'. The authors also reported a 4.1% reduction in hospital admissions although this was not statistically significant. Of the eight studies in the official evaluation that looked at health outcomes, this was the only one that found a positive impact and it was the primary piece of evidence cited by Public Health Scotland when it issued its final evaluation report in June 2023 stating that 'MUP has had a positive impact on health outcomes' (Public Health Scotland 2023: 14).

Upon release of the final report, the Scottish Government (2023) issued a press release stating that 'researchers said that "robust, independent evaluation" and the best-available, wide-ranging evidence drawing on 40 independent research publications, showed that MUP has been effective in its main goal of reducing alcohol harm with the reduction in deaths and hospital admissions'. The press release was later amended after the chair of the UK Statistics Authority, Sir Robert Chote, wrote a letter explaining that only eight of the 40 papers had studied health outcomes, of which only one studied deaths and hospitalisations, and that 'the level of uncertainty associated with the reduction in hospitalisations and deaths was not included' in either Public Health Scotland's summary or the Scottish Government's press release. Of the other seven papers, Chote noted that that the evaluation had found 'no consistent evidence that MUP impacted on other alcohol-related health outcomes such as ambulance callouts, emergency department attendances and prescribing of medication for alcohol dependence' (Chote 2023).

FOBTs

No post-implementation review of the £2 stake limit was conducted and there has been no evaluation in the academic literature. The UK went into lockdown less than a year after the stake limit was cut and bookmakers were closed for much of the next 18 months. This makes before-and-after comparisons difficult. Table 6 shows Gross Gambling Yield (GGY) in the online and betting shop sectors, and overall. Betting shop revenue fell by £847 million in the first year of the reform while online revenue increased by £430 million. Overall gambling spend fell by £180 million (–1.25%). This was the second successive year of decline (Gambling Commission 2023).

Table 6. Gross Gambling Yields, UK (£m)

	Total	Betting (non-remote)	Online (excluding lotteries)
2016/17	13,780	3,311	4,775
2017/18	14,411	3,268	5,346
2018/19	14,367	3,262	5,305
2019/20 (£2 stake limit introduced)	14,187	2,415	5,735
2020/21	12,670	1,035	6,843
2021/22	14,164	2,128	6,324
2022/23	15,122	2,476	6,500

There can be no doubt that the fall in GGY in betting shops was primarily due to a reduction in machine gambling. GGY from B2 (FOBT) machines fell from £1,689 million in 2017/18 to zero in 2022/23 while GGY from B3 machines rose from £570 million to £1,862 million over the same period (ibid.). Interestingly, around £500 million of the substitution from B2 to B3 machines occurred in the year before the new stake limit came into force, perhaps indicating that the industry encouraged players to switch to them in advance of the change.

The number of active betting shops in the UK fell from 8,304 in March 2019 to 5,931 in March 2024. This was a decline of 29%, much larger than the decline of 6% in the rest of the land-based sector (i.e. arcades, bingo and casinos combined) and more than the 5–15% forecast by modellers commissioned by the anti-gambling coalition. The number of FOBTs in the UK fell from 32,798 to just seven between 2018/19 and 2021/22, and then to zero. Overall, GGY from machine betting in bookmakers fell from a peak of £1,834 million in 2017/18 to £1,241 million in 2022/23 (a decline of 32% in cash terms) (ibid.).

The impact of COVID-19 restrictions notwithstanding, it is clear that the £2 stake limit led to a total collapse in revenue from B2 machines which was largely, but not entirely, offset by a large rise in B3 machine revenue. It may have also contributed to the rise in online gambling revenue shown in Table 6 which would be consistent with the prediction that the FOBT reform would lead to significant displacement towards online gambling.

Figure 19 shows the problem gambling rate between 1999 and 2024 using data from the British Gambling Prevalence Survey (1999–2010) and the Health Survey for

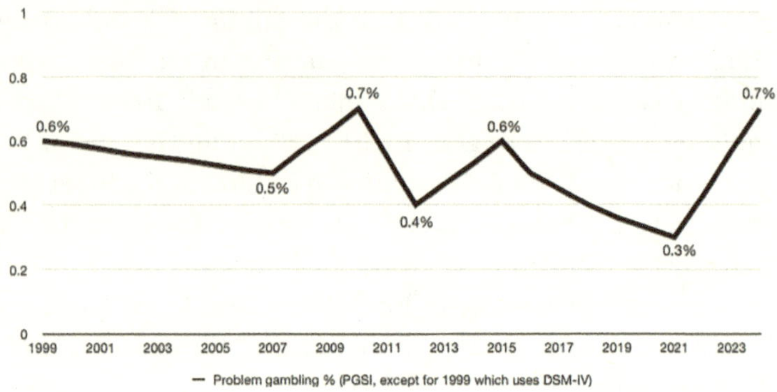

Figure 19. Problem gambling prevalence Great Britain/ England 1999–23

England (2012–24). The data fluctuates from year to year and the numbers are small with wide confidence intervals, but there is no obvious trend after 2019 or in the whole time series. The Adult Psychiatric Morbidity Survey also shows no change in the number of problem gamblers between 2018 and 2024, with a prevalence rate of 0.4% in both years. This is not consistent with the prediction of some campaigners who predicted a decline in problem gambling, such as Tracey Crouch who said in 2018:

> On the impact on problem gamblers, we expect this decision to have a significant impact on the reduction of problem gambling.

Summary

There is no strong evidence that any of the four policies had the desired effect. The exogenous shock of COVID-19 makes evaluating the efficacy of minimum pricing, the FOBT reform and, to some extent, the sugar tax unusually difficult, but while there is good evidence that MUP led to a reduction in alcohol sales and the sugar levy led to less sugar being consumed from soft drinks, the impact on health outcomes is less clear. In Scotland between 2018 and 2022, alcohol-related deaths only fell below baseline in one year (2019) and childhood obesity in England (and the UK) was above baseline in every year. With the exception of Wyper et al.'s modelling study, the official evaluation of MUP suggested that the policy had little if any positive effect on public health and public order. The only evidence that the sugar tax and MUP had a positive impact on health comes from modelling studies using assumptions about counterfactuals that are open to debate. In the case of the sugar tax, even this evidence is confined to two different sub-groups of children in two studies.

While the plain packaging evaluation claimed success, it largely overlooked the primary outcomes (smoking rates and cigarette sales) in favour of the same subjective, survey-based evidence that had been used to promote the policy in the first place. The suggestion that plain packaging had an impact on the smoking rate in 2016, when few smokers had seen a plain pack in real life, strains credibility. The only study in the PIR that looked at tobacco sales found no impact from plain packaging.

Although three of the four policies underwent official evaluation, neither the plain packaging PIR nor the sugar tax evaluation was truly independent since they both involved known advocates of the policy, some of whom had previously published research showing the policies would be effective. Several members of the Sheffield team were involved in one part of the MUP evaluation, but only as part of a larger working group. The FOBT reform was not evaluated at all and to date there has been no full evaluation or PIR of the sugar tax. The FOBT stake reduction clearly led to a large decline in expenditure on gambling machines in bookmakers and a decline in the number of betting shops. It may also have led to a small decline in gambling expenditure overall, but the raw data is too ambiguous for firm conclusions to be drawn about this or about the impact on problem gambling rates.

PART THREE

PRESSURE

9 EVIDENCE-BASED POLICY OR POLICY-BASED EVIDENCE?

Were the policy decisions in these four case studies driven by evidence? Those who produced the research certainly felt that they had contributed. The Research Excellence Framework website includes case studies from several universities showing their impact on the sugar tax and MUP campaigns. Academics from Oxford University, including Mike Rayner, Adam Briggs and Peter Scarborough – all of whom were on the sugar tax evaluation team – took credit for 'Creating a favourable policy environment for new sugary drinks taxes' through their modelling and evaluation studies and also through their close links with researchers and politicians in Mexico where a sugar tax became a 'catalyst for similar adoptions by other countries' (University of Oxford 2021: 3). They also took credit for 'Changing public attitudes towards sugary drinks taxes' by appearing on television programmes such as *Jamie Oliver's Sugar Rush*, saying:

> University of Oxford research contributed directly to the introduction of sugary drinks taxes in the UK, Ireland and Mexico and indirectly to the introduction of similar taxes around the world. (ibid.: 1)

Academics from Cambridge University, including Oliver Mytton, Jean Adams and Martin White – who were also on the sugar tax evaluation team – similarly outlined their role in 'Making the case for the sugar levy' and 'Fuelling sustained government action on sugary drinks'. Their study of an experimental sugar 'tax' in Jamie Oliver's restaurants (Cornelsen et al. 2017) was, they said, 'important in establishing that an additional tariff on sugary drinks could reduce sugar consumption' (University of Cambridge 2021: 1). They also reported that they had 'forged productive collaborations with leading charities and other influencing bodies to secure impact' and that 'Cambridge research was extensively cited in the key policy documents leading to the introduction of the Soft Drinks Industry Levy in the UK' (ibid.: 3).

The Sheffield Alcohol Research Group (SARG) filed an impact case study in 2014, saying that their Sheffield Alcohol Policy Model (SAPM) model 'played a central role in informing the UK and Scottish Governments' policy decisions to introduce minimum unit pricing (MUP) as a central feature of their alcohol strategies' (University of Sheffield 2014: 2).

> The Sheffield Alcohol Research Group (SARG)'s strategy for impact is one of ongoing engagement with policy stakeholders, from developing policy-relevant research questions through to responding rapidly and flexibly to the timescales of the policy debate. (ibid.)

SARG claimed that the model also influenced England's Chief Medical Officer Liam Donaldson whose 2009 Annual

Report 'lobbies strongly for MUP' and was 'used directly by NICE in making recommendations in June 2010 for minimum pricing' (ibid.: 3). They noted that the UK government's Impact Assessment of 2012 'drew heavily on SAPM results' (ibid.: 2).

This seems to confirm the influence of these researchers on the policy debates discussed in Chapters 4 and 5. I have argued that policymakers were presented with packages of evidence comprising theoretical studies, recent real-world precedents and expert opinion. On the face of it, this seems a good foundation for evidence-based policy and, if our analysis of media and parliamentary references is any indication, it was persuasive. Politicians were particularly impressed by apparently successful policy experiments in other countries. But closer inspection of the 'superstar' studies and the evaluations of the policies after the event provide grounds for caution and scepticism about the evidence itself.

None of the most influential evidence had the rigour of a randomised controlled trial. At the theoretical level, the campaigns for MUP and the sugar tax each hinged on a single model and, therefore, on the assumptions that had been fed into it. The theoretical justification for plain packaging came from a far larger body of research, albeit dominated by a small group of activist-academics, based on survey findings which rarely transcended the obvious. The theoretical basis of the FOBT stake reduction used solid data to show that heavy gambling losses on B2 machines became less common at lower stakes but, as the Gambling Commission acknowledged, there was no way of knowing what the substitution effects would be and, therefore, what the impact on overall gambling losses ('harm') would be.

In principle, questions about theory could be resolved by observing what happened in practice, but the 'real world' evidence cited for plain packaging and the sugar tax studied neither the primary outcome measure (the prevalence of smoking and obesity respectively) nor indicative secondary measures (cigarette sales and overall calorie consumption). One 'real world' study of MUP looked at the primary outcome of alcohol-specific deaths but it underwent so much modelling and adjustment that it bore little relationship to the actual experience in the Canadian province in question. Claims about the sugar tax in Mexico also depended to a significant degree on a hypothetical counterfactual and, therefore, on the assumptions of the authors. The most cited 'real world' study for plain packaging (Wakefield et al. 2013) was little better than the survey-based evidence produced before implementation in that it could only measure stated intentions. The 'real world' studies for MUP and the sugar tax used hard data and both used an interrupted time series but neither had a control group.

This is not to say that regression models are invalid or that confounding factors should not be controlled for. It is possible for a preventive measure in population health to make an outcome *better than it would have been* even if the outcomes stayed the same or worsened after the measure was introduced. Nevertheless, there is inherently more uncertainty about an adjusted estimate than an unadjusted figure taken from hard data and there is an important qualitative difference between the claim that 'the rate of A fell by n%' and the claim that 'the rate of A *would have fallen* by n% had it not been for X, Y and Z'.

As a matter of empirical fact, the following statements are untrue:

> 'We know from the experience in Mexico that a 10% levy on sugary drinks has led to a 6% reduction in consumption.' – Sarah Wollaston MP.

> 'Sugar tax in Mexico cuts sales of sugary drinks by 12%' – *The Telegraph.*

> 'In British Columbia a 32% reduction in alcohol related deaths was seen only one year after minimum price increases came into effect.' – Royal College of Physicians of Ireland.

As discussed in Chapter 7, there never was a 32% reduction in alcohol-related (or alcohol-specific) deaths in British Columbia, nor was there a 10% increase in the 'minimum price'. There was not even a minimum price, as a British audience would understand the term.

There never was a 6% reduction in sugary drink sales in Mexico, let alone a 12% reduction. In a study published after the sugar tax was announced in the UK, Colchero et al. (2016b) showed the trend in sugary drink sales between 2007 and 2015. They peaked in 2011 at 167 litres per capita and had fallen slightly to 166 litres per capita by 2013. In 2014, the first year of the sugar tax, they fell to 162 litres per capita. This is a decline of 2.4%, not 6%. As for the claim that sales had fallen by 12% by the end of the first year of the tax, Colchero et al. (2016b) show that per capita consumption in 2015 was 161 litres per capita. Compared to 2013, that is 3% lower.

Whilst it can be argued that minimum pricing in British Columbia and the sugar tax in Mexico were more successful in achieving their objectives than a simple before-and-after analysis might suggest, the fact remains that the claims made in the 'real world' studies were liable to be misunderstood as facts of history rather than as comparisons with counterfactuals. This matters because policymakers expect significant policy changes to produce visible and tangible benefits. Alcohol-specific deaths falling by a third after a relatively small increase in the minimum price would be so impressive that policymakers might be inclined to put their reservations to one side, ignore the costs to consumers and introduce the policy. It was, therefore, important for them to understand that this never happened. Similarly, it is not trivial to note that the actual reduction in sugary drink sales in Mexico in the first two years of the sugar tax was 75% smaller than was claimed and that obesity rates continued to rise.

A sophisticated policymaker might understand the conditional nature of claims based on counterfactuals and accept that, while the observable impact of a policy might not be as dramatic as the models suggest, the benefits are still worth pursuing. This then raises the question of how reliable the models are, but that is something almost no politician or journalist would be capable of assessing even if the models were less opaque.

Superficially, the plain packaging campaign came closest to following the rational model of evidence-based policymaking (see Table 7). It involved two systematic reviews encompassing dozens of peer-reviewed papers followed by

Table 7. Evidence gathering before and after implementation

	Evidence review	Impact assessment prior to decision	Impact assessment after decision	Post-implementation review	Other evaluation
Plain packaging	Yes	Yes	Yes	Yes	Yes
Sugar tax	Partial	No	No	No	Yes
Minimum pricing	No	Yes (England)	Yes (Scotland)	Yes	Yes
FOBTs	No	Yes	Yes	No	No

more peer-reviewed studies addressing policymakers' concerns, an independent review from a well-regarded clinician and two Impact Assessments. In terms of its formal structure, policymakers could not have expected much more and yet it produced a policy that was underwhelming when put into practice.

In this instance, quantity of evidence was a substitute for quality. The Impact Assessments based the bulk of their estimates on the subjective opinion of a group of tobacco control academics whose best guess was that plain packaging would reduce the smoking rate by 1–3% (Pechey et al. 2013). The final decision was heavily influenced by the subjective opinion of Cyril Chantler who cited several studies from the field of psychology which, upon closer inspection, did not support his argument. Chantler then inserted a figure of a 2% decline into the debate, perhaps derived from Pechey et al. (2013) but quite possibly pulled out of thin air. Neither figure could have been based on more than a hunch, but by the time of the April 2014 HoC debate, MPs were citing Chantler's estimate of what would happen if 2% fewer children started smoking as if this were a science-based prediction of what would actually happen under plain packaging:

> Jane Ellison: Sir Cyril points out that if this rate of smoking by children were reduced by even 2%, it would mean that 4,000 fewer children took up smoking each year... As a Health Minister, I regularly answer parliamentary questions and letters from colleagues throughout the House on issues that affect far fewer children than 4,000 a year.

> Fiona Bruce: Does she [Ellison] agree that if 4,000 children a year can be discouraged from taking up smoking there will be a double public health win—not only better health outcomes for those 4,000, but the release of funds for the health treatment of others in their generation for illnesses and disease? Those funds would otherwise have to be used, in time, to treat many of those 4,000 for smoking-related diseases.

The most heavily cited study during the campaign was based on a telephone survey (Wakefield et al. 2013) which seemed to suffer from residual confounding and sampling bias. Its authors made selective use of their adjusted models and exaggerated the importance of statistically insignificant findings. Like Young et al. (2014), which was also touted as 'real world' proof that plain packaging made smokers want to quit, its findings could plausibly be explained by the concurrent introduction of a new batch of graphic warnings and was unable to show a link between self-reported intentions and subsequent behaviour.

Is this nit-picking? Are we in danger of indulging in the *Nirvana fallacy* and making the perfect the enemy of the good? I don't think so. More robust research methods were available had policymakers demanded them. It is sometimes claimed that population-level public health policy does not lend itself to randomised controlled trials and yet economists have successfully used RCTs to test complex social policies, notably Duflo, Banerjee and Kramer's Nobel Prize- winning work on development economics and several large-scale field studies into the Universal Basic Income. RCTs have been used to test a variety of public health interventions, such as mandatory sex education and speed cameras. Although Chantler repeatedly insisted that it would be impossible and unethical to conduct a randomised controlled trial to study plain packaging, a small number of relevant RCTs have since been conducted. In the UK, Maynard et al. (2015: 1) found 'no evidence that pack type had an effect on either of the primary measures [number of cigarettes smoked and volume of smoke inhaled]' although they did find the usual self-reported attitudinal changes, such as rating the pack more negatively and 'rating the health warning as more impactful'.

Two RCTs from the USA have since strongly suggested that self-reported attitudinal changes cannot be used as a proxy for meaningful behavioural change in this particular field of research. Although both were principally aimed at evaluating graphic warnings on cigarette packs, the packs used were based on Australian plain packs and had no corporate branding, logos or colours. The first of these studies (Strong et al. 2021) found that the use of plain packs with graphic warnings 'appears to decrease positive perceptions of cigarettes and increase quitting cognitions in the short term' but 'there was no evidence of increased quitting or reduced consumption' (ibid.: 9). The second RCT, from the same research group, found that the packs were associated with a tendency for smokers to conceal their packs, but that '[n]either smoking prevalence nor consumption differed by group at any point in the study' (Pierce et al. 2022: 2). Moreover, the 'pack-hiding behaviour' was associated with the graphic warnings rather than the removal of brand imagery (ibid.: 11). This is significant since evidence that smokers concealed their packs more after plain packaging was introduced in Australia (Zacher et al. 2014) was cited as evidence that the policy was effective by Chantler and various public health groups.

More imaginative research methods were also available for the other policies. With regards to FOBTs, the RGSB (2017: 4) noted that 'it might be possible to pilot a [stake] reduction in a defined geographic area (or even different levels of reduction in different areas)', but this was never acted on. Alternatively, a randomised controlled trial in a laboratory or quasi-natural environment would have been relatively straightforward if policymakers had wanted to see what effects a stake reduction would have on behaviour, but no such research was commissioned. The study by Parke et al. (2014) came closest to this and was one of very few pieces of relevant, high-quality evidence mentioned in the FOBT debate, but it was not designed to examine the effect of lower stakes on problem gamblers nor on gambling losses in general.

With the sugar tax, Jamie Oliver's restaurants were used to assess the impact of a voluntary 'tax' on sugary drinks, but the methodology was weak. The opportunity could have been taken to conduct a randomised observational experiment in which half the restaurants had a 'tax' and the other half did not. Instead, the only study of Oliver's self-imposed 'tax' used a simple before-and-after comparison in a chain whose proprietor had well known views about sugary drinks and whose voluntary 'tax' was well publicised. Meanwhile, an RCT looking at the effect of reducing the sugar content of food and soft drinks was published during the course of the campaign but was completely ignored by PHE and the government. It found that reformulation led to less sugar being consumed but no change in body weight (Markey et al. 2015).

The absence of a control group was a substantial but common flaw in the evidence in all four policy debates. With MUP, British Columbia could have been compared to other Canadian provinces, but instead it was compared to a counterfactual. Mexico could have been compared to other Central American countries, but this never seems to have been considered. Had the British government been more patient, it could have compared smoking rates in Australia with those in other countries. Post-implementation, the only evaluation that used a control group (England) was Public Health Scotland's evaluation of MUP.

With MUP, it would have been possible to conduct a local trial before nationwide implementation. Indeed, the Sheffield team subsequently modelled the impact of MUP in several English regions (Brennan et al. 2022). That study did not attempt to model the impact of out-of-region shopping which could have significantly undermined the effect and caused other problems. However, if a local trial was deemed unsuitable and modelling was the only option, other teams should have been commissioned to provide their own modelling or to critique the original Sheffield research. Instead, MUP research – mostly funded by the government – became virtually a closed shop.

This was a common problem. In all four of our case studies, evidence production was dominated by small groups of often partisan researchers (or, in the case of FOBTs, researchers commissioned by interest groups). In three of the case studies, the same researchers were then commissioned to evaluate the policy afterwards. The teams in Sheffield and British Columbia cornered the market in MUP research. Crawford Moodie and his associates dominated plain packaging research in the UK while Melanie Wakefield's team did likewise in Australia. Mike Rayner's team at Oxford University were responsible for the modelling of the UK sugar tax, worked with campaigners to introduce it, and were then commissioned to evaluate it. The Campaign for Fairer Gambling funded nearly all the anti-FOBT research.

A special supplement about plain packaging published in *Tobacco Control* in March 2015[39] illustrates the incestuous nature of the research and evaluation process. It included nine new studies, all of which featured Melanie Wakefield as co-author, along with an editorial by Gerard Hastings and Crawford Moodie stating that 'Plain packaging in Australia has been a casebook example of effective tobacco control' and that 'governments which do not act on plain packaging today will have a bigger problem to tackle tomorrow' (Hastings and Moodie 2015). Hastings and Moodie had been early advocates of the policy, writing

[39] https://tobaccocontrol.bmj.com/content/24/Suppl_2

an article titled 'Plain packaging: a time for action' in 2010 (Moodie and Hastings 2010) and co-authoring both Stirling Reviews. Melanie Wakefield was another longstanding supporter of plain packaging and by 2015 had been commissioned by the Australian Government Department of Health to evaluate its impact, an appointment later emulated in Britain when Moodie was commissioned by the Department of Health to produce a systematic review for the PIR. Wakefield was so keen for her research to be disseminated to policymakers that she flew to London in April 2013 to share the provisional findings of Wakefield et al. (2013) with the Department of Health (Gadher and Leake 2013).

The anti-FOBT coalition of religious organisations, former problem gamblers and rival sectors of the gambling industry had an obvious bias, but there was also a strong suggestion of bias among some of the MUP researchers, with their links to the neo-temperance Kettil Bruun Society (see Chapter 5), and in sugar tax research with the divinely inspired Reverend Mike Rayner (see Chapter 4). There were also professional biases. An academic who has published a model showing that a policy will work will rarely be eager to admit in an evaluation that it has not.

There are clear risks in having politically charged corners of the academic literature dominated by a narrow band of researchers, especially when findings depend to a significant extent on the assumptions they feed into models and their subjective interpretation of evidence in systematic reviews. At the least, there is a danger of groupthink. One of the Stirling Review authors, Ann McNeill, argued in 2014 that the normal requirements of proof of efficacy should be inverted when it came to policies such as plain packaging.

> As with all tobacco control policies, the burden of proof for effectiveness of 'standardised tobacco packaging' lies with the tobacco control community, in line with a desire for evidence-based public health. This desire could be questioned. Arguably, when a product kills one in two of its regular users, the burden of proof should lie elsewhere: policy makers should err on the side of protecting the health of the public when introducing preventive measures (in this case by removing attractive tobacco packaging) unless there is strong evidence that such measures could increase harm.' (McNeill et al. 2014: 704)

Melanie Wakefield, the most prolific plain packaging researcher of all, argued in an article titled 'Welcome to cardboard country' that any loss in consumer surplus resulting from plain packaging should be seen as a benefit rather than a cost:

> In the case of a deadly product such as tobacco, there is no place for powerful branding imagery on packs if it serves to promote greater subjective enjoyment of smoking (Wakefield et al. 2011).

Academics who took moral positions of this kind had little incentive to value the potential welfare costs to consumers of their policies, and they regarded any cost to industry as a benefit. This attitude was reflected to some extent in the Impact Assessments for plain packaging and MUP, both of which acknowledged the potential for a loss of consumer welfare but failed to monetise it. A cost-benefit analysis will always look more attractive if it counts intangible benefits and ignores intangible costs. In the unusual case of FOBTs, the Impact Assessment assumed that there would be welfare benefits from the reform but failed to monetise them. It therefore estimated that lowering the stake limit would incur a large net cost, and yet the policy proceeded nonetheless.

It goes without saying that many opponents of the four policies also had their own biases. Because of the logic of collective action discussed in Chapter 2, there was little organised grassroots opposition from consumers and it was the affected industries who were most vocal. They had some strong arguments at times, as the evaluations later showed, but they rarely backed them up with fresh or credible research. The tobacco, alcohol and bookmaking industries commissioned their own studies, often from economic consultancy firms, but regardless of their quality, they rarely had an impact. When they were mentioned in the media, it was often disparagingly. None of them was published in peer-reviewed journals and many of them were taken offline once the policy battle was over. This was particularly true of the FOBT campaign which was, to some extent, a battle between rival factions of the gambling industry in which both sides used the 'industry tactic' (as public health academics see it) of commissioning research favourable to their argument and having it published in the grey literature.

Industry-funded research was always tainted in the eyes of public health campaigners who encouraged politicians and the media to treat it with great caution. This was an intractable problem, but it could have been partially overcome by appealing to the authority of peer review.

Some prestigious journals refuse to publish studies funded by tobacco companies, but even for this most toxic of industries, there were plenty of journals that would have published robust research had the industry chosen that route. The study by Kaul and Wolf (2014) which reported no impact on smoking rates from plain packaging in Australia was independently reviewed after complaints from anti-smoking campaigners and found to have no fundamental flaws. Although there was 'some space for improvement and some of the interpretations by Kaul and Wolf might be challenged', the academic reviewer saw no reason why it could not have been published as something more high profile than a working paper (Jann 2015: 45).

Opponents of the other three policies had even less reputable research evidence to work with. Research commissioned by the ABB tended to focus on the economic damage a £2 stake limit would do to the bookmaking industry, but while this was of some concern to DCMS, many people saw it as a benefit rather than a cost.[40] The alcohol industry was somewhat more effective in commissioning research from the CEBR challenging the Sheffield model and emphasising the cost of minimum pricing to consumers. The British Soft Drinks Association, whose members were divided on the sugar tax issue, produced no evidence favourable to its 'Can the Tax' campaign that was cited by the media or in the HoC.

[40] CFFG spokesman Matt Zarb-Cousin (2019) later wrote that 'the Association of British Bookmakers commissioned online adverts during the government's gambling review which argued that a £2 cap on FOBTs would lead to the "closure of betting shops". This not only restated our eminently reasonable position, it foregrounded our ultimate objective while attempting to argue against it.'

In terms of quantity and prestige, the evidence presented by the public health interest groups in favour of plain packaging, the sugar tax and MUP was much more impressive than that of their opponents. The quality of the evidence notwithstanding, it would be understandable if politicians at least *believed* that they were 'following the science' by siding with the public health groups. And yet there are a number of reasons to believe that policymaking in all four areas was not driven purely, or even primarily, by evidence. Since we do not have a window into policymakers' souls, this cannot be proved categorically but, as the Campaign for Fairer Gambling (2013: 20) said in a response to one public consultation: 'Where evidence is imperfect for whatever reason, there is no excuse for not relying on logic.' We know what the classic model of evidence-based policymaking is supposed to look like and we are therefore able to see divergences from it.

Plain packaging

1. When the government put plain packaging on hold in July 2013, its stated reason was that it wanted to wait until the 'emerging impact of the decision in Australia can be measured' (Gadher and Leake 2013), but it commissioned the Chantler Review just four months later when the only notable evidence to have appeared from Australia was Wakefield et al. (2013). If there was insufficient evidence to proceed in July 2013, very little had changed by November. Even in April 2014, when Chantler published his report, the data needed to draw firm conclusions was unavailable. Australian smoking prevalence data was not expected to be published until

October 2014[41] and there was no tobacco sales data to speak of (the debate about the Australian Bureau of Statistics' data did not begin until the summer).

2. Not only was there little evidence to test whether plain packaging had worked in Australia when Chantler conducted his review, but Chantler believed such evidence might never be available. He argued that data from Australia could not prove or disprove the efficacy of plain packaging 'because a number of things have happened together, including tax rises. Disentangling and evaluating these will take years, not months' (Chantler 2014: 5). In the event, Chantler's report did not discuss the Australian experience at length, except in relation to the illicit trade which he had not been asked to review. Despite having demanded evidence of efficacy from Australia, the government described his findings as 'compelling' and announced that it was 'minded' to introduce plain packaging.
3. The timing of the final decision in February 2015 suggests that political considerations played a large role. In April 2014, the government announced that it was 'minded to introduce regulations to provide for standardised packaging of tobacco products, subject to a short consultation'.[42] Although public health minister Jane Ellison said 'I want to move forward as swiftly as possible',[43] the six-week consultation did not open until

---

[41] In the event, it was published in July 2014, still too late to be included in Chantler's report.

[42] https://www.gov.uk/government/news/government-response-to-tobacco-standardised-packaging-review

[43] https://www.gov.uk/government/speeches/chantler-report-on-standardised-packaging-of-tobacco-products

late June and the consultation summary report was not published until February 2015. In the intervening ten months, the Prime Minister refused to be drawn on whether he supported the policy and whether it would go ahead.

Plain packaging did not feature in the Queen's Speech in May 2014 and the Prime Minister refused to say whether he personally supported it as late as January 2015 when he announced that there would be a free vote on the matter before the election. This, again, was in contrast to his public health minister, Jane Ellison, who said, 'Having considered all the evidence, I believe that the policy is a proportionate and justified response to the considerable public health harm from smoking tobacco.'[44] It should be noted that free votes are typically held when an issue is seen as a matter of conscience involving policies about which reasonable people disagree.

The prevarication by the Prime Minister suggests that he was open to the possibility of rejecting plain packaging even at a late stage. Despite the 'compelling' evidence of the Chantler review, nearly a year elapsed before the parliamentary vote. It was widely reported that Cameron wanted the vote to be held before the next general election in May 2015 to avoid the issue hovering over him during the election campaign. Possible reasons for this are discussed in the next chapter.

[44] https://www.telegraph.co.uk/news/politics/david-cameron/11361515/David-Cameron-orders-pre-election-vote-on-plain-cigarette-packs.html

Sugar tax

1. As with plain packaging, the timing of the sugar tax announcement suggested short-term political motivations. When Public Health England's evidence review was published in October 2015, the government insisted that it had no plans for a sugar tax. A spokesperson for David Cameron said that he 'doesn't see a need for a tax on sugar'.[45] On 7 January 2016, six weeks after the Health Select Committee report and a day after Colchero et al. (2016a) was published in the *British Medical Journal*, the Department of Health insisted that the 'government position has not changed and we have no plans for a sugar tax.' And yet a sugar tax was announced in the Budget two months later. No significant new evidence was published in the interim.
2. The sugar tax introduced by George Osborne differed significantly from the sugar tax that had been modelled. Experts repeatedly claimed that a tax on sugary drinks would need to raise prices by at least 20% to have a measurable impact on obesity (e.g. Mytton et al. 2012; BMA 2015). This advice was ignored in favour of a rate that was, in practice, around half the minimum 'evidence-based' level. Briggs et al. (2013) had modelled a 20% excise tax (with a 10% sales tax modelled in the sensitivity analysis). Instead, George Osborne introduced a two-tiered tax on industry based on sales volumes charged per litre. In practice, there

[45] https://www.theguardian.com/society/2015/oct/22/sugar-report-delayed-jeremy-hunt-tax-radical-action-obesity

was a pass-through rate of 31% and the average price of sugary drinks increased by around 3% (Scarborough et al. (2020: 12). Even if there had been 100% pass-through, as the Briggs model assumed, prices would only have risen by around 10%.

3. The mechanism by which the sugar tax was supposed to reduce obesity fundamentally changed between the production of the evidence and the government's announcement. Modelling studies, the PHE report and the Mexico study all focused on the price effect whereas the government's stated aim when it announced the Soft Drinks Industry Levy was to encourage manufacturers to reduce the sugar content of their drinks. Using taxes to encourage soft drink reformulation had been barely mentioned in the peer-reviewed literature prior to March 2016. (As it transpired, reformulation had a far greater impact on sugar consumption from soft drinks than the price increase *per se*. According to an independent analysis, more than 80% of the reduction in sugar consumption from soft drinks was due to reformulation rather than reduced consumption of soft drinks (Dickson et al. 2021)).
4. Although the sugar tax was explicitly introduced in the name of children's health and was part of the childhood obesity plan, Briggs et al. (2013) modelled the impact of a sugar tax on adults, not children. Colchero et al. (2016a) looked at the impact of the Mexican sugar tax on households rather than on children. Of the eleven experimental studies discussed in the Public Health England review, only one involved children.

Minimum pricing

1. Scotland went ahead with MUP but England did not. Since the evidence for the policy was very similar in both nations, at least one of them had a policy that was not 'evidence-based'. Factors unrelated to evidence must have driven policy in either England or Scotland, and possibly in both.
2. The British government not only declined to introduce MUP but abruptly changed its mind about it. Having said that it was 'committed to introducing a minimum unit price for alcohol in England and Wales' (Home Office 2012a: 6) in 2012, citing evidence from the Sheffield model and producing an Impact Assessment which found that the benefits exceeded the costs, the government announced in July 2013 that the public consultation had 'not provided evidence that conclusively demonstrates that Minimum Unit Pricing (MUP) will actually do what it is meant to ... In the absence of that empirical evidence, we have decided that it would be a mistake to implement MUP at this stage' (Home Office 2013: 3). The evidence base did not significantly change in this period, and advocates would argue that it became stronger with the publication of studies from Canada. With reports in the press about resistance from some cabinet ministers, including the Home Secretary, it seems likely that political pressure led to a reassessment of the evidence.
3. By contrast, the SNP were committed to MUP before there was any evidence for the policy at all. Its 2008 discussion paper supported the policy, but cited no evidence for it, as none existed (Scottish Government 2008: 19–20). The consultation document did not

request evidence but instead invited views on 'the proposed principles on which a minimum pricing scheme for alcohol products should be established' (ibid.: 20).

4. If the logic of MUP is accepted, a minimum price of 50p is no more 'evidence-based' than a minimum price of 60p or 70p. As Jeremy Browne said to Sarah Wollaston in a HoC debate:

> The logic of their argument, as I have just said, is why stop at 45p? If we had a £1 minimum unit price, the health case would be made all the more strongly.[46] (Hansard 2013)

The Sheffield models projected better health and social outcomes as the minimum price increased. In 2012, the Scottish government made it clear that it would await the next iteration of the Sheffield model before making a decision on what the minimum price should be. That model projected 60 fewer deaths in the first year at 50p and 182 fewer deaths at 70p (Meng et al. 2012: 60). Despite the additional putative benefits of a 70p minimum price, the government chose to set it at 50p. This was, presumably, because anything more would have been politically unpopular and could have been seen as excessive and regressive, but no evidence to justify this trade-off was presented.

5. Not only did the Westminster government reject MUP while the Scottish government embraced it, but for several years the Scottish Labour Party opposed MUP

[46] He added: 'The Government have to balance all kinds of competing concerns and other, also compelling, concerns about the affordability of alcohol for people on low incomes.'

while the Labour Party in England supported it. The Scottish Liberal Democrats opposed MUP while the Liberal Democrats in England supported it. Since all these politicians had access to the same evidence, it is difficult to explain such contradictions without reference to domestic politics, with opposition parties on both sides of the border rejecting or endorsing MUP for party political reasons.

FOBTs

1. Peer-reviewed research was almost entirely absent from the campaign to reduce the stake limit. Both sides relied on commissioned 'grey literature' research from third parties, much of which was wiped from the internet after 2019 and some of which was not made available to the public even at the time. Although the bookmakers commissioned some (unpublished) research estimating how many betting shops would close if stakes were reduced, no modelling was carried out to estimate the impact on problem gambling rates or gambling losses.
2. The best evidence/expert opinion came late in the day from the RGSB and Gambling Commission, but it was essentially ignored by DCMS. The stake limit that was introduced was what campaigners had demanded from the outset, but it was not what the evidence implied. RGSB explicitly said of a £2 stake limit that 'we would find it difficult to regard so strong an action as being proportionate on the basis of the existing evidence' and that it 'could create a variety of unintended

and potentially harmful consequences' (ibid.: 39). The Gambling Commission was less strident but its recommendation that the stake limit be 'at or below £30' implied a limit closer to £30 than to £2, with its own evidence suggesting that it should be between £16 and £50. Like the RGSB, the Commission noted that a 'very low limit' would amount to *de facto* prohibition since FOBTs would no longer be commercially viable. Although it did not explicitly advise against this, it warned that 'removing a popular product from the high street would be a significant change, and any restriction on freedom of choice requires careful consideration' (Gambling Commission 2018a: 9). Insofar as DCMS's decision was evidence-based, it was based on a unique interpretation of raw data and an argument that had never been used by activists, academics or the arm's length bodies during the course of the campaign.

3. As with setting a minimum price for alcohol, the exact stake limit could never be wholly 'evidence-based'. As RGSB (2017: 4) noted, there was 'no evidenced-based way of determining any uniquely correct new level.' Moreover, it emphasised that it was impossible to 'predict the effect of a reduction in maximum stakes with any confidence' (ibid.: 32) and that while it was likely that a large stake reduction would have a marked impact on gambling behaviour, 'the nature of the shift [towards substitute gambling activities], and the effect on overall harm, are impossible to predict' (ibid.: 32).
4. The Impact Assessment was unable to quantify any benefits of the policy and therefore gave its net benefit as a *cost* of over £4 billion over ten years. The policy was nevertheless introduced.

Summary

Taken together, there are many reasons to think that the classic model of evidence-based policy was not followed in any of the four case studies. They all saw prevarication and U-turns from the British government and there was a sense that the government could go in either direction right up until the final decision was made. Even campaigners for the sugar tax were surprised when George Osborne announced it in March 2016,[47] and the size of the stake cut on FOBTs defied the expectations of the markets. The Westminster government's abrupt U-turn on MUP, despite a firm commitment to introduce it, was as much of a shock as its equally abrupt U-turn on the sugar tax, which it had repeatedly insisted would not be introduced.

The policymaking process in each of the four case studies can be described, at best, as 'evidence-informed'. The advice of independent experts commissioned by the government was followed in the case of plain packaging but effectively ignored in the case of FOBTs. Public Health England's advice was heeded by the Cameron government with regards to plain packaging and the sugar tax but not minimum pricing. With the sugar tax, the government deferred to experts insofar as the tax was introduced but ignored them insofar as the tax was not set at the level experts insisted was necessary to reduce obesity. In the case of the sugar tax and the FOBT reform, the policy that was introduced was based on a different rationale to that assumed by researchers and experts. Minimum pricing was

[47] 'I didn't think we would ever get it,' said Jamie Oliver. 'I never thought we were going to get this.' ('"We did it!" Jamie Oliver welcomes surprise sugar tax announcement', *The Herald* 16/3/16)

adopted in Scotland before there was any evidence to speak of and rejected in England as more evidence supportive of the policy emerged. Opposition to MUP in both countries tended to follow party lines.

Politicians who supported plain packaging, MUP and the sugar tax were given packages of evidence to cite, including peer-reviewed studies and 'real world' data from other countries, and yet most MPs chose to ignore them in the HoC debates and instead referred to anecdotes, personal opinion and intuition. There was a tendency to talk about the scale of the problem and the urgent need to address it rather than assess the efficacy of the policy proposal. When evidence was cited, it was often cited incorrectly or misattributed. The FOBT case study shows that while a package of evidence could be useful to supporters of a cause, it was not a necessary condition of success. Conversely, the failure of the minimum pricing campaign in England showed that such a package of evidence was not a sufficient condition of success.

As I shall argue in the following chapter, the significant and multiple divergences from the classic model of evidence-based policymaking can all plausibly be explained by politics, both in the narrow sense of party political interests and intraparty fighting, and in the broader sense of public pressure and political presentation. Given the pressure put on them by the various interest groups, the government acted in its rational self-interest, regardless of the evidence, in all four case studies.

10 GETTING THE BARNACLES OFF THE BOAT

Although there are many reasons to think that decision-makers were not principally led by the evidence in any of the case studies, the U-turns, indecision and inconsistencies also suggest that they were not ideologically committed (or opposed) to any of the policies. If, as I contend, they were not generally waiting for evidence to dictate their decision and they were not strongly committed *a priori* to the policy, they must have been swayed by something other than research and personal conviction.

The policy decisions can best be understood by looking at the political pressures and incentives at work. The principal goal of any government is to be re-elected. It is in the interest of politicians to be popular, or at least not too unpopular. Political capital can be spent on unpopular policies if the government strongly believes that they will be beneficial (and will therefore pay off politically in due course), but when politicians are largely indifferent, the political benefits of acting must be greater than the political costs of acting. In this chapter, we will look at the political costs of action and inaction.

Public approval

The popularity of each of the four policies can be measured, albeit imperfectly, by nationwide surveys conducted during the course of the campaigns. With the notable and telling exception of MUP in England, they all enjoyed at least a plurality of support by the time the final decision was made.

Plain packaging

Plain packaging had absolute majority support from the British public from at least 2012, according to YouGov surveys. An early survey conducted by ASH found that 50% of respondents had no opinion, presumably because they had never heard of the idea, but from 2012 to 2014 around 60% of respondents supported it. By January 2015 – the month before the House of Commons vote – only 13% of respondents were undecided and 72% were in favour.

Sugar tax

Public opposition to a sugary drinks tax was not insubstantial but seems to have faded by 2016. ComRes surveys

Table 8. Support/oppose plain packaging

	Support	Oppose	Don't know
February 2008 (YouGov)	43%	17%	50%
August 2012 (YouGov)	62%	11%	27%
July 2013 (YouGov)	58%	26%	16%
March 2014 (YouGov)	64%	11%	25%
January 2015 (YouGov)	72%	15%	13%

Table 9. Support/oppose soft drinks levy

	Support	Oppose	Don't know
2014 (ComRes)	35%	51%	14%
October 2015 (ComRes)	54%	43%	3%
October 2015 (CATI)*	57%	42%	2%
January 2016 (BMG)*	44%	33%	18%

**Includes food (e.g. 'Do you support or oppose new tax on food and drinks which contain high levels of sugar?')*

found that only 35% of respondents supported such a tax in 2014, but this had risen to 54% by October 2015.

October 2015 was a crucial month for the sugar tax debate, with the Health Select Committee holding oral sessions on childhood obesity with the high-profile celebrity chef Jamie Oliver, whose *Jamie's Sugar Rush* documentary had been broadcast the previous month. It also saw the publication of Public Health England's evidence review on sugar. From this point, all surveys found that a sugar tax was supported by more people than opposed it. A further survey carried out in 2017, after the announcement but before implementation, found that 70% of 18–64-year-olds supported the tax (Adams et al. 2021).

Minimum pricing

In January 2011, YouGov found that 47% of Britons supported MUP and 44% were opposed. The following year, it found that support and opposition were equally split, with 46% for each.

Table 10. Support/oppose minimum unit pricing (UK)

	Support	Oppose	Don't know
January 2011 (YouGov)	47%	44%	9%
March 2012 (YouGov)	46%	46%	8%

Although only two relevant surveys could be identified, an academic study published in 2012 also found that MUP lacked widespread support. Based on 28 focus groups in the north of England, it concluded:

> There was little evidence to suggest that people would support the introduction of a minimum price per unit of alcohol policy. (Lonsdale et al. 2012: 1)

One of its authors told the *Guardian*:

> 'In concordance with our expectations, participants did express negative views of the minimum price per unit,' said Hagger. 'They were sceptical of its effects. They found the idea unfair to sensible drinkers and perceived that it might create or exacerbate other social problems – increases in crime or drug abuse where people who were heavily dependent might turn to crime to fund their alcohol abuse.' (Jha 2011)

Focus group research commissioned by the Home Office and carried out in England and Wales also concluded that MUP was 'unpopular' and was perceived to be ineffective (Banerjee et al. 2010: 55). In addition, a January 2013

ComRes survey found that 55% thought that MUP would be ineffective and only 38% thought it would be effective. Politicians in Westminster sensed this public mood, as a member of the Alcohol Health Alliance told Thom et al. (2016: 15):

> They [MPs] feel it's not effective, or that it penalises moderate drinkers and as we are in a particularly sensitive time in terms of recession and so on, that people aren't going to tolerate it. So it's seen as an unpopular political move.

Importantly, however, opinion was more favourable in Scotland. In 2015, 41% of Scots were in favour of MUP and only 33% were opposed. By 2019, 50% were in favour and only 28% were opposed (Ferguson et al. 2020: 9).

It is possible that public opinion in England changed after 2013. A survey commissioned by Public Health England in 2015 found that 52% of Britons supported MUP and only 25% were opposed (Fuller and Simpson 2015). This finding is surprising given the results of earlier surveys but since no surveys have been conducted since, it is not clear whether it was an outlier. For our purposes, the important point is that around half of English adults who had an opinion on MUP were opposed to it in 2012 when the policy was under serious consideration in Westminster.

FOBTs

According to survey evidence, FOBTs were extremely unpopular from at least 2014 onwards. A YouGov survey in May 2014 found that only 4% were opposed to banning the machines completely. A further YouGov survey reported by the *Daily Mail* found that 48% thought FOBTs should not be in betting shops and 60% believed the maximum stake should be reduced to £2. Both surveys included a large number of 'don't knows', but after the maximum stake was reduced in April 2019, a YouGov survey found that 85% of respondents approved of the change and only 9% were opposed. This suggests that the vast majority of those who were undecided in 2014 had become opposed to FOBTs by 2019.

Taking all the survey evidence together, we can see a correlation with policy outcomes. The only policy that did not have relative majority support was UK-wide MUP. This, of course, was the only policy that was rejected by policymakers in Westminster.

Table 11. Support/oppose FOBT stake limit of £2

	Support	Oppose	Don't know
2014 (YouGov)*	58%	4%	38%
2014 (YouGov)	60%	6%	34%
2019 (YouGov)	85%	9%	6%

**Question refers to a ban on fixed odds betting terminals*

Table 12. Public opinion before the policy decision was taken

	Support	Oppose
Minimum pricing (UK)	46%	46%
Sugar tax	44%	33%
Minimum pricing (Scotland)	41%	33%
Plain packaging	72%	15%
£2 FOBT stake	60%	6%

It is notable that the British government's change of heart about the sugar tax occurred a few months after public opinion had shifted in its favour. It is also striking that FOBTs were hugely unpopular, with a majority wanting not just to reduce the stake to £2 but to ban them outright. By the time the decisions were taken on FOBTs and plain packaging, public opinion had been strongly in favour of action for some time and there was little opposition.

Risks of failure

For politicians dealing with low salience issues, a lack of strong opposition is crucial. As one policy actor told John W. Kingdon (1995: 151): 'If too many people get angry, it's not worth it.' And while it is important for a policy to have majority support among the electorate in the short term, the more far-sighted politician does not want to support a policy that will become unpopular after implementation. They want to be assured that the policy will not backfire or become an embarrassment. For the uncommitted policymaker, fear of failure may be a greater motivator than hope of success. As subsequent evaluations showed, it was always going to be difficult to prove whether any of the four policies made a positive difference, but negative consequences, such as a booming black market or an increase in certain criminal activities, might have been more obvious. Aware of these concerns, opponents exploited *status quo bias* and warned of unintended consequences: a rise in counterfeit cigarettes, gamblers switching to unregulated websites, drinkers switching to drugs, etc. Opponents of plain packaging and FOBT reform warned the government that it would lose tax revenue. Opponents of MUP and plain packaging warned that the policies would be illegal. Only the sugar tax lacked plausible unintended consequences of any significance.

Policymakers took many of these concerns seriously. Impact Assessments for plain packaging acknowledged that there was a risk of the tobacco black market growing and tobacco duty revenues declining. There is little doubt that Philip Hammond was concerned about a decline in gambling duty revenue resulting from the FOBT reform. It is telling that these policies were only introduced once such concerns had been dealt with. In the case of FOBTs, Hammond increased remote gaming duty on online casinos from 15% to 21% in the Budget of October 2018 to help offset the tax losses from gambling machines. Cyril Chantler addressed the illicit trade issue in his report on plain packaging, despite not being asked to focus on anything other than the health impact, and concluded that there was little to worry about. HMRC carried out an assessment in August 2014 which found 'no evidence to suggest the introduction of standardised packaging will have a significant impact on the overall size of the illicit market' (HMRC 2014: 4). Similarly, the chair of the Royal College of Psychiatrists in Scotland told Scotland's Health and Sport Committee that he was 'sceptical' of the notion that drinkers 'might switch the kind of alcohol they drank or replace drink with drugs' (Scottish Parliament 2012: 41).

The threat of lawsuits hung in the air for plain packaging and MUP, but decision-makers knew that these would take years to be resolved and they would not be blamed for the outcome if the industry's lawsuits succeeded. The World Trade Organisation began looking at plain packaging in May 2014 and did not reach a final judgement until

2020 when it ruled against the tobacco industry. It was not an impediment in the meantime. The industry, having already lost a case in Australia, followed through on its promise to go to the High Court in London in December 2015 where it filed another ultimately unsuccessful case. The Scotch Whisky Association's case against MUP seemed more robust but was ultimately thrown out in 2017 after going back and forth between Scotland, Luxembourg and England.

As we have seen, politicians were particularly interested in how each of the policies fared in other countries. As one academic told Katikireddi et al. (2013: 493) with regards to minimum pricing, 'there's no doubt that everyone is much happier with a real-life experience, well evaluated, than a model'. This may be because 'real world' experience seems more solid, tangible and comprehensible than theoretical, experimental and modelled evidence, but politicians would have also observed that the policies had been introduced legally elsewhere without a significant public backlash and without any obvious negative consequences. The evidence that the policies had achieved their goal in other countries may have been disputed, but implementation was clearly possible and there seemed to be few negative political repercussions from doing so.

Risks of inaction

Having established that there was little for politicians to fear from introducing each of the policies, except MUP in England, we now turn to the costs of inaction. What did they stand to lose if they did nothing? In each case, there was substantial, and often overwhelming, political pressure for the government to act. The pressure came, naturally enough, from pressure groups but also from opposition parties, the media and, as the opinion polls suggest, the public.

Plain packaging

There is always pressure on governments to do more to tackle smoking, especially underage smoking. In March 2013, campaigners started using Cancer Research UK's claim that 207,000 children start smoking every year. This figure became inextricably bound up with the plain packaging policy. It is indicative of how important framing was to the debate that this statistic was cited in more media reports than any piece of evidence apart from the Chantler Review and Wakefield et al. (2013). It was cited in the HoC debates 19 times, more than *any* piece of evidence, including the Chantler Review.

The political pressure intensified in July 2013 after the government put plain packaging on hold, saying that it would wait for evidence to emerge from Australia. It was immediately alleged that David Cameron's advisor Lynton Crosby had encouraged him to ditch the policy. Since Crosby's public affairs company, Crosby Textor, had Philip Morris International among its clients, it was rumoured that Cameron had capitulated to indirect lobbying from the tobacco industry.

This was swiftly exploited by the opposition. In a press release, Diane Abbott, the shadow public health minister, said:

> This is deeply concerning, because behind all the chaos, confusion and dither, it's clear that Lynton Crosby and the government's friends in big business are pulling the strings, and public health is being quietly ditched by this government. (Clark 2014a: 136)

Andy Burnham, Labour's shadow health secretary, said:

> David Cameron promised to get tough on smoking and alcohol abuse but instead has caved in to big business and vested interests. (ibid.: 126)

In the four months between the government putting plain packaging on hold and commissioning the Chantler Review, three debates about the policy were held in the House of Commons. Labour leader Ed Miliband called Cameron the 'Prime Minister for Benson and Hedge funds' and wrote to the Cabinet Secretary to demand an inquiry 'to establish public confidence about the activities of Mr Crosby'.[48] Although Cameron strongly denied these claims, the Crosby story appeared regularly in the media for two weeks until Crosby himself explicitly denied having ever discussed the issue with him. This was still not enough to quell suspicions about industry influence, and these claims, though unsupported by evidence, had an impact on public opinion. A YouGov poll in July 2013 found that '60% of respondents feel the government has been leant on by tobacco companies' (Gadher and Leake 2013).

---

[48] https://www.bbc.co.uk/news/uk-politics-23338997

When David Cameron put plain packaging on hold in July 2013, it was reported to be part of Lynton Crosby's strategy to 'get the barnacles off the boat', a phrase that was understood to mean getting rid of unnecessary policies and focusing on what the *Guardian* described as 'core issues that resonated with voters' (Doward 2014b). Within months, largely thanks to Crosby's presence in government, plain packaging had become a barnacle that could only be scraped off the boat by capitulating to the anti-smoking pressure groups.

Minimum pricing

History has shown that the political repercussions for Westminster politicians from not introducing MUP were negligible. After the government put the policy on indefinite hold, the media lost interest and calls for it to be introduced across the UK were largely confined to a few public health groups. In 2015, Ian Gilmore, chair of the Alcohol Health Alliance, lamented that 'all major political parties in Westminster remain anxious about MUP being a "vote-loser"' (Gilmore 2015: 6).

The U-turn in July 2013 was reported to be the result of a 'cabinet revolt' led by Home Secretary Theresa May. According to the *Guardian* in March 2013:

> May, the former health secretary Andrew Lansley, and the education secretary, Michael Gove, have all opposed the proposals on grounds that the impact on living standards would be unacceptable.
>
> The proposals have also been rejected by the Mayor of London, Boris Johnson, as regressive. (Wintour 2013)

The U-turn was condemned by the Alcohol Health Alliance and a few other health groups, who accused the government of caving in to alcohol industry lobbying, but claims about undue industry influence, which were echoed by Sarah Wollaston and Tracey Crouch, did not taint the government in the same way as similar claims about the tobacco industry in the plain packaging campaign. The cost of inaction on MUP was therefore minimal. Without significant public pressure to introduce the policy, there was little political capital to be earned from doing so.

In Scotland, however, the political incentives and 'institutional geography' were different. As Brownlow (2022) argues, the economic benefits of devolution can be difficult to attain and this is especially true when a devolved administration has limited control over taxation (in Scotland, most taxes, including corporation tax, are set in Westminster). In the absence of full independence, the devolved administration acted as an additional layer of government which, from 2011, was controlled by Scottish nationalists who saw devolution as a stepping-stone to their overriding political objective of secession. While MPs in London had to divide their time debating a wide range of issues, the institutional geography of Scotland meant that MSPs could only usefully focus on certain policy areas, such as health and education. Politically constrained in many ways, the SNP was always likely to flex its legislative muscles when given the chance to diverge from the rest of the UK.

Moreover, Scotland had a bigger problem with alcohol than the rest of the UK – its rate of alcohol-specific deaths was twice that of England's – while having no control over alcohol duty. MUP was one of the few ways in which it could affect the price of alcohol. With the SNP eager to take a visibly different path to England, alcohol regulation became one of the 'cultural faultlines' (Rodríguez-Pose and Gill 2005: 408) dividing Holyrood from Westminster. While many Conservative politicians were wary of 'nanny state' measures, the SNP was more openly paternalistic and explicitly endorsed the whole-population approach to alcohol discussed in Chapter 5. While MPs in England worried about the impact on the majority of 'responsible drinkers', the Scottish government took the view that everybody would have to drink less if alcohol-related harm was to decline. For them, the impact on moderate drinkers was a feature rather than a bug of MUP.

MUP offered the SNP the opportunity to not only distinguish itself from the rest of the UK, but to make its mark on the world. Scotland had previously assumed the role of pioneer by introducing a smoking ban in March 2006, more than a year before the rest of the UK. With MUP, it had the opportunity to be a global trailblazer. SNP politicians were aware of the attention this would get them and pro-MUP campaigners exploited the desire for national prestige with flattery. Under the heading 'The world is watching', Scotland's Health and Sport Committee reported in 2012 that:

One further consequence [of introducing minimum pricing], arguably a welcome one, was the international coverage the Bill was receiving. Professor [Tim] Stockwell informed the Committee that the Bill was being written about in such publications as *The Huffington Post*, the *Chicago Tribune* and the *Washington Post*. He said:

> 'What you are doing is being looked at across the world.'

Dr [Peter] Rice also remarked that colleagues elsewhere in the UK and beyond were interested in what was happening here. He told the Committee:

> ... the Royal College of Physicians in London has consistently presented Scotland as a model of where it would like to head in its discussions with the UK Government.

The Cabinet Secretary told the Committee that it was 'a thoroughly good thing' the world was watching, and she said:

> I know that, on alcohol, many countries regard Scotland as a leader in our public health approach, as we were rightly regarded when the previous administration brought in the ban on smoking in public places. Northern Ireland, the Republic of Ireland and England are looking closely at what we are doing on minimum pricing. I am firmly of the view that where Scotland leads, other countries will follow. (Scottish Parliament 2012: 41)

It therefore seems reasonable to conclude that the SNP's championing of MUP was not solely motivated by health concerns. It is telling that Labour and the Liberal Democrats, both of whom opposed Scottish independence, also opposed MUP, and still more telling that those same parties supported MUP in England. As Katikireddi et al. (2014: 8) conclude:

> The story of MUP illustrates the complexity of the policy process and highlights the limitations

> of seeing policymaking as purely determined by evidence (evidence-based policy) rather than evidence as one important influence on policy.
>
> ... much of the MUP story does not relate to evidence but rather political and institutional factors which should not be ignored by researchers and practitioners seeking to influence the policy process.

FOBTs

FOBTs were so unpopular by 2017 that there was no danger of a popular backlash against any clampdown. The vast majority of voters had never played the machines and several newspapers were actively campaigning against them. As with plain packaging, the government risked being seen as being in the pocket of an unpopular industry if it failed to act.

The only risk was to HMRC, which expected to lose several hundred million pounds of machine gaming duty per annum, but this was resolved by increasing duty on another unpopular form of gambling. The Treasury's resistance to reducing the FOBT stake limit before October 2019 was driven by concerns about a six-month shortfall in gaming tax revenue rather than any fondness for the machines or the industry. Explaining this to the House of Commons Treasury Committee (2018: 6), Philip Hammond said 'I have absolutely no love for these machines, I think they are terrible things – but the Government have to manage this process in an orderly and sensible way'. When the FOBT reform was brought forward to April 2019, Hammond brought the remote gaming duty rise forward to the same date.

Sugar tax

With regards to the risks of inaction, the sugar tax campaign is something of an exception and, as usual, the exception offers an insight into the policymaking process. Although there was a constant drumbeat of support for a sugar tax from campaigners and sections of the media in 2016, it was not at a crescendo when George Osborne announced the new levy on 16 March.

The government was arguably under the most pressure in October 2015 after the Health Select Committee hearings, Jamie Oliver's television documentary and the Public Health England report, and then again in January 2016 after the publication of Colchero et al. (2016a), Ma et al. (2016) and a letter from a number of influential health organisations calling for the introduction of a sugar tax. There was a slight softening of the Prime Minister's attitude after the second period of pressure when he said, 'I don't really want to put new taxes on anything, but we do have to recognise that we face potentially in Britain something of an obesity crisis'.[49] But the government had weathered both storms and nothing happened in February or March to explain the sudden and unexpected announcement of a sugar tax in that year's Budget.[50]

[49] https://www.bbc.co.uk/news/uk-politics-35256647

[50] The only new piece of evidence to emerge in this period was the estimate from Cancer Research UK and UK Health Forum (2016) of how many cases of obesity would be prevented by a 20% sugar tax.

It was political pressure of another kind that explains why the sugar tax was announced when it was and, perhaps, why it was announced at all. Having presided over six years of 'austerity', the government was supposed to have eliminated the structural current budget deficit by 2015/16. Not only had it failed to do this, but Osborne was going into a Budget knowing that he would have to announce worse economic growth forecasts and higher debt forecasts than he had announced in his November statement a few months earlier.

In the absence of a high-profile policy such as a sugar tax, it would have been the revised forecasts, along with new cuts to disability living allowance, that would have led the news. While it cannot be proven that this was Osborne's motivation, it was the sugar tax that instead dominated the news cycle on Budget day and it was the view of many people at the time that it was Osborne's 'rabbit from the hat', a reference to Osborne's tendency to announce unexpected measures, usually tax *cuts*, in previous Budgets. The sugar tax featured heavily on the front page of the *Independent* ('A spoonful of sugar tax'), the *Mirror* ('Sugar and spite'), the *Telegraph* ('Osborne sugars the pill'), the *i* ('Sugar tax sweetens the pill') and the *Scotsman* ('Osborne's bid to sweeten economic warnings'). Online headlines included 'Sugar tax the big rabbit in Osborne's budget' (Sky News) and 'Sugar tax surprise in Budget – but growth forecasts cut' (BBC). As many of these headlines indicate, the general view was that the sugar tax was some good news to help offset, or distract from, the bad news. It was a sign of how much public opinion had shifted that it was considered good news at all.

11 A PUBLIC CHOICE PERSPECTIVE

If the conscientious use of robust evidence was not decisive in any of the four case studies, it is not a surprising or controversial conclusion to reach. The academic literature on politics, research dissemination, public health and economics largely agrees that policymaking is a messy business, that solid evidence is neither sufficient nor necessary for legislation to pass, that politicians make political decisions rather than evidence-based decisions, and that the rational model of policymaking is never attained in the real world.

A more realistic model, mentioned in Chapter 2, is the multiple streams approach of John W. Kingdon (1995) in which a problem rises to the top of the political agenda, a list of possible solutions is narrowed down to one feasible policy, and the policy is tested in the water of political and public opinion. Although Kingdon did not set out any iron laws or testable predictions, there are three notable differences between what he observed in his case studies and what we have seen in ours.

Firstly, Kingdon presents a policy's progression from idea to legislation as a ponderous slog involving many years of frustration and setbacks. Politicians and policy entrepreneurs can wait decades for the stars to align. Softening up the public for a new policy is a gradual and uncertain process with victory often only earned after a long battle of ideas. It would, wrote Kingdon, 'be exceedingly surprising if wholly new ideas suddenly appeared on the scene in the policy primeval soup and immediately received a serious hearing' (ibid.: 141).

This is consistent with the theory of incrementalism outlined by Lindblom and Cohen (1979) but it was not the experience of the public health interest groups in our case studies. Of the four policies, only one (plain packaging) had been around for more than a decade by the time it became government policy. The Campaign for Fairer Gambling came up with the £2 stake policy in 2013. It immediately received 'a serious hearing' and became policy five years later. Minimum pricing was first advocated by SHAAP in 2007. Within two years it had been included in the Scottish government's Framework for Alcohol and by 2012 it was in the Alcohol (Minimum Pricing) Act, its implementation only delayed by legal issues. 'Soda taxes' were first discussed as public health measures in the USA in around 2008 but there was barely a ripple of agitation for them in the UK until 2012 when Mytton et al. (2012) published their editorial in the *British Medical Journal*. Plain packaging had a longer history and could be traced back to a policy proposal in Canada in the late 1980s which soon faded from view and did not appear on the UK's political radar until 2008 when it was mentioned in a public consultation on tobacco control.

In each case, it took only a few years for the policies to not only be implemented but, with the exception of the sugar tax, to be implemented exactly as the campaigners demanded. There were no compromises and no watering down by industry stakeholders.

Secondly, Kingdon found that issues were typically put on the agenda as a result of 'focusing events' or changes in routine indicators or, in some cases, feedback from government officials and voters. Focusing events, such as the Hillsborough disaster and the Grenfell Tower fire, have often led to a change in policy in the UK but there was nothing comparable in our case studies. There was no crisis or high-profile event, such as the death of a celebrity or child, to push the issues up the agenda, nor were most of the indicators going in the wrong direction. Smoking prevalence was going down while rates of alcohol-related mortality, childhood obesity and problem gambling were broadly static.

With the possible exception of alcohol, none of the issues discussed in our case studies was a priority for politicians or the public at the start of the decade. The Conservative Party's election manifesto of 2010 included several anti-alcohol policies, but not MUP. Smoking and obesity each received one passing mention and gambling was not mentioned at all. Labour's manifesto did not mention obesity or gambling and the only references to alcohol and tobacco appeared in one short paragraph:

> The ban on smoking in public places will be maintained. Wherever necessary, we will act to protect children's health from tobacco, alcohol and sunbeds. (Labour Party 2010: 43)

The Liberal Democrat manifesto supported MUP in principle, but did not mention obesity, gambling or smoking. And yet by the end of 2014 all of these issues *except alcohol* had been pushed towards the top of the political agenda in Westminster and the government was under intense pressure to make a decision about policies it had not devised and which had largely been forced upon it.

Thirdly, and most importantly, Kingdon found that interest groups could be significant policy actors but chiefly because they blocked policy reforms rather than initiated them. This may be true of financially self-interested groups, such as business associations and trade unions, but it is emphatically not true of the public health interest groups in our case studies who not only successfully promoted their policy solutions, but raised their issues up the agenda in the first place *and* created the public mood and momentum required for their ideas to become law. *The public health interest groups dominated all three of Kingdon's political streams.*

Activism

Despite the lack of focusing events, getting these issues up the agenda was not difficult. Smoking, alcohol-related harm, childhood obesity and problem gambling were not new problems to be solved. Various efforts had been made to tackle them in the past and policymakers needed no persuading that they were legitimate targets for government action. Politicians were familiar with the topics, and the media knew from experience that the public were interested in them. In the case of smoking, in particular, the question was not whether there should be more regulation but what the next regulation should be. The public health interest groups only needed to market their new policies and show that they were the 'best buys' at that moment in time. In practice, this required the implicit or explicit suggestion that cigarette packaging, cheap alcohol, sugary drinks and FOBTs were the most pressing problems in each of the policy areas.

Public health interest groups increased the salience of their issues in a variety of ways. Both the anti-obesity and anti-gambling groups focused on what was perceived to be a newly discovered threat to the nation: sugar was presented as 'the new tobacco' and FOBTs were portrayed as 'the crack cocaine of gambling'. The anti-smoking coalition appealed to new knowledge, portraying cigarette packaging as a hitherto unrecognised trigger of youth smoking, while the anti-alcohol coalition focused on minimum pricing as a novel solution to a longstanding problem.

These groups also found fresh ways to frame the problems. Cancer Research UK produced a new estimate of how many children took up smoking every year and projected that the sugar tax would prevent 3.7 million cases of obesity over ten years. Although the routine data showed that the problems in question were in decline or flatlining, the public were given the impression that they were spiralling out of control. Statistically insignificant fluctuations in the estimated rate of problem gambling provided opportunities for the media to claim every few years that the number of 'gambling addicts' had doubled.[51] Obesity models predicted extraordinarily high rates of obesity in the future unless the government acted. In Scotland, policymakers were shown a graph of liver cirrhosis mortality rates between 1950 and 2002 which showed a huge rise since 1990 but did not show the steep decline after 2002. One civil servant later said that this was 'the single most compelling graph

[51] In 2013, the *Independent* reported that the number of problem gamblers had 'doubled in six years to almost 500,000'. In 2016, the *Times* reported that the number of problem gamblers had 'almost doubled in three years from 0.4% of the population to 0.7%, the equivalent of 336,000 people'. Such claims are mutually incompatible.

that we showed ministers' during the MUP campaign (Katikireddi et al. 2014: 5).

An important observation from Kingdon (1995: 142) is that issues are more likely to rise up the agenda 'if a solution is attached'. In all four case studies, the public health interest groups had a policy 'solution' from the outset. The whole purpose of getting the issue up the agenda was to promote the policy. Over time, the policies became synonymous with the problem.

Finally, the public health interest groups used press releases, television documentaries, peer-reviewed studies, petitions, media appearances, public gatherings and celebrity endorsements to create a national mood that was sympathetic to their policies. Persistent campaigning eroded public opposition to the policies until politicians felt safe to act. The exception was MUP in England, which was announced by David Cameron before campaigners had 'softened up' the public. Based on 26 interviews with non-industry policy actors, Hawkins and McCambridge (2020: 323) argue that the campaign failed because public health activists were taken by surprise and had not had time to roll the pitch.

> The fact the policy was not widely trailed before its announcement meant that not just policymakers, but the wider policy community were unprepared for its landing. Health NGOs and advocates which would be expected to support the policy and defend it publicly had not had the opportunity [to] develop coherent media and influencing strategies around the announcement. This was crucial in a context in which the public still needed to be convinced about the merits of the policy.

The dominance of a single interest group pushing for new legislation at all three stages (or streams) of the policy-making process and achieving their goals in such a short space of time is unusual. The literature on real world policymaking built up by scholars such as Kingdon and Lindblom suggest a slower and more chaotic process in which other policy actors have a greater role, there is more compromise and much is left to serendipity. With the caveat that he was writing about US politics, Kingdon (1995: 21) observed that the administration, which is to say the president, his staff and his political appointees, were very powerful policy actors in agenda-setting and policy formulation, but in our case studies we find the government on the back foot, reacting to policy demands from pressure groups and dealing with issues that were not its priorities.

Conceptually, it is important to distinguish two forms of activism: lobbying and campaigning. In the political economy, as in the public health literature, lobbying is given great importance, as if all that needs to be done to instigate or prevent legislation is to give large sums of money to smooth-talking public affairs professionals and watch policymakers crumble. Lobbying is certainly one approach used by pressure groups, but other strategies include disseminating research, commissioning surveys, writing op-eds, holding demonstrations, participating in media interviews, briefing journalists and holding public events. Through public-facing activity of this kind, activists can help mould opinions in the media, academia and among the general public, thereby putting pressure on policymakers. Activities designed to change public opinion were almost certainly more important than traditional lobbying in our case studies – and changing public opinion was a prerequisite for policy adoption.

In the final analysis, lobbying was no match for campaigning, and persuasion was no match for pressure. Lobbyists from industry sought to *persuade* politicians of their arguments but had no power to put *pressure* on them. Indirectly, they could threaten them with the prospect of reduced tax revenues, black market activity and job losses, but these relied on arguments that could be dismissed and, even if accepted, could be seen as a risk worth taking to save thousands of lives. By contrast, the public health interest groups, which included highly regarded charities such as Cancer Research UK, framed the issue in such a way that the government was at risk of being seen to be in the pocket of the gambling industry and 'Big Tobacco' if it did not proceed with the FOBT reform and plain packaging, and would be seen as not caring about the health of children if it did not proceed with the sugar tax. (It was perhaps to the detriment of the minimum pricing campaign that it was never able to convincingly portray MUP as a child-centred policy and could not persuade the public that the alcohol industry was as odious as 'Big Tobacco'.)

The public health interest groups were well aware that the public had little sympathy with their most vocal opponents. When the Australian government passed plain packaging into law in 2011, the Health Minister Nicola Roxon publicly described it as a 'very courageous step'.[52] In private, however, she told an activist-academic that 'this was a no-brainer, being really bold, taking on big tobacco. How do you lose, even if you lose? Big tobacco... everyone

[52] https://edition.cnn.com/2012/08/15/world/asia/australia-tobacco-packaging/

hates them... so really, having a fight with them can't hurt.'[53] Looking back on the FOBT campaign, Matt Zarb-Cousin of the CFFG wrote: 'The most effective campaigns focus attacks on their opponent, which is often the sector that is resistant to the campaign's objective. This allows the decision-maker, such as a government minister, to ride to the rescue and earn political capital' (Zarb-Cousin 2019). By framing the debate as 'people versus profit', the public health interest groups appealed to the *intentions heuristic* mentioned in Chapter 2. If they genuinely believed that industry had some kind of hold over the government, they would not have spent so much time reminding policymakers that the industry was opposed to their policies. By the 2010s, the idea that standing up to any of these industries required political bravery was anachronistic at best. All the meaningful pressure came from the other side.

Policymaking under pressure

Analysis of each of the four campaigns leads to the conclusion that decision-makers were acting in response to *pressure*: pressure from the media, from the public, and from other political parties. Underpinning and driving this pressure were the public health interest groups, i.e. *pressure groups*. Moreover, the course and outcome of all four campaigns can be explained by reference to the rational self-interest of politicians, of the interest groups and of the public themselves. Since the policymaking process

[53] https://www.croakey.org/simon-chapman-honoured-as-skeptic-of-the-year-a-good-time-to-look-back-on-the-historic-tobacco-plain-packaging-campaign/

was dominated at every level by the public health interest groups, we shall begin with them.

Interest groups

In the analysis of pressure group politics set out by Mancur Olson in *The Logic of Collective Action,* small, concentrated interest groups prevail over large, diffuse interest groups because the individuals who make up the larger group do not have a sufficient incentive *as individuals* to mobilise. *As a group,* they would gain collective benefits from lobbying in their collective interest, but the benefits to the individual are smaller than the marginal cost of taking political action. Should a policy entrepreneur form an organisation to represent the interests of the large group, individuals will benefit regardless of whether they contribute personally and their contribution as one voice among many would be too small to make a measurable difference to the cause. Since each of these individuals is faced with the same (dis)incentives, the group suffers a free rider problem and remains politically inactive. Members of a small interest group, by contrast, have strong incentives to mobilise because the benefits of a change in policy accrue to fewer people and are worth more to each individual. A member (or leader) of a small group has a greater say in the group's activities and their political cause will be materially affected if they withdraw their contribution, thereby making it less tempting to free ride.

When discussing interest groups, political scientists, including public choice academics, tend to focus on rent-seeking lobby groups who stand to gain financially from government action. A typical textbook example is the trade association that wants tariffs to protect its members from competition. The industry is highly motivated to lobby for the tariffs while millions of consumers, who will be disadvantaged by the resulting higher prices, do not have a strong enough incentive, *as individuals*, to mobilise in their collective interest. It is conflicts of this kind, involving financially self-interested groups lobbying for obvious collective benefits, that were the focus of George Stigler's seminal paper 'The Theory of Economic Regulation' (Stigler 1971) which heavily influenced scholars such as Peltzman (1976) and Becker (1983).

This theory can explain the existence of such groups as the Association of British Bookmakers and the British Soft Drinks Association. It also explains why there was little or no organised grassroots opposition to such policies as minimum pricing and the sugar tax. But can it explain the public health interest groups? On the face of it, their very existence poses a challenge to the public choice account; firstly, because they overcame the free rider problem and secondly because they had no self-interested collective benefits to lobby for. Their objectives could be described as paternalistic and possibly even altruistic, but they were not obviously selfish or self-interested in the layman's sense of the word.

All things being equal, lobby groups formed exclusively to change the self-regarding behaviour of other people do not appear to have what John Ferejohn termed a 'thick-rational' motive. 'Thick-rationality' assumes that individuals 'value the same sorts of things: for example, wealth, income, power, or the perquisites of office' (Ferejohn 2000: 396). These are predictable motivations for human behaviour because they are, to a greater or lesser extent, universal.

A 'thin-rational' account, by contrast, assumes that individuals rationally pursue their goals, but that those goals can be anything and can only be discerned by observing the person's revealed preferences. Olson acknowledged the existence of thin-rational motives (in religion and philanthropy, for example) but shied away from them in his analysis because they have little predictive power.

Are there thick-rational incentives that can explain how pressure groups with a fundamentally paternalistic agenda become prominent political actors? One possibility, *pace* Olson, is that they offer selective incentives, such as price discounts and networking events, which attract paying members who provide the financial resources for the organisation to lobby as a sideline. This is certainly true of some of the groups that supported the policy campaigns, such as the British Medical Association (a trade union), the Salvation Army (a religious group) and the Royal College of Physicians (an elite association for medical professionals), but it is not true of the single-issue pressure groups such as ASH and Action on Sugar. These are not membership organisations and they do not offer ancillary benefits that might attract supporters.

Another possibility is that their agenda is fundamentally altruistic and their existence is therefore no more difficult to explain than the existence of groups that campaign against the death penalty or raise money for disaster relief. This is difficult to sustain, however. If coercive paternalism is altruistic, it is a particularly aggressive and punitive form of altruism, arguably a form of 'pathological altruism' ('behaviour in which attempts to promote the welfare of another, or others, results instead in harm' (Oakley 2013: 10,408)) with the harm going unnoticed by its advocates

(Bonell et al. 2015). But if paternalism requires coercion, it is objectively not altruistic, at least not in the view of mainstream economics. Unless there is clear evidence of market failure, economists assume that people optimise their wellbeing by pursuing their preferences, including the preference to drink sugary drinks and play electronic roulette. Public health campaigners might consider these to be the wrong choices but, as Littlechild and Wiseman (1986: 162) note, 'the notion that preferences might simply be "wrong" (as opposed to misinformed) is outside the market failure framework as normally conceived.'

Those who use regulation or taxation to make it more difficult for adults to satisfy their preferences therefore make their lives worse, not better. Of course, it is very possible that single-issue public health campaigners do not share the assumptions of economists, but it is notable that the general public do not see their activities as altruistic either. The British public donate large sums of money to unambiguously altruistic causes such as animal welfare and poverty relief, but they almost never donate to the single-issue pressure groups mentioned in our case studies. Despite having a high public profile and claiming that their policies would save many thousands of lives, registered charities such as ASH and Alcohol Focus Scotland received risibly small donations from the public and inspired virtually no voluntary activism. This suggests that the public do not see coercive paternalism as a 'good cause' and do not think it would be altruistic to give their time or money to those who advocate it.[54]

[54] For a longer discussion of the possible motives of public health pressure groups, see Snowdon (2025a).

It could be argued that the natural supporters of such causes are able to free-ride on state-funded pressure groups and that government funding crowds out voluntary donations, but there is no evidence for this proposition. In the case of ASH, the government only stepped in with funding after attempts to raise money from the general public failed. For years thereafter, ASH intended to become financially self-supporting, but in its grant application to the Department of Health in 1993 acknowledged that 'Anti-smoking activity is not a popular cause for donors' (ASH 1993). There were no grassroots lobby groups of any stature campaigning against sugar or gambling before Action on Sugar and the CFFG were founded, and although the temperance movement has historically enjoyed broader public support, it has usually been an adjunct to religious institutions which offer members selective incentives (e.g. salvation).

A further argument against the altruism theory is that altruism by definition requires selflessness. If an individual benefits from an action, it is not altruistic. This leads us towards to real reason why small, concentrated public health pressure groups exist and thrive in Britain. Public health advocacy has been professionalised since the 1970s, largely because of funding from the government. The individuals working for groups such as ASH, Alcohol Focus Scotland and Action on Sugar were full-time employees of small, professional organisations. The question of why they participated in political activism is no more puzzling than the question of why a butcher chops meat. It was their job. Unlike the members of Olson's latent interest groups, their contributions required no sacrifice. On the contrary, being salaried, the benefits of their advocacy outweighed the costs even if they enjoyed no psychological reward from achieving their goals. Their position was quite different from that of a grassroots volunteer whose activism would have required a significant opportunity cost and often direct financial costs (such as travelling to protests).

The public health interest groups did not need to attract members nor raise donations from the public. Some of the most prominent groups were overwhelmingly funded by the state, including Alcohol Concern, Alcohol Focus Scotland and SHAAP in the minimum pricing debate. At the height of the plain packaging campaign, a number of regional anti-tobacco campaign groups, such as FRESH North-East, Smokefree North-West and Smokefree South-West were receiving hundreds of thousands of pounds in funding from NHS primary care trusts.[55] In 2010/11, ASH and Alcohol Concern received £220,500 and £300,000 from the Department of Health respectively. Alcohol Concern also received £250,000 from the Welsh Assembly. These sums dwarfed the £15,365 in donations and legacies ASH received from the public and the £4,729 in donations and £13,115 in membership fees received by Alcohol Concern.[56] In the same year, ASH Wales received £18,023 in donations and £173,000 from the Welsh Assembly.

The phenomenon of state-funded lobby groups has received little attention in the public choice literature, perhaps because it was rare in the 1960s and 1970s when the field evolved. Olson (1971: 149) mentions the Farm Bureau,

[55] Information about regional anti-tobacco quangos were obtained under the Freedom of Information Act. Smokefree South-West was given £468,462 in 2011/12 specifically for its campaign on plain packaging.

[56] By 2013, Alcohol Concern had ceased to be a membership organisation to focus more on campaigning.

which was created by the US government to lobby for the interests of farmers, but this was an unusual example at the time. By 1983, however, Jack L. Walker had noted a proliferation of new 'citizens groups' in the USA and found that 89% of them been set up with the help of funding from the government, foundations, wealthy individuals or other associations. He concluded that 'group leaders learned how to cope with the public goods dilemma not by inducing large numbers of new members to join their groups through the manipulation of selective benefits, but by locating important new sources of funds outside the immediate membership' (Walker 1983: 397) and found that interest groups funded by the state were much more likely to support greater government intervention than those that did not (ibid.: 402). This significant development helps explain why successive campaigns have been fought over fundamentally paternalistic issues despite there being no large group of voters who significantly benefits from them. The very existence of many of the core paternalistic interest groups in our case studies was only made possible by funding from the state. Voluntary donations from the public were typically too small to employ a single member of full-time staff, let alone run an office and finance a campaign.

In addition to state-funding, several of the paternalistic pressure groups received funding from large charities. Action on Sugar was created by the charity Consensus Action on Salt and Health (CASH) which only received £860 in public donations in 2011/12 but received £30,000 from the British Heart Foundation and £200,000 from the Marcela Trust. ASH received sizeable grants from the British Heart Foundation and Cancer Research UK. The Institute of Alcohol Studies – a key player in the Alcohol

Health Alliance – received grants from the European Commission but got the bulk of its income from the Alliance House Foundation, a charity set up to 'spread the principles of total abstinence from alcoholic drinks' whose income comes from property investments built up by its nineteenth century forebear, the United Kingdom Alliance for the Suppression of the Traffic in All Intoxicating Liquors. The Children's Food Campaign was wholly funded (and founded) by the charity Sustain using a grant from the British Heart Foundation. Sustain campaigned for a range of food and farming policies and received £71,980 in voluntary donations in 2010/11 from a total revenue of over £2 million. Its biggest donors were the European Commission, the Greater London Authority and the Big Lottery Fund.[57]

The charities that funded these pressure groups did not stand to gain financially from the introduction of policies such as plain packaging. Large charities such as the British Heart Foundation presumably felt that supporting small advocacy groups was consistent with their mission, but the result was that public donations were diverted towards causes of which donors may not have approved in ways that they were unlikely to be aware of.

Activist-academics had economic incentives that were at least as strong as those of the pressure group employees, but with the additional motivation of wanting to demonstrate the impact of their research. Higher education

[57] All figures from the Charity Commission. The Marcela Trust is a grant-making charity named after the wife of Octav Botnar, the founder of Datsun UK (later Nissan UK). It owns 95.5% of the share capital of OMC Investments Limited (formerly Nissan UK Limited). Its reasons for donating heavily to CASH are not known; its stated charitable objective is vague: 'The charity provides support to selected causes in line with the charity's objectives.'

rewards prolific academics who publish in high impact journals and whose research is heavily cited. The Research Excellence Framework defines impact as 'the effect on, change or benefit to the economy, society, culture, public policy or services, health, the environment or quality of life, beyond academia.'[58] Such a system positively encourages academics to engage in high profile, winnable policy campaigns. The political battles discussed in this book were not only demonstrably winnable, but attracted sustained media attention and gave researchers access to some of the world's top journals, including the *Lancet* and *British Medical Journal*.

Very few of the primary policy actors on either side of the debates were not financially remunerated for their advocacy, but among them we might include Professor Ian Gilmore (Alcohol Health Alliance), Professor Graham MacGregor (Obesity Health Alliance/Action on Sugar) and Derek Webb (CFFG/Stop the FOBTs), all of whom participated in the campaigns at some expense to themselves and as an adjunct to their professional careers. Their contributions do not conflict with a public choice account, however, since they were not mere foot soldiers helping out a worthy cause but were political entrepreneurs running high-profile campaigns and enjoying enhanced status as a selective benefit (Salisbury 1969). They all had a controlling stake or a decisive say in their own pressure group and could enjoy the prestige and power that is bestowed on leaders. If, as Olson argued, individuals are disinclined to join large pressure groups because they will have a negligible say in the group's operations, this clearly does not apply to those who

[58] https://www.ref.ac.uk/guidance-on-results/guidance-on-ref-2021-results/

created and directed the core pressure groups in our case studies. Olson's theory would be on shakier ground if these groups attracted a mass membership and drew sizeable donations from the general public but, as we have seen, they did not.

None of this discounts the possibility that some policy actors were driven by selfless motivations or by 'thin-rational' incentives. Kingdon (1995: 123) notes that some campaigners 'simply like the game. They enjoy advocacy, they enjoy being at or near the seat of power, they enjoy being part of the action'. Such a description perhaps fits Jamie Oliver, although as a celebrity whose business revolved around his own brand, the publicity he received could be considered more in line with rational self-interest of a narrower kind. Derek Webb is a more unusual case since, by his own account, he was motivated by a desire to settle a score ('rather than sue I backed a campaign to make my point' – see Chapter 6). Revenge can be rational and self-interested if it serves the purpose of being a deterrent. Whether it was a deterrent in this instance is an open question, but revenge can be comfortably accommodated into a utility function insofar as the individual enjoys psychological benefits from pursuing and achieving that goal.

Overall, it is striking how few policy actors behaved in ways that cannot be explained by thick-rational motivations. In anticipation of the charge that this is an unduly cynical analysis, it should be stressed that there is no suggestion that the policy entrepreneurs from the public health side did not believe in their cause. It is reasonable to assume that they all cared about the issues and some of them cared deeply. Several activist-academics addressed the issues with conspicuous fervour. But the question that concerns us here is how political activity comes about and why some issues rise up the agenda while others do not. Passion is not a sufficient explanation. There are seldom enough selfless true believers with time on their hands to wage a sophisticated political campaign for years, especially when they stand to gain little or nothing from it. Even true believers need to pay the bills and most individuals need to be compensated for their time. The availability of resources is what turns a concerned citizen into a policy actor. In our case studies, the resources overwhelmingly came not from the public but from elite sources: the government, large charities and (in the case of the anti-gambling coalition) a multi-millionaire.

As a result, small coalitions of professional activists who did not represent any collective interest (in the economic sense) prevailed over a very large (but latent and unorganised) group of consumers. The concentrated public health interest groups did not claim to represent non-consumers, but rather to be acting on behalf of 'public health' in the same way as campaigners for myriad causes claim to be acting in the public interest. They often had motivations that were neither purely altruistic nor selfless, but their self-interest was not as blatant as that of the industry-led groups. The policy changes imposed a relatively small cost on millions of individuals financially (in the case of the sugar tax and MUP) or in terms of utility (plain packaging and FOBTs) while a small group of activists and academics enjoyed the benefits of enhanced prestige, publicity and the glow of success, which helped secure further grants, commissions and donations, without which there may have been no agitation for paternalistic policies at all.

Bureaucrats

For government departments and the Scottish government, activist groups acted as outriders, helping to legitimise new policy proposals through active campaigning that would otherwise not exist because of the free rider problem and the lack of collective benefits. In England and Wales, the funding mostly came from the Department of Health and reflected the policy priorities of those who worked in that department rather than necessarily being the priorities of the government as a whole. The grants awarded were so tiny in the context of the overall health budget that it is doubtful whether the Health Secretary, let alone the Prime Minister, was even aware of them.

Why would bureaucrats agree to sponsor such groups? Two public choice frameworks help answer that question. In the Baptists and Bootleggers scenario identified by Yandle (1983), the interests of commercial entrepreneurs and moral entrepreneurs temporarily align. Politicians are persuaded by Baptists to introduce laws that align with the latter's moral values while Bootleggers enjoy the financial benefits that indirectly and unintentionally accrue. The broader public pay the cost. In our case studies, the professional paternalistic lobby groups played the part of both Baptist and Bootlegger. They were, so to speak, 'Bootlegging Baptists' using moral, economic and quasi-altruistic arguments to persuade politicians to introduce certain policies, but also to persuade politicians that their pressure groups were essential stakeholders without whom further progress could not be made. Since improvements in public health were seen to be reliant on political activity, state funding of political activist groups was considered to be a valid use of public health funds. Any attempt to withdraw funding was portrayed not only as a step backwards for the health of the nation but as an attempt to 'gag' an important stakeholder and an attack on democracy itself.[59] Much the same pitch could be made to wealthy donors and large charities.

As in the classic scenario, it is the broader public who paid the price for Baptist activity, firstly through costs that the policies imposed on consumers, but secondly through the cash grants that were delivered directly to the Bootlegger. The twist is that the Baptist and the Bootlegger are one and the same.

What did the government stand to gain from this? Here it is useful to view elected officials, bureaucrats and interest groups as being engaged in a symbiotic relationship sometimes referred to as an Iron Triangle. In the classic model, interest groups offer support to the bureaucracy and votes to politicians in exchange for special favours, access and friendly legislation. This model can be directly applied to public health policymaking in the UK, with direct funding from the state as an additional benefit for the interest groups. Budget-maximising bureaucrats want a constant stream of new policies to implement (Niskanen 1968) and encourage support from 'civil society' for policies favoured by their department (but not necessarily by the executive). Government employees, says Daniel B. Klein (1994 101), 'like to see their agency's actions as the cause of achievement, and themselves the cause of the agency's actions.'

[59] In the European Union, where state-funding of NGOs is common, a proposal to ban environmental groups from using EU grants to lobby politicians has been described as a 'gag order' and 'a dangerous challenge to democracy' (Gros et al. 2025).

The bureaucrat may personally approve of their cause (and can support it at no financial cost to themselves)[60] or may simply feel that the group's agenda broadly aligns with their political mission (the same applies to the large charities). Governments have a habit of setting ambitious goals and leaving the civil service to work out how to achieve them. In the UK, there are longstanding targets to halve childhood obesity by 2030 and to bring the smoking rate below 5% by the same year. These targets do not necessarily imply coercive paternalism, but some bureaucrats may see taxes and regulation as the best way to achieve them and would welcome some external pressure to push politicians in that direction.

Since the paternalistic public health groups were not mere lobbyists but were public-facing campaigners, they could shift public opinion in favour of policies that were favoured by the bureaucracy and/or the government. In a sense, these groups were controlled opposition within the Iron Triangle. They may have made life uncomfortable for politicians at times by making excessive demands, but this only served to make whatever political settlement emerged look like a moderate compromise. In 1974, the Minister of Health, David Owen, told ASH:

> The facts of life are that Government in this area will respond to pressure, and I, instead of acting defensively on the pressure that you will put me under, am coming to you with a different message,

[60] At the time of writing, a former director of research and policy at Alcohol Change UK (the successor to Alcohol Concern) is the policy lead on alcohol and gambling at DHSC, and a former Institute of Alcohol Studies employee is the Head of Excise at the Treasury.

> which is to say 'Put me under as much pressure as you like' (Berridge 2007: 167).

David Simpson, ASH's CEO in the 1980s, later recalled that:

> It was a curious form of brinkmanship, having in one's daily work to attack the government that was funding you. But this was expected, and encouraged, so that there was a lot of cooperation behind the scenes' (Simpson 1998: 211).

As these quotes suggest, financial arrangements between the political elite and political agitators can be mutually beneficial and it is in the political self-interest of both parties for them to continue.

Industry

The motive of the commercial actors in our case studies is plain enough: the pursuit of profit. This applies to the businesses that supported the public health policies, such as Bacta in the FOBT campaign and the pub companies in the MUP campaign, as much as it does to the large corporations that opposed them. We have seen evidence of industries using all of the political strategies listed by Savell et al. (2014; 2016). Coalitions were formed, research was commissioned, opponents were attacked, politicians were lobbied and lawsuits were filed. Has the public health perspective on policymaking discussed in Chapter 2 therefore been vindicated? The answer is yes, but with the heavy caveat that the public health framing is only trivially true. The public health groups also formed coalitions, attacked their opponents, commissioned research and followed most of supposed 'tobacco playbook' to the letter.

In our case studies, industry was generally defeated, but there is nothing in the public health perspective to explain why. The major flaw in the public health approach is that it has no predictive power whatsoever. The tactics are said to be the same across industries and across different campaigns, and yet the outcomes vary enormously. In retrospect, public health academics can attribute policy wins to sound evidence and strong advocacy while attributing defeats and delays to industry lobbying, but this merely turns lobbying into the *deus ex machina* of political science. Political entrepreneurs would not spend so much time and money lobbying if it had no impact – although Lucas and Tasić (2015: 236) argue that 'the primary function of lobbying may be to cement and maintain ties among people who already agree with one another'– but whilst public health academics portray it as being incredibly powerful (when conducted by commercial actors) the evidence in our case studies suggests that it is often rather ineffective.

The public health narrative is incomplete because it largely ignores other interest groups and it pays little attention to the incentives of policymakers themselves. The binary framing of policymaking as 'public health' versus industry provides a David and Goliath narrative that flatters the public health lobby when they win and consoles them when they lose, but it is simplistic and ultimately fatuous. Rent-seeking industries may clash or collude with the public health interest groups at different times and there are often differences of opinion within each industry. In the past, elements of the tobacco industry have lobbied against e-cigarettes and for higher tobacco taxes. Parts of the alcohol industry have lobbied for minimum pricing, and elements of the gambling industry have lobbied for anti-gambling legislation. These are textbook examples of the Bootleggers and Baptists phenomenon, but they attract little attention in the public health literature. Nor is much attention paid to the influence of wealthy benefactors on the public health side, such as Michael Bloomberg, who has given hundreds of millions of dollars to organisations to lobby for sugary drinks taxes and e-cigarette flavour bans; organisations that would be termed 'front groups' if public health academics opposed them. But even if the literature gave a full account of *all* the commercial and ideological players in these policy debates, it would have little explanatory power unless it analysed the incentives of decision-makers themselves. In a democracy, that requires looking at the public.

The public

As Olson's theory would predict, individual consumers who would be negatively affected by each of the policies did not find it worth their while to mobilise.[61] As George Ade reflected during Prohibition in the USA: 'The non-drinkers had been organising for fifty years and the drinkers had no organisation whatever. They had been too busy drinking'

[61] The negative consequences of paternalistic lifestyle regulation include the financial costs of paying 'sin taxes' (and minimum prices), stigmatisation, inconvenience, and loss of consumer surplus. Welfare costs may arise when consumers are driven away from their first preference, as in the case of the *de facto* ban on FOBTs, or when their consumption is made less enjoyable, as in the case of plain packaging (see the quote from Melanie Wakefield in Chapter 9 for an explicit acknowledgement of the latter).

(Okrent 2010: 83). Olson's crucial insight about the paradox of participation explains why there was so little grassroots opposition to the public health interest groups (and indeed why these groups had so little organised grassroots *support*). In our case studies, some consumers were prepared to voice their opposition in low-cost ways (more than 100,000 people signed a petition against plain packaging, for example), but they otherwise had little option but to free ride on the unsuccessful campaigns of often divided industries.

Those who did not consume the product in question had even less reason to get involved since the external benefits of each policy, which mostly consisted of the dubious promise of slightly reduced public expenditure, would be spread very thinly, and so they sat it out. The dearth of voluntary donations to the public health interest groups and the lack of grassroots activism for their causes are an indication that while the general public may have taken a view of each of the policies, they did not feel strongly about them. Despite the intense agitation against FOBTs, the Gambling Commission (2018a:7) found that only 1.2% of the public mentioned gaming machines when asked their views about gambling. A survey conducted in 2014 found that only 3% of respondents mentioned plain packaging when asked to name three policies they would like to see included in the manifestos of political parties at the next General Election (Clark 2014b). A further survey conducted the following year asked respondents to rate a range of policies on a scale of importance from 0 to 10 and found that plain packaging received the lowest score of 3.51, well below the second lowest rated policy of 'regulating the future of the fracking sector' which scored 6.10 (FOREST 2015).

Since most people did not smoke or play FOBTs, apathy towards these policies was a rational response for the majority. Nevertheless, when asked in surveys, people were much more likely to support the policies than to oppose them or express no opinion (with the exception of MUP). Why? One could argue that they were persuaded by the academic evidence that the policies would work. This seems unlikely given voters' incentives to remain rationally ignorant about matters in which they have no selfish interest (Tullock 1984), but even if true, it does not answer the question. Why should someone who does not consume a product care whether a policy to stop other people consuming it is effective?

As with the pressure groups, industry groups and bureaucrats, there is no need to look beyond rational self-interest to explain the views of the public. The sugar tax effectively transferred money from those who consumed sugary drinks to those who did not. A reduction in smoking and heavy drinking was widely assumed to cut NHS costs, thereby lowering taxes or providing better treatment to those who do not drink heavily or smoke. Cutting the stake on FOBTs was assumed to reduce the number of high street betting shops, thereby freeing up commercial property for shops that might be of more benefit to non-gamblers and, in the opinion of many, lifting the character of the high street. It was also argued that money not spent on FOBTs would have a greater multiplier effect if spent on other goods and services.

Whether or not these assumptions were realistic is beside the point. It should be stressed again that the vast majority of the public were not actively involved in campaigning for or against any of the policies and their 'support' amounted to no more than expressing an opinion when asked by a pollster. The putative benefits of the policies to individuals who did not consume the products may have been negligible, but the cost of agreeing with the policies was zero (and since all the campaigns involved alleged social evils, social desirability bias encouraged support for the policies). Like the politicians, the public did not need to be convinced that the policy would work so long as they had no reason to believe that they would be adversely affected if the policy failed. So long as there was *some chance* that they would benefit, however indirectly, from fewer people using a product that they themselves did not consume, they had a self-interested reason for supporting the policy.

Interest groups on both sides of the debate knew that externality arguments were important in swaying individuals who would otherwise be disinterested. Research commissioned by the CFFG emphasised the supposed benefits to the economy of a stake reduction. Economic savings were modelled in the Sheffield reports. Supporters of the sugar tax stressed that the revenue raised would be used to pay for free breakfasts and sports facilities in schools. Public Health England claimed that plain packaging would produce an economic benefit of £500 million a year. The putative costs to the NHS of smoking, drinking and obesity were cited routinely.

Perceived self-interest can therefore explain why so many members of the public supported the policies. Perhaps more importantly, it explains why so few people opposed them. This is a subtle but important distinction. Effective campaigning by the public health groups polarised the debate as 'industry versus health' and made support for their policies the high-status option. Lacking an obvious self-interested reason to oppose the policies, support became the default option for disinterested non-consumers of the product. This does not preclude the possibility of paternalism, misguided altruism or simple prejudice playing a part, nor does it preclude the possibility of the policies being evidence-informed in some sense. But rational self-interest offers a sufficient explanation for both public support and public opposition.

As for consumers, there were no grassroots organisations promoting (or opposing) their interests. In line with Olson's theory, there were some groups formed for other reasons, such as the Campaign for Real Ale, which participated in policy debates that concerned their members, and there were concentrated interest groups from industry that may have reflected consumers' views to some extent, but millions of consumers went largely unrepresented. If they felt strongly, they could participate in low-cost methods of expressing their views, such as responding to public consultations, but the vast majority did not even do that.

Table 13 shows how many people were regular users of each product at the time of the policy decision alongside the number who were opposed to the policy in the last survey before the decision (in Westminster) was made.[62]

There is a clear relationship between prevalence of use and opposition to the relevant policy. FOBTs had the fewest users and the fewest opponents of the stake reduction.

[62] The figure of 53% for sugary drinks comes from a 2017 survey analysed by Adams et al. (2021). As it excludes people aged 65 and over, it is certainly higher than the overall adult population prevalence hence it is marked '<53%'. The other figures come from the ONS (alcohol, tobacco) and the Gambling Commission (FOBTs).

Table 13. Prevalence of use and public support for the related policy

	Regular consumers	Opposition to the related policy
Alcohol	58% (past week)	46%
Sugary drinks	<53% (past week)	33%
Tobacco	17% (current smoker)	15%
FOBTs	1.5% (past month)	6%

Alcohol had the most regular users and minimum pricing encountered the most public opposition. This, again, suggests that public opinion was largely driven by self-interest. Some regular drinkers of alcohol and sugary drinks supported MUP and the sugar tax respectively, but this does not necessarily mean they were acting against their interests. Some drinkers of alcohol may have assumed, in some cases correctly, that a 50p minimum price would not affect them, and some drinkers of sugary drinks may have been happy to see reformulation of their preferred brands. Some users of any of the products may have welcomed paternalistic regulation because they wanted a commitment device. But overall, the pattern is clear: the fewer consumers, the less resistance.

Politicians

The incentives faced by politicians were discussed in the previous chapter in which I argued that the government was keen to avoid unnecessary political risks. This is consistent with the view of Cairney and Zahariadis (2016: 89)

that 'policymakers decide who to trust, and what information to use, to help them develop a sense of risk associated with any decision. They then decide what level of risk is acceptable, given the potential reward'. In our case studies, the evidence is unavoidably circumstantial, but it suggests that the government was neither ideologically committed nor opposed to any of the four policies. Instead, it was forced to make a decision once the policies had been put on the political agenda and pressure had been applied. With the exception of MUP, the policies faced relatively little opposition from the general public and were broadly supported by much of the media. The most vocal opponents were industry groups, libertarians and some Conservative backbenchers, none of whom were politically powerful. Without a compelling reason to *not* go ahead with the policy, all the pressure was on the government to proceed.

As with the public and the pressure groups, there are few examples of selfless altruism among the politicians who campaigned for these policies. Altruism requires some degree of sacrifice, but politicians on both sides of the debates were simply doing their job and many of them were doing it in a way that demonstrated to their constituents that they were men and women of firm purpose. Public opinion was such that it took no great bravery to take the decisions that were taken. It would have been courageous if David Cameron had gone into the 2015 election as a committed opponent of plain packaging or if Theresa May had made a robust defence of FOBTs, but this never seemed likely. The only MP who could be said to have suffered for her beliefs was Tracey Crouch who resigned as sports minister in protest at the supposed delay to the FOBT reform. She may have believed that her long-term political interests were better advanced by being seen as a conviction politician than by being a junior minister in Theresa May's beleaguered minority government, but even if we accept that she resigned on principle and paid a cost for her beliefs, her case stands out because it is so unusual.

By the time the decisions were made on plain packaging, the sugar tax and FOBT reform, the pressure on the government had reached a critical threshold. In the case of plain packaging and FOBTs, the tipping point had been reached long ago. From a public choice perspective, the relevant question about these two policies is not 'why did politicians introduce them?' but 'why didn't politicians introduce them sooner?' As discussed in Chapter 10, the most plausible answer is that the government had genuine concerns about losing tax revenue that had to be addressed before it committed itself. There were no such concerns about the sugar tax, which raised revenue, but public opposition needed to wane before the government could confidently proceed. Minimum pricing was not expected to raise revenue and was not particularly popular with voters and so it was abandoned in Westminster but not in Scotland, where public support was stronger and nationalist politicians had additional motivations.

Is this 'government by opinion poll'? In the sense that the elected government responded to what it thought voters wanted, it could be described as such, although the opinion polls cannot be fully separated from the media coverage of the issues or the campaigns and lobbying efforts of the time, all of which contributed to a perceived national mood. It could be argued that the government merely happened to be of the same mind as the majority of the public, but this is not consistent with David Cameron's early support for minimum pricing and initial opposition to the sugar tax, both of which were firm and unequivocal, nor is it consistent with his prolonged ambivalence about plain packaging. The phrase 'government by opinion poll' implies some kind of direct democracy. That would be a huge overstatement, but 'government by opinion poll' is a more apt description of the policymaking process in our four case studies than 'evidence-based'.

The value of evidence

I have argued that the outcomes of all four campaigns can be explained in terms of public choice economics and rational responses to pressure in a democracy. So where does this leave the use of evidence?

In a broad sense, research was profoundly important. A large body of evidence built up over decades had persuaded politicians that all four issues – smoking, obesity, alcohol and gambling – were worthy targets of government intervention. This is in keeping with Carol Weiss's ideas about the 'enlightenment function of social research'. Weiss (1977) argued that academic research has its greatest influence in the long-term battle of ideas, slowly changing minds and shaping attitudes. It should not be taken as a given that a Conservative government, which publicly championed personal liberty and free markets, would be so willing to introduce fundamentally paternalistic policies that were opposed by businesses. It did so, in part, because research evidence had created a climate of opinion favourable to state intervention.

Evidence was important in a narrower sense too. It may not have played a large role in the ultimate decision-making, but it was important as part of the political campaigns.

The 'real world' evidence served a useful purpose in reassuring politicians. It showed that the policies could be implemented legally, cheaply and without unleashing a significant public backlash. Whether or not the policies 'worked' was irrelevant from this perspective, but if they were later shown not to have worked, politicians could absolve themselves from blame by saying, with some justification, that they had been following the science.

Modelling studies also served a useful political purpose. Based on interviews with policy entrepreneurs, politicians and civil servants who were closely involved with the MUP campaign in Scotland, Katikireddi et al. (2016) concluded that the Sheffield model was highly influential even though it may not have changed anybody's mind. They argue that it 'served a rhetorical function. Its existence helped policy makers to present a rhetorical argument to a variety of audiences' (ibid.: 533).

None of the policies under discussion were particularly complex. As shown in Table 14, there were simple reasons to think that they would work and simple reasons to think that they would *not* work. Politicians and laymen alike only needed what Lindblom and Cohen (1979: 82) called 'ordinary knowledge' to make a judgement about the likely outcomes. As one politician who was sceptical about MUP told Katikireddi et al. (2013: 493–4), rather than 'being blinded by some study that's been carried out in an ivory tower', they preferred to use 'what I call sort of logic and human nature and my observation of human nature over a period of time, and I just don't accept that it [MUP] will make any great difference to people's behaviour.'

People often form judgements based on first principles or 'common sense' and then seek out evidence to confirm their gut instinct. Lindblom and Cohen suggested in 1979 that some evidence is 'contracted for or otherwise produced in order to display the rationality of decisions reached through ordinary knowledge' and that such evidence allows stakeholders to not only rationalise their decision but to argue their way towards the decision (Lindblom and Cohen 1979: 82). For those who supported MUP, the Sheffield model validated their assumptions and offered a way of explaining how the policy would work to those who were undecided.

Table 14. Intuitive arguments for and against each policy

	Will work	Will not work
Plain packaging	Reducing the appeal of tobacco packaging will reduce the appeal of the product and therefore sales.	Tobacco packaging is not the reason why people start smoking or continue smoking.
Sugar tax	Increasing the price of sugary drinks will reduce consumption of sugar and therefore obesity.	A small reduction in sugary drink consumption will not have a measurable impact on obesity.
Minimum pricing	Increasing the price of cheap alcohol will reduce consumption of alcohol.	Heavy drinkers will always find the money to buy alcohol.
FOBTs	A *de facto* ban on FOBTs will prevent problem gamblers losing money on them.	Problem gamblers will lose all their money regardless of which gambling products are available.

The same applies to the modelling of the sugar tax and the FOBT reform as well as the numerous studies showing that people found plain packaging less appealing than conventional cigarette packaging. Although the latter finding seems trivially obvious and it did not prove that reduced appeal would lead to lower rates of smoking, it confirmed a link in the chain of reasoning that explained how plain packaging *could* work and gave it the stamp of academic authority.

> Evidence was also important in the campaigns because, quite simply, some evidence is better than no evidence. As one Scottish civil servant told Katikireddi et al. (2016: 527): 'Minimum unit pricing would never have flown if we hadn't had something, you know, to kind of back it up.'

As discussed in Chapter 1, the push for evidence-based policy in the UK since the 1990s has created a system of public consultations, impact assessments and official evaluations that is intended to keep new policies grounded in evidence. In academia, this is buttressed by the checks and balances of peer review, meta-analysis and systematic review. Providing research evidence to support a policy has become, at the very least, a box that must be ticked. Plain packaging was rejected by the Labour government in 2008 because 'there is no evidence base that it actually reduces the number of young children smoking'.[63] When Theresa May rejected MUP in 2013, she did not say that it was because she and her allies had won an internal battle with

---

[63] https://hansard.parliament.uk/commons/2008-12-16/debates/08121646000017/Smoking

the Prime Minister over a potentially unpopular policy, but because the consultation had 'not provided evidence that conclusively demonstrates that Minimum Unit Pricing (MUP) will actually do what it is meant to' (Home Office 2013: 3).

The policy changes may not have been driven by evidence, but it would have been a major hindrance to the public health interest groups if they had been unable to provide any evidence at all. In that sense, evidence was essential to all of the campaigns.[64]

Essential, but not sufficient. For the campaign to succeed, it required broad public support (or, more importantly, the absence of strong public opposition). Evidence played a significant role in influencing the national mood and keeping the issues on the agenda. Studies from public health academics were expertly disseminated to the media by press release, often accompanied by quotes from the authors urging the government to proceed with the policy. The media 'hits' from the five outlets analysed in previous chapters are shown below. Figure 20 shows the number of mentions of evidence related to plain packaging from the start of 2013 until the conclusion of the campaign in March 2015. Figure 21 shows the number of mentions of evidence related to the sugar tax between the start of 2015 and the conclusion of the campaign in March 2016. In each case, we see regular references to evidence in the media and various peaks of interest which were sometimes triggered by political events and at other times triggered by the publication of the evidence itself.

[64] It was a legal necessity in the case of MUP in Scotland where an iteration of the Sheffield model was the key piece of evidence used to win the EU legal case against the Scotch Whisky Association.

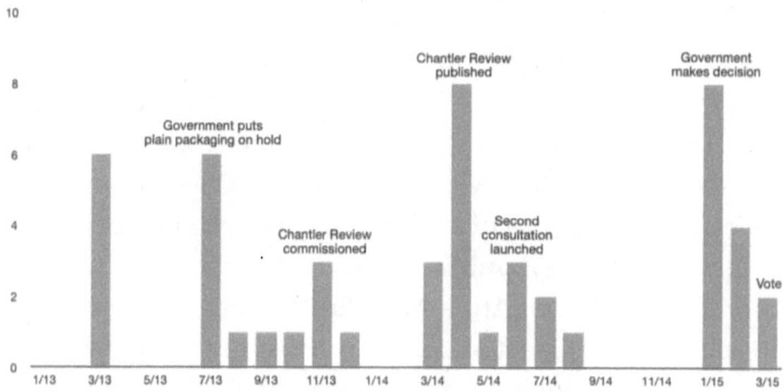

Figure 20. Media references to evidence related to plain packaging

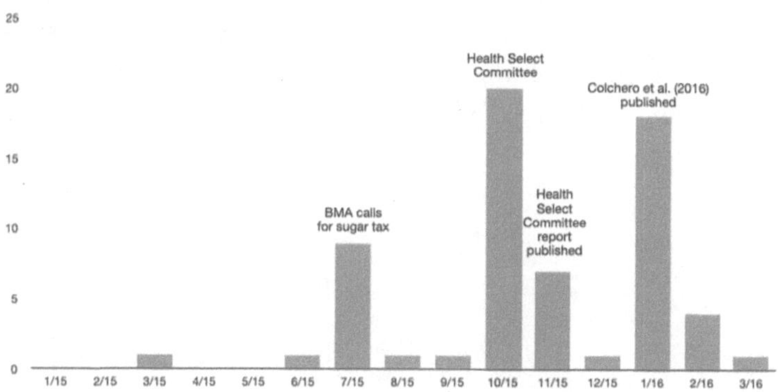

Figure 21. Media references to evidence related to the sugar tax

However, as the next graphs show, evidence made up only a small part of the media coverage. Figure 22 shows the mentions of plain packaging evidence and the number of articles mentioning Lynton Crosby in relation to plain packaging. Media interest in this angle began when plain packaging was absent from the Queen's Speech in May 2013 and exploded when the policy was officially put on hold in July 2013. Over the whole period, articles mentioning Crosby's alleged involvement appeared three times more often than mentions of any form of research evidence. The *Guardian/Observer* published 31 such articles in a single month (July 2013). After April 2013, there were only two months when at least once article mentioning Crosby in relation to plain packaging was not published, as compared to eight months when no articles mentioned evidence related to plain packaging. This only came to an end after the government committed itself to plain packaging (subject to a free vote) in January 2015.

Figure 23 shows mentions of sugar tax evidence in blue and the number of articles mentioning Jamie Oliver's support for a sugar tax in green. Oliver's campaigning for the tax began in earnest in August 2015. From then until the

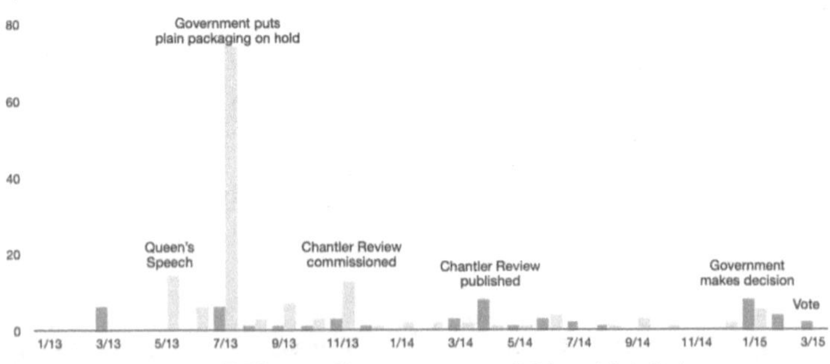

Figure 22. Media references to evidence related to plain packaging/Lynton Crosby

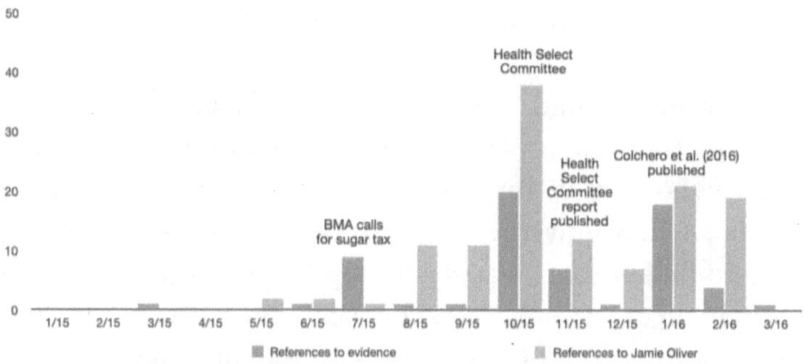

Figure 23. Media references to evidence related to the sugar tax/Jamie Oliver

end of the campaign, articles referencing his support for the tax were published more than twice as often as mentions of any form of evidence. Some of these mentions were in passing (as were some of the mentions of evidence) and not all were complimentary towards Oliver, but these graphs illustrate how much of the media coverage was driven by personalities and political controversy.

Plenty of other examples of non-evidence-based media coverage could be cited: Sarah Wollaston's claim that the sugar review was being 'suppressed'; the news that a tobacco company had given MPs tickets to the Chelsea Flower Show; numerous stories of problem gamblers losing large sums of money on FOBTs; cabinet revolts; politicians resigning or threatening to resign. Human interest stories and the hint of political scandal made up a very large share of the media coverage. (Interestingly, it is difficult to find similar examples pertaining to minimum pricing whose media coverage tended to focus on academic evidence and the legal battle with the Scotch Whisky Association. This may partly explain why that campaign failed in Westminster).

Journalists had their own incentives, of course. Some of them were openly in favour of certain policies, but even those who were disinterested needed to produce stories at a time when newsrooms were increasingly short-staffed due to falling sales. Press releases from campaign groups and medical journals could be easily rewritten to produce instant copy. The disproportionate media coverage of evidence that supported the public health coalitions can be largely explained by them simply being more prolific. Stories about undue industry influence tapped into familiar narratives and appealed to *availability bias* while the very nature of the fast-moving modern media (and social media) encouraged *action bias*. Regardless of whether they had any ideological commitment to the public health side, the media had significant influence in exerting pressure on politicians to act.

In addition to stories driven by personalities and perceived scandals, eye-catching statistics repeatedly framed the problem: the 570 children who started smoking every day, the nine spoonfuls of sugar in a can of *Coca-Cola*, the one in five children leaving primary school obese, the £18,000 that could be lost on a roulette machine in an hour, the beer being sold cheaper than water. None of this counted as lobbying, nor was it evidence in an academic sense – and much of it was contestable – but it was all part of an emotional campaign that appealed to large sections of the public, drove media interest and applied pressure to the government.

CONCLUSION

Through an analysis of 348 references to evidence in five media outlets and 69 references to evidence in fourteen House of Commons debates, we have identified common themes among four campaigns for lifestyle-related public health regulation in the UK between 2008 and 2018. With the exception of the anti-FOBT campaign, which had little involvement from the public health establishment, each policy debate was dominated by two 'superstar' studies which were cited far more often than other pieces of research. These were accompanied by evidence reviews by respected individuals or institutions which concluded that the policy was likely to be effective. Taken together, these documents represented a 'package of evidence' that emerged chronologically showing (a) how the policy would work in theory, (b) how the policy had recently worked in another country, and (c) that the policy had the blessing of experts. Although the evidence for the FOBT reform was scanter, an approximation of a package of evidence was constructed from (a) simple modelling, (b) an evaluation of how a related reform had worked in the recent past, and (c) expert advice from the Gambling Commission.

Each of the three elements of the package of evidence helped to reassure policymakers. The provision of a theoretical framework, usually comprising modelling, offered empirical support from academics for a layperson's intuitive reasons for thinking that the policy would have the desired effect. Since none of the policies were complicated, this provided confirmation of the policymaker's 'ordinary knowledge' or 'common sense'. This was followed by evidence from other countries apparently showing that the policies had worked in practice and – importantly from the politician's perspective – that they could be introduced without a significant public backlash. Finally, expert evidence reviews supporting the policy reforms appealed to authority and provided cover for policymakers who could claim to be 'following the science' even if the policy failed. In the absence of compelling, peer-reviewed evidence from opponents of the policies, these packages of evidence exerted pressure on decision makers to capitulate to the public health interest groups.

The most heavily cited evidence was not necessarily the strongest evidence – significant flaws in methodology and analysis are readily apparent and the primary outcomes of smoking, obesity and problem gambling prevalence were never studied in the 'real world' research – but they helped to tell a story about how an intervention could work in theory and in practice. The 'real world' experience of policy implementation in other countries seemed to be particularly persuasive in the case of the sugar tax and plain packaging, with relatively frequent mentions not only in the media and the House of Commons but also in the most influential government documents and expert reviews. Politicians were highly deferential to statistical modellers in the minimum pricing debate, especially in Scotland, and their confidence in the modelling was bolstered by (misleading) claims about the effect of social referencing pricing in Canada.

An underlying assumption of this book is that when supporters (or opponents) of a policy cite evidence, it is because they believe it to be persuasive, but that does not necessarily mean that anybody was persuaded by it. Like the proverbial drunk's use of a lamppost, evidence can be used more for support than illumination. Although the Westminster government prevaricated over all of the policies we have reviewed and changed its mind about at least two of them, it is far from obvious that the U-turns occurred as a result of evidence. On the contrary, there were so many departures from the classic model of evidence-based policymaking that it is difficult to interpret the final decisions as being wholly, or even mostly, driven by research. Aside from the weaknesses of the evidence itself, we have noted the timing of often abrupt decisions which appear to reflect short-term political anxieties; discrepancies between the sugar tax, as implemented, and the modelling behind it; the effective dismissal of expert advice in the FOBT reform; the different political decisions on MUP in England and Scotland; the split in opinion on MUP between the Liberal Democrats and Labour on either side of the Scottish border; the near-absence of evidence for the FOBT reform; the reluctance to wait for hard data on plain packaging from Australia; the sidelining of the most relevant and methodologically sound evidence in the sugar tax debate; the preference for anecdotes, *ad hominem* arguments and framing devices over evidence in the HoC debates, and much more.

If, as I have argued, the policymaking process was not driven by careful deliberation of academic research evidence, how do we explain the success of the public health interest groups' campaigns? It bears repeating that we do not have a window in policymakers' souls and, given the subject matter of this book, we must be especially careful about drawing firm conclusions from circumstantial evidence, but my findings are consistent with the hypothesis that politicians will succumb to pressure on low-salience issues unless they believe that the policy will be broadly unpopular or will conspicuously backfire. Once the public health interest groups had put the policies on the agenda, the government could not put off a decision forever. As pressure mounted due to well-orchestrated campaigns which included the production and dissemination of research evidence as one of several devices to generate publicity and force the government's hand, it became a question of whether the costs of continued inaction outweighed the costs of acting. The policies became 'barnacles on the boat' that needed to be scraped off, either by implementing them or by rejecting them. With the exception of minimum pricing in England, which had significant public and political opposition, the government in Westminster concluded that the reputational risks of inaction were greater than the political, economic and legal risks of acting. This could be inferred from the results of opinion polls, the tone of media coverage and the fact that the policies had already been tolerated, if not embraced, by the public in other countries. By and large, this judgement has been vindicated. Although the evidence that any of the policies achieved their objective is mixed at best, there has been no significant political blowback from introducing them. Latent interest groups of disgruntled consumers have remained latent.

Are the findings generalisable to policymaking more broadly? Clearly not. In Kingdon's case studies and in many other studies in political science, pressure groups do not dominate all three policy streams in the way we have seen here. Policies typically take a long time to gestate or are manifesto commitments, neither of which apply to our case studies. When policies have been developed by the government itself, rather than being thrust upon it by pressure groups, politicians have a higher tolerance for short-term unpopularity. When policies are popular with the public, or at least with a key voting demographic, politicians are more willing to ignore expert opinion.

But in the field of lifestyle-related public health regulation in the UK, other examples give support to the tentative conclusions of this book. They include the campaigns for the smoking ban (2007) and the tobacco display ban (2012), both of which were co-ordinated by ASH and accompanied by evidence showing how the policy would work in theory and how it had worked in practice in another country (Ireland and Canada respectively), with an emphasis on the absence of negative unintended consequences (pub closures and increased illicit tobacco sales respectively). The tobacco display ban was broadly popular with the public and there were no strong political reasons for the government *not* to proceed. The smoking ban was more controversial, and the results of opinion polls depended on how the question was framed. ASH activists later said that they would have lost the campaign if the government had believed that a ban 'would be unpopular with a significant minority of voters' (Arnott et al. 2007: 426–7), but Tony Blair evidently concluded that the political risks of acting were limited. The concentrated interest group of the pub trade had been neutralised (see Chapter 3) and the precedent in Ireland, which had a similar pub culture, suggested that the ban was enforceable. It could be argued that there was no overwhelming political pressure for the Labour government to introduce a 'comprehensive' smoking ban in 2007, although it should be noted that the policy was delivered by a Prime Minister looking for a legacy (Blair left office a few days before it came into effect) and its official justification was not paternalistic (it was framed as being about protecting workers from secondhand smoke).

The first major development in the field of lifestyle-related public health policy after the period covered in this book occurred in July 2020 when a slew of anti-obesity laws was suddenly announced, including an online and pre-watershed television advertising ban, a ban on volume price discounts and restrictions on where HFSS (high in fat, sugar and salt) food can be placed in supermarkets. A familiar coalition of activists, including the Obesity Health Alliance and Jamie Oliver, had been lobbying for these policies for years and they had been endorsed by Public Health England. With echoes of minimum pricing, they were adopted by David Cameron before being abandoned by his successor Theresa May. When Boris Johnson became Prime Minister, they were assumed to be incompatible with his more libertarian instincts and yet they became part of a new obesity strategy a year after he took office.

Since most of the restrictions on HFSS food had not been introduced in any other country, there was no 'real world' evidence to cite, and there were few relevant experimental studies in the academic literature. There were expert reviews from PHE and Henry Dimbleby, although the latter's National Food Strategy was not published until after Johnson's announcement. With no 'superstar' studies and no modelling aside from some calculations in a 2019 Impact Assessment, there was no 'package of evidence' of the kind we have seen in our case studies. It is difficult to argue that evidence was decisive.

Two related events provide a better explanation. Firstly, Johnson had been hospitalised with COVID-19 three months earlier and explicitly blamed this on him being 'too fat'.[65] Johnson's hospitalisation provided a focusing event which made the issue more salient for the nation and for the Prime Minister personally. Secondly, the UK had one of the world's highest cumulative death rates from COVID-19 in July 2020 and obesity was a known risk factor for COVID-19 mortality. New anti-obesity policies were unlikely to have an impact before the pandemic subsided, but the new strategy signalled that the government was taking action and it helped shift attention away from its own policy failures in controlling the virus.

The sudden resurrection of anti-obesity policies in July 2020 is therefore consistent with the theory that lifestyle-related public health policymaking in the UK can be better explained by short-term political pressure than sober analysis of academic evidence. It is noteworthy that when the COVID-19 pandemic began to subside, the government's enthusiasm for the anti-obesity policies waned. When the economy became a more pressing issue during the period of high inflation in 2022–23, the ban on volume price discounts for HFSS food was postponed, first by Liz Truss and then again by Rishi Sunak. Johnson himself had postponed the advertising ban in 2022 on economic grounds and it was postponed again (to 2025) by Sunak. The introduction of the advertising ban was also repeatedly delayed, including by the Labour health secretary Wes Streeting in 2025.

---

[65] https://www.theguardian.com/world/video/2020/jul/27/i-was-too-fat-boris-johnson-launches-uk-obesity-reduction-drive-video

But for a brief moment in 2020, COVID-19 opened an unexpected window of opportunity for policies that had been floating around for some time. It is a reminder of the 'messiness, accident, fortuitous coupling, and dumb luck' that Kingdon (1995: 206) associates with policymaking. Serendipity cannot be ignored in our case studies either. Would the plain packaging campaign have ended differently if David Cameron had not hired Lynton Crosby in 2012, or if Crosby had no association with the tobacco industry? Would the sugar tax have been introduced if George Osborne had a good story to tell about the economy in 2016? In these parallel universes, it is possible that the policies might not have been introduced when they were, but the political incentives suggest that they would have been introduced sooner or later, as they were in several other countries.

In October 2023, the British government returned to the issue of smoking when Prime Minister Rishi Sunak announced a permanent ban on the sale of tobacco products to anyone born after 2008, thereby introducing incremental prohibition. There was no 'superstar' study, but the three components of a package of evidence could be discerned. Firstly, the policy had already become law in another country (New Zealand). Secondly, there was proof of concept, albeit tenuously, from 2007's increase in the purchase age for tobacco from 16 to 18 which one study found was accompanied by a 30% reduction in smoking prevalence among 16- and 17-year-olds (Fidler and West 2010). Thirdly, the policy had been recommended in an expert review by Javed Khan in 2022 (Khan 2022).

Although New Zealand's incremental tobacco ban had been passed by Parliament and put into legislation in

December 2022, it would be several years before anybody over the age of 17 would be prohibited from buying cigarettes. The New Zealand experiment could not yield any evidence until 2027 at the earliest and yet it was cited as a precedent for the UK decision. This is a significant fact if, as I have suggested, such international precedents are of interest to politicians because they demonstrate that a potentially controversial policy is politically feasible rather than necessarily effective. Equally significant is the fact that the policy polled well, particularly with those who had voted Conservative in 2019. Surveys conducted days before the announcement found that it was supported by over 70% of the public, with fewer than a quarter opposed.[66]

It should be acknowledged that there are also counterexamples showing that public health interest groups do not always get their way. In New Zealand, where modelling had been cited as evidence that the incremental tobacco ban would work (Ait Ouakrim et al. 2024), a change of government led to the policy being dropped in November 2023, shortly after Sunak's announcement, partly because of fears about losing tax revenue. In the UK, campaigns for a ban on advertisements for gambling and alcohol have so far failed and successive governments in the last fifteen years have generally ignored demands from the public health lobby to increase alcohol duty in real terms. The anti-smoking lobby has enjoyed a series of policy wins but has failed to pressure the government into introducing a levy on tobacco companies despite a levy on the gambling industry being announced in 2023 after a campaign spearheaded by Clean Up Gambling, the successor to the CFFG,

[66] For example: https://yougov.co.uk/topics/health/survey-results/daily/2023/09/25/cbec9/2

and Gambling With Lives (which began receiving funding from the Gambling Commission in 2020).

Nothing in this book suggests that public health interest groups should *always* prevail. Four conditions typically need to be met in addition to the application of pressure:

- *some* evidence of efficacy must be presented
- public opposition must be limited
- the policy must be revenue-raising or close to revenue-neutral
- policymakers must be assured that it will not cause major social or economic problems.

The failure of the anti-alcohol lobby to raise alcohol duty can be explained, as with the failure of MUP in Westminster, by the large number of drinkers who would be displeased by it, including many politicians.[67] The failure of the anti-smoking lobby to introduce a tobacco industry levy can be explained – and *has* been explained by HMRC – by a levy being 'entirely equivalent to an increase in the specific tax that currently exists on tobacco products' (because the tobacco companies would raise their prices if they had to pay a levy) (HM Treasury 2015: 6). Since ASH had already succeeded in persuading the government to raise tobacco duty by the rate of inflation plus 2% every year, the revenue-raising aim of the levy had been achieved by simpler means. By contrast, gambling companies cannot generally raise their prices (because players choose how much to stake) and so a levy was seen as being more

[67] Neo-temperance academic Robin Room complained in 2004 that 'Westminster itself is a very wet environment, and is thereby congenial to alcohol industry interests.' (Room 2004: 1,087)

suitable. And although surveys suggest that a substantial majority of people would support further restrictions on gambling and alcohol advertising, the government is likely to be more aware of the economic downsides for culture and sport. However, as new restrictions on HFFS food advertising show, none of these policy proposals can be ruled out in the future if circumstances change.

If this analysis is correct, a paternalistic public health policy that meets the four conditions listed above has a strong chance of being introduced in the UK at the present time. It can expect little opposition from those who will not be personally disadvantaged by it and even consumers who will incur a cost will not mobilise for the reasons given by Olson (1971). There is little evidence that the government (as distinct from some vocal MPs) had strong feelings about any of the policies in our case studies, nor were the public greatly exercised by them, but the public health interest groups were highly motivated and had the resources to carry their campaigns while consumers remained unorganised. Hearing little opposition from the public, the government gauged the public mood and acted accordingly. The squeaky wheel got the grease.

For the most part, the political campaigns discussed in this book did not end in victory for the small, concentrated interests of big business, as Olson's theory might imply and as more recent economists such as Luigi Zingales (2017) might have expected, but nor did they conclude with an unambiguous defeat of corporate power. The paternalistic interest groups were not interested in correcting the kind of market failures that might arise from oligopolistic commercial behaviour (Acemoglu and Robinson 2013). Insofar as the industries could be described as oligopolies, their market dominance was scarcely weakened by any of the policies. Plain packaging arguably benefited incumbent tobacco companies by raising yet another barrier to entry in a market that was already almost impregnable while MUP raised prices in a way that would have been illegal if the drinks manufacturers had colluded to introduce it voluntarily. Plain packaging had the potential to reduce industry profits and the FOBT reform clearly *did* reduce bookmakers' profits, but the soft drinks industry sold more drinks after the sugar tax was introduced (Rogers et al. 2023a) and Scottish drinkers spent more money on alcohol after MUP was introduced (Frontier Economics 2023). Although public health lobbyists often used anti-industry rhetoric, controlling industry was a secondary consideration and they were not at all interested in making markets more competitive. Their primary aim in regulating the industries was to control the behaviour of consumers.

Once it is understood that the public health groups had a financial interest in achieving the policy wins, not because they stood to gain directly from the policies but because they were being paid to advocate as part of an open-ended campaign of paternalistic lifestyle regulation, the facts fit an Olsonian account remarkably well. The fact that such groups were incentivised to *campaign* rather than to achieve limited policy goals provides a public choice explanation for the existence of 'mission creep' and 'the slippery slope' in this area of public health activism. So long as the money is available from either the state or from wealthy benefactors, the groups must find new dragons to slay.

And that is exactly what happened after the campaigns discussed in this book finished. ASH moved on to lobbying for a generational tobacco sales ban, Alcohol Focus Scotland shifted its attention to an alcohol advertising ban, and Action on Sugar called for the sugar tax to be extended to food and milkshakes. The APPG on FOBTs was disbanded and replaced with the APPG on Gambling-Related Harm – later renamed the APPG on Gambling Reform – with a much wider remit. The anti-smoking, anti-alcohol, anti-obesity and anti-gambling groups called for a levy on the tobacco, alcohol, food and gambling industries respectively. The CFFG and Stop the FOBTs were shut down and replaced by Clean Up Gambling and the Coalition to End Gambling Ads, both funded by Derek Webb. The three ASH groups began calling for more regulation and taxation of e-cigarettes. The Obesity Health Alliance campaigned for a ban on HFSS advertising online and, once that was achieved, for the ban to be extended and for mandatory food reformulation.

Where does it end? Mancur Olson's theory addressed an important misconception: that interest groups in a pluralist society balance each other out and if any faction grows too strong and makes outrageous demands, latent groups will organise to restore equilibrium (Olson 1971: 121). This idealistic theory of a self-correcting political ecosystem, most famously articulated by David Truman (1951), is not what Olson observed in practice and it is not what we saw in our case studies. A public choice analysis helps explain why small, paternalistic pressure groups, given modest but sufficient resources, prevail over large groups of consumers, but since these groups have an interest in permanent disequilibrium, it implies that the process will go on indefinitely unless consumers take collective action (which would, in Olson's account, require them to coalesce around selective benefits of some kind).[68]

For those who are of a liberal disposition, this is not a happy conclusion to reach. It implies a 'tyranny of the majority' (Mill 1987: 62) in which politicians are hostages to small pressure groups manipulating public opinion almost without end. It suggests that minorities can expect to suffer at the hands of the majority if most people have no self-interested reason to defend the activities in question. It is always possible that more far-sighted voters will become concerned that if they allow a succession of special interest groups to restrict or ban the pleasures of other people, it will not be long before their own pleasures are under attack. This could lead to an Ostrogorski Paradox in which 'the fulfilment of the majority's preferences can make everyone worse off' (Widerquist 2003: 328).

Since individuals are sometimes in the majority and sometimes in the minority, it may be in the long-term interest of the majority to defend minorities on principle. This is why defenders of free speech defend the right of people to say things that they personally find objectionable and it may explain why some MPs opposed plain packaging, the sugar tax and the FOBT reform despite being personally unaffected by the policies and despite their party and constituents generally supporting them. Fearing that a precedent is being set, an individual may feel that the surest way to avoid a ban on sugary drinks is to prevent a ban on cigarettes, despite disapproving of smoking themselves. The problem is that, in the absence of selective benefits or external funding, such individuals have insufficient

[68] See Snowdon (2025b) for a discussion of how this could be achieved.

incentives to mobilise as a collective political force and the small, concentrated paternalistic groups therefore tend to prevail.

Scholars of political science and rational choice economics have tended to overlook pressure groups whose objectives are fundamentally paternalistic, and the phenomenon of state-funded interest groups instigating policy campaigns that would otherwise not exist has received little academic attention. The patterns identified in this book may not apply to policymaking in general, but they may be generalisable to a sub-set of policy-making that could be described as paternalistic lifestyle regulation. There is no reason, in principle, why they should not apply to any committed group of activists that has the opportunity and resources to apply pressure on government.

REFERENCES

Acemoglu, D. and Robinson, J. A. (2013) Economics versus Politics: Pitfalls of Policy Advice. *Journal of Economic Perspectives* 27(2): 173–92.

Action on Smoking and Health (ASH) (1993) Application to the Department of Health for renewal of Section 64 Core funding. ASH Archive: Wellcome Library.

Adams, J., Pell, D., Penney, T. L., Hammond, D., Vanderlee, L. and White, M. (2021) Public acceptability of the UK Soft Drinks Industry Levy: repeat cross-sectional analysis of the International Food Policy Study (2017–2019). *BMJ Open* 11: e051677.

Ahmed, M. (2017) Unlikely duo behind the multimillion hit facing British bookmakers. *Financial Times* 30 September.

Ait Ouakrim, D., Wilson, T., Waa, A. et al. (2024) Tobacco endgame intervention impacts on health gains and Māori:non-Māori health inequity: a simulation study of the Aotearoa/New Zealand Tobacco Action Plan. *Tobacco Control* 33: e173–e184

All Party Parliamentary Group on Fixed Odds Betting Terminals (APPG on FOBTs) (2017) Fixed Odds Betting Terminals – Assessing the Impact. January.

Allami, Y., Hodgins, D., Young, M., Brunelle, N., Currie, S., Dufour, M., Flores-Pajot, M. and Nadeau, L. (2021) A meta-analysis of problem gambling risk factors in the general adult population. *Addiction* 116(11): 2,968–77.

Andalón, M. and Gibson, J. (2017) The 'Soda Tax' is Unlikely to Make Mexicans Lighter: New Evidence on Biases in Elasticities of Demand for Soda. IZA Institute of Labor Economics Discussion Paper No. 10765.

Andreoni, J. (1990) Impure Altruism and Donations to Public Goods. *The Economic Journal* 100(401): 464–77.

Angus, C. and Ally, A. K. (2015) Modelling the potential impact of duty policies using the Sheffield Alcohol Policy Model Version 3. University of Sheffield.

Angus, C., Gillespie, D., Ally, A. K. and Brennan, A. (2015) Modelling the impact of Minimum Unit Price and Identification and Brief Advice policies using the Sheffield Alcohol Policy Model Version 3. University of Sheffield.

Angus, C., Holmes, J., Pryce, R., Meier, P. and Brennan, A. (2016a) Model-based appraisal of the comparative impact of Minimum Unit Pricing and taxation policies in Scotland. An adaptation of the Sheffield Alcohol Policy Model version 3. University of Sheffield.

Angus, C., Holmes, J., Pryce, R., Meier, P. and Brennan, A. (2016b) Alcohol and cancer trends: Intervention Studies. University of Sheffield and Cancer Research UK.

Archer, E. and Arjmandi, B. (2021) Falsehoods and facts about dietary sugars: a call for evidence-based policy. *Critical Reviews in Food Science and Nutrition* 61(22): 3,725–39.

Arnott, D. and Willmore, I. (2006) Smoke and mirrors. *Guardian* 19 July.

Arnott, D., Dockrell, M., Sandford, A. and Willmore, I. (2007) Comprehensive smoke-free legislation in England: how advocacy won the day. *Tobacco Control* 16: 423–8.

Association of British Bookmakers (ABB) (2013) The Truth about Betting Shops and Gaming Machines – ABB submission to DCMS Triennial Review. April.

Association of British Bookmakers (ABB) (2018) Association of British Bookmakers submission to the Department for Digital, Culture, Media & Sport Consultation on proposals for changes to Gaming Machines and Social Responsibility Measures. January.

Atherton, F. and Beynon, C. (2019) Is gambling an emerging public health issue for Wales, UK? *Journal of Public Health* 41(4): 858–63.

Australian Bureau of Statistics (2014) 5206.0 Australian National Accounts: National Income, Expenditure and Product Table 8. Household Final Consumption Expenditure (HFCE) [downloaded 12 March 2015]

Australian Institute of Health and Welfare (2014) National Drug Strategy Household Survey detailed report 2013. Drug statistics series no. 28. Cat. no. PHE 183. Canberra: AIHW.

Babor, T., Caetano, R., Casswell, S., Edwards, G., Giesbrecht, N., Graham, K., Grube, J., Grunewald, P., Hill, L., Holder, H., Homel, R., Osterberg, E., Rehm, J., Room, R. and Rossow, I. (2010) *Alcohol: No Ordinary Commodity: Research and Public Policy*. Oxford: Oxford University Press.

Banerjee, J., Squires, J. and Parkinson, T. (2010) Public Perceptions of Alcohol Pricing. BDRC Continental.

Barnes, R., Johnston, H., MacKenzie, N., Tobin, S. and Taglang, C. (2018) The effect of ad hominem attacks on the evaluation of claims promoted by scientists. *PLOS One* 13(1): e0192025.

Baron, J. (2018) A brief history of evidence-based policy. *Annals of the American Academy of Political and Social Science.* 678(1): 40–50.

Barry, B. M. (1970) *Sociologists, Economists and Democracy.* London: Collier-Macmillan.

Bayly, M., Scollo, M. and Wakefield, M. (2015) No lasting effects of plain packaging on cigarette pack retrieval time in small Australian retail outlets. *Tobacco Control* 24(e1): e108–9.

BBC (2012) Old, Drunk and Disorderly? (television documentary). *Panorama*. First aired on 16 September 2012.

Becker, G. S. (1983) A Theory of Competition Among Groups for Political Influence. *Quarterly Journal of Economics* 98(3): 371–400.

Beede, P. and Lawson, R. (1992) The effect of plain packages on the perception of cigarette health warnings. *Public Health* 106: 315–22.

Berridge, V. (2007) *Marketing Health: Smoking and the Discourse of Public Health in Britain, 1945–2000*. Oxford: Oxford University Press.

Black, N. (2001) Evidence based policy: proceed with caution. *British Medical Journal* 323: 275–9.

Blank, L., Baxter, S., Woods, H. B. and Goyder, E. (2021) Interventions to reduce the public health burden of gambling-related harms: a mapping review. *Lancet Public Health* 6: e50–63.

Blaszczynski, A. (2013) A critical examination of the link between gaming machines and gambling-related harm. *Journal of Gambling Business and Economics* 7(3): 55–76.

Block, J., Chandra, A., McManus, K. and Willett, W. (2010) Point-of-purchase price and education intervention to reduce consumption of sugary soft drinks. *American Journal of Public Health* 100(8): 1,427–33.

Bonell, C., Jamal, F., Melendez-Torres, G. J. and Cummins, S. (2015) 'Dark logic': theorising the harmful consequences of public health interventions. *Journal of Epidemiology and Community Health* 69: 95–98.

Borland, R., Wilson, N., Fong, G. T. et al. (2009a) Impact of graphic and text warnings on cigarette packs: findings from four countries over five years. *Tobacco Control* 18: 358–364.

Borland, R., Yong, H-H., Wilson, N. et al. (2009b) How reaction to cigarette packet health warnings influence quitting: Findings from the ITC Four Country survey. *Addiction* 104(4): 669–75.

Brennan, A., Purshouse, R., Taylor, K. and Rafia, R. (2008) Independent review of the effects of alcohol pricing and promotion – Part B: Modelling the potential impact of pricing and promotion policies for Alcohol in England: results from the Sheffield Alcohol Policy Model version 2008(1–1). University of Sheffield.

Brennan, A., Meng, Y., Holmes, J., Hill-McManus, D. and Meier, P. (2014) Potential benefits of minimum unit pricing for alcohol versus a ban on below cost selling in England 2014: modelling study. *British Medical Journal* 349: g5452.

Brennan, A., Angus, C., Pryce, R., Buykx, P., Henney, M., Gillespie, D., Holmes, J. and Meier, P. (2022) Effectiveness of subnational implementation of minimum unit price for alcohol: policy appraisal modelling for local authorities in England. *Addiction* 118(5): 819–33.

Breton, M. O., Britton, J., Huang, Y. and Bogdanovica, I. (2018) Cigarette brand diversity and price changes during the implementation of plain packaging in the United Kingdom. *Addiction* 113: 1,883–94.

Breton, M. O., Britton, J., Brown, J., Beard, E. and Bogdanovica, I. (2021) Was the implementation of standardised tobacco packaging legislation in England associated with changes in smoking prevalence? A segmented regression analysis between 2006 and 2019. *Tobacco Control* 32: 195–204.

Briggs, A., Mytton, O., Kehlbachder, A., Tiffin, R., Rayner, M. and Scarborough, P. (2013) Overall and income specific effect on prevalence of overweight and obesity of 20% sugar sweetened drink tax in UK: econometric and comparative risk assessment modelling study. *British Medical Journal* 347: f6189.

British Heart Foundation (2013) UK cigarette health warnings 'not up to the job' 7 October: https://www.bhf.org.uk/what-we-do/news-from-the-bhf/news-archive/2013/october/standardised-packs

British Medical Association (BMA) (2015) Food for thought: promoting healthy diets among children and young people. July.

Brownlow, G. (2022) Institutional Geography Once More? Devolution Economics Northern Ireland Style. *National Institute Economic Review* 261(1): 34–47.

Bruun, K., Edwards, G., Lumio, M., Mäkelä, K., Pan, L., Popham, R. E., Room, R., Schmidt, W., Skog, O., Sulkunen, P. and Österberg, E. (1975) *Alcohol control policies in public health perspective*. The Finnish Foundation for Alcohol Studies, Volume 25 Forssa.

Budd, A., Bishop, D., Bose, M., Dean, P., Gray, J., Hoddinott, J., Marks, P., Nathan, S., Weekes, A., and Wolff, J. (2001). *Gambling Review Report*. London: Department for Culture, Media and Sport.

Bulmer, M. (1986) *Social Science and Social Policy*. London: Allen & Unwin.

Cabinet Office (1999a) *Modernising Government*. London: The Stationery Office.

Cabinet Office (1999b), Professional Policy Making for the Twenty-first Century: A Report by the Strategic Policy Making Team. September.

Cairney, P. and Zahariadis, N. (2016) Multiple streams approach: a flexible metaphor presents an opportunity to operationalize agenda setting processes, in Zahariadis, N. (ed.) *Handbook of Public Policy Agenda-Setting*. Cheltenham: Edward Elgar Publishing: 87–105.

Cairney, P. and Oliver, K. (2017) Evidence-based policymaking is not like evidence-based medicine, so how far should you go to bridge the divide between evidence and policy? *Health Research Policy and Systems* 15(35): 1–11.

Campaign for Fairer Gambling (CFFG) (2013) FOBT Research Report. 18 June: https://web.archive.org/web/20170408104349/http://fairergambling.org/wp-content/uploads/2013/08/Fairer-Gambling-Report-19062013v2.pdf

Campos, P., Saguy, A., Ernsberger, P., Oliver, E. and Gaesser, G. (2006) The epidemiology of overweight and obesity: public health crisis or moral panic? *International Journal of Epidemiology* 35: 55–60.

Cancer Research UK and the UK Health Forum (2016) Short and Sweet: Why the government should introduce a sugary drinks tax. February.

Capacci, S., Allais, O., Bonnet, C. and Mazzocchi, M. (2019) The impact of the French soda tax on prices and purchases. An ex post evaluation. *PLOS One* 14(10): e0223196.

Carl, N. (2017) *Lackademia: Why Do Academics Lean Left?* London: Adam Smith Institute.

Carter, S. and Chapman, S. (2006) Smokers and non-smokers talk about regulatory options in tobacco control. *Tobacco Control* 15: 398–404.

Carter, O., Mills, B., Phan, T. and Bremner, J. (2012) Measuring the effect of cigarette plain packaging on transaction times and selection errors in a simulation experiment. *Tobacco Control* 21: 572–7.

Centre for Addictions Research of BC (2013) Alcohol-Related Deaths in British Columbia. University of Victoria. https://www.uvic.ca/research/centres/cisur/assets/docs/report-alcohol-related-deaths.pdf

Centre for Economics and Business Research (CEBR) (2009) Minimum Alcohol Pricing: A targeted measure? June.

Chamary, J. V. (2021) WHO Finally Admits Coronavirus Is Airborne. It's Too Late. *Forbes,* 4 May.

Chantler, C. (2014) Standardised packaging of tobacco: Report of the independent review undertaken by Sir Cyril Chantler. April.

Chatrou, M., Maes, S., Dusseldorp, E. and Seegers, G. (1999). Effects of the Brabant smoking prevention programme. A replication of the Wisconsin programme. *Psychology and Health* 14: 159–178.

Chote, R. (2023) Response from Sir Robert Chote to Sandesh Gulhane MSP – minimum unit pricing. UK Statistics Authority, 29 August. https://uksa.statisticsauthority.gov.uk/correspondence/response-from-sir-robert-chote-to-sandesh-gulhane-msp-minimum-unit-pricing/

Clarence, E. (2002) Technocracy Reinvented: The New Evidence Based Policy Movement. *Public Policy and Administration* 17(3): Autumn.

Clark, S. (2014a) Hands off our packs: Diary of a political campaign. Cambridge: Berforts Information Press.

Clark, S. (2014b) Poll: little support for plain packaging. 8 September: http://taking-liberties.squarespace.com/blog/2014/9/8/poll-little-support-for-plain-packaging.html

Cochrane, A. (1972) *Effectiveness and Efficiency: Random reflections on health services*. London: The Nuffield Provincial Hospitals Trust.

Colchero, M. A., Salgado, J. C., Unar, M., Hernandez-Avila, M., Velasco-Bernal, A., Carriedo, A. and River-Dommarco, J. A. (2013) Impuesta al refresco. *Mexican National Institute of Public Health Blog*: https://web.archive.org/web/20131024053555/https://www.insp.mx/epppo/blog/2946-imp-refresco.html

Colchero, M. A., Popkin, B., Rivera, J. and Ng, S. W. (2016a) Beverage purchases from stores in Mexico under the excise tax on sugar sweetened beverages: observational study. *British Medical Journal* 352: h6704.

Colchero, M. A., Guerrero-López, C., Molina, M. and Rivera, J. A. (2016b) Beverages Sales in Mexico before and after Implementation of a Sugar Sweetened Beverage Tax. *PLOS One* 11(9): e0163463.

Collin, J., Hill, S. E., Eltanani, M. K., Plotnikova, E., Ralston, R. and Smith, K. E. (2017) Can public health reconcile profits and pandemics? An analysis of attitudes to commercial sector engagement in health policy and research. *PLOS One* 12(9): e0182612.

Collins, B., Capewell, S., O'Flaherty, M., Timpson, H., Razzaq, A., Cheater, S., Ireland, R. and Bromley, H. (2015) Modelling the Health Impact of an English Sugary Drinks Duty at National and Local Levels. *PLOS One* 29 June: https://doi.org/10.1371/journal.pone.0130770

Collins, P., Barr, G. and Scott, L. (2016) Report on results of research into the likely effects of substantially reducing the maximum stake of £100 per 20-second spin on Category B2 electronic gambling machines in UK betting shops. Bacta. https://web.archive.org/web/20170705035501/https://bacta.org.uk/downloads/Research_Results_into_Effects_of_B2_Stake_Reduction.pdf

Conolly, A., Fuller, E., Jones, H., Maplethorpe, N., Sondaal, A. and Wardle, H. (2017) Gambling behaviour in Great Britain in 2015: Evidence from England, Scotland and Wales. NatCen. August.

Coraiola, D. and Derry, R. (2019) Remembering to Forget: The Historic Irresponsibility of U.S. Big Tobacco. *Journal of Business Ethics* 166(2): 233–252.

Cornelsen, L., Mytton, O., Adams, J. et al. (2017) Change in non-alcoholic beverage sales following a 10-pence levy on sugar-sweetened beverages within a national chain of restaurants in the UK: interrupted time series analysis of a natural experiment. *Journal of Epidemiology and Community Health* 71: 1,107–12.

Courtright, D. T. (2004) Drugs Wars: Policy hots and historical cools. *Bulletin of the History of Medicine* 78(2): 440–50.

Critchlow, N., Stead, M., Moodie, C., Eadie, D. and MacKintosh, A. (2019) Introduction of Standardized Tobacco Packaging During a 12-Month Transition Period: Findings from Small Retailers in the United Kingdom. *Nicotine and Tobacco Research* 21: 871–8.

Curnock, E., Robinson, M., McCartney, G., Craig, N., and Beeston, C. (2012) Monitoring and Evaluating Scotland's Alcohol Strategy: preliminary descriptive analysis of the impact of the quantity discount ban on off-trade alcohol sales in Scotland. Edinburgh: NHS Health Scotland.

Dale, I. (ed.) (2000) *Labour Party General Election Manifestos, 1900–1997*. London: Routledge.

Daube, M. and Chapman, S. (2014) The Australian's dissembling campaign on tobacco plain packaging. *Medical Journal of Australia* 201(4): 191–2.

DCMS (2012) The Gambling Act 2005: A bet worth taking? First Report of Session 2012–13 (1). July.

DCMS (2013) Gambling Act 2005: Triennial Review of Gaming Machine Stake and Prize Limits. 15 January.

DCMS (2014) Gaming Machine (Circumstances of Use) (Amendment) Regulations 2015: Impact Assessment. DCMS 078. 5 August.

DCMS (2016) Evaluation of Gaming Machine (Circumstances of Use) (Amendment) Regulations 2015. January.

DCMS (2018) Government response to the consultation on proposals for changes to Gaming Machines and Social Responsibility Measures. May.

DeLeon, P. and Weible, C. (2010) Policy Process Research for Democracy: A Commentary on Lasswell's Vision. *International Journal of Policy Studies* 1(2): 23–34.

Delfabbro, P. and King, D. (2017) Prevention paradox logic and problem gambling: Does low-risk gambling impose a greater burden of harm than high-risk gambling? *Journal of Behavioural Addictions* 6(2): 163–7.

Deloitte (2011) Potential impact on retailers from the introduction of plain tobacco packaging. February.

Department of Health (2008) Consultation on the Future of Tobacco Control. 31 May.

Department of Health (2013) Consultation on standardised packaging of tobacco products: Summary report. HM Government. July.

Department of Health (2014) Impact Assessment No. 3080: Standardised packaging of tobacco products. June.

Department of Health (2015) Consultation on the introduction of regulations for standardised packaging of tobacco products: Summary report. HM Government. February.

Department of Health (2016) Childhood Obesity: A plan for action. HM Government. August.

Department of Health and Social Care (2022) Post-Implementation Review of Tobacco Legislation: The Standardised Packaging of Tobacco Products Regulations 2015. March.

Dickson, A., Gehrsitz, M. and Kemp, J. (2021) Does a Spoonful of Sugar Levy Help the Calories Go Down? An Analysis of the UK Soft Drinks Industry Levy. IZA Institute of Labor Economics IZA DP No. 14528.

Dockrell, M. (2009) Eye and heart at mortal war: coronaries and controversy in a smoke-free Scotland. *Expert Review of Pharmacoeconomics & Outcomes Research* 9(1): 23–7.

D'Onofrio, C. N., Moskowitz, J. M., and Braverman, M. T. (2002). Curtailing tobacco use among youth: Evaluation of Project 4-Health. *Health Education and Behaviour* 29: 656–682.

Doward, J. (2014a) Tobacco firms hype smuggling fears to avoid plain packaging, finds study. *Guardian,* 30 March.

Doward, J. (2014b) Delay in law on plain packs for cigarettes angers MPs. *Guardian,* 6 December.

Downs, A. (1957) An economic theory of political action in a democracy. *Journal of Political Economy* 65(2): 135–150.

Duffy, J. (2013) The price of a drink – too exactly? Flawed evidence for minimum pricing. *Significance* April: 23–27.

Eagan, K., Stolzenberg, E. B., Lozano, J. B., Aragon, M. C. Suchard, M. R. and Hurtado, S. (2014) *Undergraduate Teaching Faculty: The 2012–14 HERI Faculty Survey.* Los Angeles: Higher Education Research Institute.

Edwards, R., Peace, J., Russell, M., Gifford, H., Thomson, G. and Wilson, N. (2012) Qualitative exploration of public and smoker understanding of, and reactions to, an endgame solution to the tobacco epidemic. *BMC Public Health* 12: 782.

Embrett, M. and Randall, G. E. (2014) Social determinants of health and health equity policy research: Exploring the use, misuse, and nonuse of policy analysis theory. *Social Science & Medicine* 108: 147–55.

Ferejohn, J. (2000) Rationality and Interpretation: Parliamentary Elections in Early Stuart England. In *Culture and Politics: A Reader* (Crothers, L. and Lockhart, C. (eds)) London: Palgrave MacMillan.

Ferguson, K., Beeston, C. and Giles, L. (2020) Public attitudes to Minimum Unit Pricing (MUP) for alcohol in Scotland. Public Health Scotland. September.

Fidler, J. and West, R. (2010) Changes in smoking prevalence in 16–17-year-olds versus older adults following a rise in legal age of sale: findings from an English population study. *Addiction* 105(11): 1,984–8.

Field, M., Munafò, M. and Franken, I. (2009) A Meta-Analytic Investigation of the Relationship Between Attentional Bias and Subjective Craving in Substance Abuse. *Psychological Bulletin* 135(4): 589–607.

Flegal, K. (2021) The obesity wars and the education of a researcher: A personal account. *Progress in Cardiovascular Diseases* 67: 75–9.

Fletcher, J. M., Frisvold, D. E. and Tefft, N. (2014) Non-Linear Effects of Soda Taxes on Consumption and Weight Outcomes. *Health Economics* 24(5): 566–82.

Ford, A., MacKintosh, A., Moodie, C., Richardson, S. and Hastings, G. (2013) Cigarette pack design and adolescent smoking susceptibility: a cross-sectional survey. *BMJ Open* 3: e003282.

FOREST (2015) Poll: plain packaging not a priority says British public. 11 February. https://www.forestonline.org/news-comment/headlines/poll-plain-packaging-not-priority-says-british-public/

Francesconi, M. and James, J. (2021) None for the Road? Stricter Drink Driving Laws and Road Accidents. *Journal of Health Economics* 79: 102487.

Freeman, B., Gartner, C., Hall, W. and Chapman, S. (2010) Forecasting future tobacco control policy: where to next? *Australian and New Zealand Journal of Public Health* 34(5): 447–450.

Frontier Economics (2023) Minimum Unit Alcohol Pricing: Impacts on the alcoholic drinks industry in Scotland: final report. January.

Fuller, E. and Simpson, I. (2015) British Social Attitudes: Attitudes to alcohol. NatCen Social Research.

Gadher, D. and Leake, J. (2013) Hole opens in No 10's tobacco 'smokescreen'. *Sunday Times,* 21 July.

Gambling Commission (2016) Participation in gambling and rates of problem gambling – England 2016: Statistical report. April.

Gambling Commission (2017) New data to inform government gambling review: https://web.archive.org/web/20170213222828/https://www.gamblingcommission.gov.uk/news-action-and-statistics/news/2017/New-data-to-inform-government-gambling-review.aspx

Gambling Commission (2018a) Review of gaming machines and social responsibility measures – formal advice. March.

Gambling Commission (2018b) Participation in gambling and rates of problem gambling – England 2016. April.

Gambling Commission (2022) Industry Statistics. November 2022. https://www.gamblingcommission.gov.uk/statistics-and-research/publication/industry-statistics-november-2022

Gambling With Lives (2020) Gambling with Lives – Supplementary written evidence (GAM0131). House of Lords Select Committee on the Social and Economic Impact of the Gambling Industry: https://committees.parliament.uk/writtenevidence/2093/pdf/

Garde, A., Byrne, S., Gokani, N. and Murphy, B. (2018) A child rights-based approach to food marketing: A guide for policy makers. UNICEF, April 2018.

Gibson, J. and Kim, B. (2019) Quality, quantity, and spatial variation of price: Back to the bog. *Journal of Development Economics* 137: 66–77.

Gilbert, N. (1997) Advocacy Research and Social Policy. *Crime and Justice* 22: 101–48.

Gilmore, I. (2015) A minimum unit price: the 'holy grail' of alcohol policy. *Clinical Medicine* 15: 5–6.

Goyder, E., Blank, L., Baxter, S. and van Scalkwyk, M. (2020) Tackling gambling related harms as a public health issue. *Lancet Public Health* 5(1): e14–15.

Green, D. P. and Shapiro, I. (1994) *Pathologies of Rational Choice Theory: A critique of applications in political science.* New York: Yale University Press.

Gros, M., Guillot, L. and Griera, M. (2025) Europe's conservatives target green NGO financing rules. *Politico,* 22 January.

Griffith, R. and Leicester, A. (2010) The Impact of Introducing Minimum Pricing on Alcohol in Britain. Institute for Fiscal Studies Briefing Note 109.

Haghpanahan, H., Lewsey, J., MacKay, D., McIntosh, E., Pell, J., Jones, A., Fitzgerald, N. and Robinson, M. (2019) An evaluation of the effects of lowering blood alcohol concentration limits for drivers on the rates of road traffic accidents and alcohol consumption: a natural experiment. *Lancet* 393(10169): 321–29.

Hancock, L., Ralph, N. and Martino, F. P. (2018) Applying Corporate Political Activity (CPA) analysis to Australian gambling industry submissions against regulation of television sports betting advertising. *PLOS ONE* 13(10): e0205654.

Hansard (2011) Alcohol (Minimum Pricing): 2 February 2011: https://hansard.parliament.uk/Commons/2011-02-02/debates/11020240000001/Alcohol(MinimumPricing)

Hansard (2012) Alcohol Strategy: 7 February 2012: https://hansard.parliament.uk/Commons/2012-02-07/debates/12020765000002/AlcoholStrategy

Hansard (2013) Alcohol: Minimum Unit Price: 14 March 2013: https://hansard.parliament.uk/Commons/2013-03-14/debates/13031445000008/AlcoholMinimumUnitPrice

Hansard (2015) Sugary Drinks Tax: 30 November 2015: https://hansard.parliament.uk/Commons/2015-11-30/debates/15113012000001/SugaryDrinksTax

Hastings, G. and Moodie, C. (2015) Death of a salesman. *Tobacco Control* 24: ii1–ii2.

Hawkins, B. and Holden, C. (2013) Framing the alcohol policy debate: industry actors and the regulation of the UK beverage alcohol market, *Critical Policy Studies* 7(1): 53–71.

Hawkins, B. and McCambridge, J. (2020) Policy windows and multiple streams: an analysis of alcohol pricing policy in England. *Policy & Politics* 48(2): 315–33.

Hayek, F. (1974) The Pretence of Knowledge. Lecture to the memory of Alfred Nobel. 11 December: https://www.nobelprize.org/prizes/economic-sciences/1974/hayek/lecture/

Head, B. W. (2010) Reconsidering evidence-based policy: Key issues and challenges. *Policy and Society* 29(2): 77–94.

Health Committee (2012). Government's Alcohol Strategy: Third report of session 2012–13 HC 132. London: Stationary Office.

Hiscock, R., Augustin, N., Branston, J. R. and Gilmore, A. (2020) Longitudinal evaluation of the impact of standardised packaging and minimum excise tax on tobacco sales and industry revenue in the UK. *Tobacco Control* 30: 515–22.

HM Government (2011) Healthy Lives, Healthy People: A call to action on obesity in England. October.

HM Government (2012) The Government's Alcohol Strategy. March.

HMRC (2014) The Introduction of Standardised Packaging for Tobacco HMRC's Assessment of the Potential Impact on the Illicit Market.

HM Treasury (2015) Tobacco levy: response to the consultation. September: https://assets.publishing.service.gov.uk/government/uploads/system/uploads/attachment_data/file/464795/PU1814_Tobacco_Levy_final_v3.pdf

Holmes, J., Meng, Y., Meier, P. S. et al. (2014) Effects of minimum unit pricing for alcohol on different income and socioeconomic groups: a modelling study. *Lancet* 83(9929): 1,655–64.

Holmes, J., Buykx, P., Perkins, A. et al. (2022) Evaluating the impact of Minimum Unit Pricing in Scotland on people who are drinking at harmful levels. University of Sheffield. 7 June.

Home Office (2011) The likely impacts of increasing alcohol price: a summary review of the evidence base. January.

Home Office (2012a) A consultation on delivering the Government's policies to cut alcohol fuelled crime and anti-social behaviour. November.

Home Office (2012b) Impact assessment: A minimum unit price for alcohol. 1 November.

Home Office (2013) Next steps following the consultation on delivering the Government's alcohol strategy. July 2013.

Horel, S. and Keyzer, T. (2021) Covid 19: How harm reduction advocates and the tobacco industry capitalised on the pandemic to promote nicotine. *British Medical Journal* 373: n1303.

House of Commons Health Committee (2010) Alcohol: First Report of Session 2009–10. 8 January 2010.

House of Commons Health Select Committee (2015) Childhood obesity – brave and bold action. First Report of Session 2015–16.

House of Commons Treasury Committee (2018) Oral evidence: Budget 2018, HC 1606. 5 November.

Hungarian National Institute for Health Promotion (2013) A népegészségügyi termékadó hatásvizsgálata [Impact assessment of the public health tax]. Budapest.

James, E., Lajous, M. and Reich, M. R. (2020) The Politics of Taxes for Health: An Analysis of the Passage of the Sugar-Sweetened Beverage Tax in Mexico. *Health Systems and Reform* 6(1): e1669122.

Jann, B. (2015) Methodological Report on Kaul and Wolf's Working Papers on the Effect of Plain Packaging on Smoking Prevalence in Australia and the Criticism Raised by OxyRomandie. March. https://www.econ.uzh.ch/static/wp/Jann-2015-03-10-Methodological-Report-on-Kaul-and-Wolf.pdf

Jha, A. (2011) Price of alcohol is 'obscenely low'. *Guardian,* 14 September.

Jones, M. D., Peterson, H. L., Pierce, J., Herweg, N., Bernal, A., Raney, H. L. and Zahariadis, N. (2016) A River Runs Through It: A Multiple Streams Meta-Review. *Policy Studies Journal* 44(1): 13–36.

Katikireddi, S. V., Bond, L. and Hilton, S. (2013) Perspectives on econometric modelling to inform policy: a UK qualitative case study of minimum unit pricing of alcohol. *European Journal of Public Health* 24(3): 490–5.

Katikireddi, S. V., Hilton, S., Bonell, C. and Bond, L. (2014) Understanding the Development of Minimum Unit Pricing of Alcohol in Scotland: A Qualitative Study of the Policy Process. *PLOS One* 19(3): e91185.

Katikireddi, S. V., Hilton, S. and Bond, L. (2016) The role of the Sheffield model on the minimum unit pricing of alcohol debate: the importance of a rhetorical perspective. *Evidence & Policy* 12(4): 521–39.

Kaul, A. and Wolf, M. (2014) The (possible) effect of plain packaging on smoking prevalence in Australia: A trend analysis. University of Zurich, Department of Economics. Working Paper No. 165.

Khan, J. (2022) The Khan Review: Making Smoking Obsolete. Office for Health Improvement and Disparities. 9 June.

Kingdon, J. W. (1995) *Agendas, Alternatives, and Public Policies.* New York: Longman.

Klein, D. B. (1994) If Government is so Villainous, How Come Government Officials Don't Seem Like Villains? *Economics and Philosophy* 10(1): 91–106.

Kopasker, D., Whybrow, S., McKenzie, L., McNamee, P. and Ludbrook, A. (2022) The effects of minimum unit pricing for alcohol on food purchases: Evaluation of a natural experiment. *SSM - Population Health* 19: 101174.

KPMG (2013) Illicit tobacco in Australia, 2013 Half Year Report. October. London: KPMG LLP.

KPMG (2014) Illicit tobacco in Australia: 2013 Full Year Report. London: KPMG LLP.

Kruger, J. and Dunning, D. (1999) Unskilled and unaware of it: How difficulties in recognising one's own incompetence lead to inflated self-assessments. *Journal of Personality and Social Psychology* 77(6): 1121–34.

Krzemieniewska-Nandwani, K., Bannister, J., Ellison, M. and Adepeju, M. (2021) Evaluation of the impact of alcohol minimum unit pricing (MUP) on crime and disorder, public safety and public nuisance. Manchester Metropolitan University.

Kypri, K., McCambridge, J., Robertson, N., Martino, F., Daube, M., Adams, P. and Miller, P. (2019) 'If someone donates $1000, they support you. If they donate $100,000, they have bought you'. Mixed methods study of tobacco, alcohol and gambling industry donations to Australian political parties. *Drug and Alcohol Review* 38(3): 226–33.

Labour Party (2010) A Future Fair For All: The Labour Party Manifesto 2010.

LaPlante, D. A., Nelson, S. E., LaBrie, R. A. and Shaffer, H. J. (2011) Disordered gambling, type of gambling and gambling involvement in the British Gambling Prevalence Survey 2007. *European Journal of Public Health* 21(4): 532–7.

Laverty, A. A., Diethelm, P., Hopkinson, N. S., Watt, H. C. and McKee, M. (2015) Use and abuse of statistics in tobacco industry-funded research on standardised packaging. *Tobacco Control* 24: 422–24.

Ledermann, S. (1956) Alcool, Alcoolisme, Alcoolisation: données scientifiques de caractère physiologique, économique et social. Paris: Presses Universitaires de France.

Leicester, G. (1999) Viewpoint: The Seven Enemies of Evidence-Based Policy. *Public Money & Management* 19(1): 5–7.

Leicester, A. (2011) Alcohol pricing and taxation policies. Institute of Fiscal Studies Briefing Note BN124. https://ifs.org.uk/sites/default/files/output_url_files/bn124.pdf

Leicester, A. and O'Connell, M. (2012) What is the impact of a 45p minimum unit price for alcohol? Institute of Fiscal Studies. https://ifs.org.uk/publications/6462

Lindblom, C. (1959) The Science of 'Muddling Through'. *Public Administration Review* 19(2): 79–88.

Lindblom, C. and Cohen D. (1979) *Usable Knowledge: Social Science and Social Problem Solving*. New Haven: Yale University Press.

Littlechild, S. C. and Wiseman, J. (1986) The Political Economy of Restriction of Choice. *Public Choice* 51(2): 161–72.

Lomas, J. and Brown, A. (2009) Research and Advice Giving: A Functional View of Evidence-Informed Policy Advice in a Canadian Ministry of Health. *Millbank Quarterly* 87(4): 903–26.

Lonsdale, A., Hardcastle, S. and Hagger, M. (2012) A minimum price per unit of alcohol: A focus group study to investigate public opinion concerning UK government proposals to introduce new price controls to curb alcohol consumption. *BMC Public Health* 12: 1,023.

Lucas, G. M. and Tasić, S. (2015) Behavioural public choice and the law. *West Virginia Law Review* 118: 199–264.

Lynn, L. (1978) *Knowledge and Policy: The Uncertain Connection*. Washington D.C.: National Academies Press.

Ma, Y., He, F., Yin, Y., Hashem, K. and MacGregor, G. (2016) Gradual reduction of sugar in soft drinks without substitution as a strategy to reduce overweight, obesity, and type 2 diabetes: a modelling study. *Lancet Diabetes and Endocrinology* 4(2): 105–14.

Mair, M. and Kierans, C. (2007) Critical reflections on the field of tobacco research: The role of tobacco control in defining the tobacco research agenda. *Critical Public Health* 17(2): 103–12.

Maniadakis, N., Kapaki, V., Damianidi, L. and Kourlaba, G. (2013) A systematic review of the effectiveness of taxes on nonalcoholic beverages and high-in-fat foods as a means to prevent obesity trends. *ClinicoEconomics and Outcomes Research* 5: 519–43.

Manning, W. G., Blumberg, L. and Moulton, L. H. (1995) The demand for alcohol: The differential response to price. *Journal of Health Economics* 14: 123–48.

Manyema, M., Veerman, L., Chola, L., Tugendhaft, A., Sartorius, B., Labadarios, D. and Hofman, K. (2014) The Potential Impact of a 20% Tax on Sugar-Sweetened Beverages on Obesity in South African Adults: A Mathematical Model. *PLOS One* 9(8): e105287.

Markey, O., Le Jeune, J. and Lovegrove, J. A. (2015) Energy compensation following consumption of sugar-reduced products: a randomized controlled trial. *European Journal of Nutrition* 55: 2,137–49.

Marston, G. and Watts, R. (2003) Tampering with the evidence: A critical appraisal of evidence-based policy-making. *The Drawing Board: An Australian Review of Public Affairs* 3(3): 143–63.

Maynard, O. M., Munafò, M. R. and Leonards, U. (2013) Visual attention to health warnings on plain tobacco packaging in adolescent smokers and non-smokers. *Addiction* 108(2): 413–19.

Maynard, O.M., Leonards, U., Attwood, A. S. et al. (2015) Effects of first exposure to plain cigarette packaging on smoking behaviour and attitudes: a randomised controlled study. *BMC Public Health* 15: 240.

McCambridge, J., Kypri, K., Miller, P., Hawkins, B. and Hastings, G. (2014) Be aware of Drinkaware. *Addiction* 109(4): 519–24.

McKee, M. and Sassi, F. (1995) Gambling with the nation's health? The social impact of the National Lottery needs to be researched. *British Medical Journal* 311(7004).

McMahon, N., Thomson, K., Kaner, E. and Bambra, C. (2019) Effects of prevention and harm reduction interventions on gambling behaviours and gambling related harm: An umbrella review. *Addictive Behaviours* 90: 380–88.

McNeill, A., Brose, L. S. and Hitchman, S. C. (2014) Commentary on Zacher *et al.* (2014): Emerging behavioural impact of packaging changes in Australia: time for action elsewhere. *Addiction* 109(5): 704–5.

Mellor, D. and Green, D. (2023) A critical review exploring science communication of nutrition and dietetic research: a case-based approach exploring methodologies. *Journal of Human Nutrition and Dietetics* 36(4): 1,468–79.

Meng, Y., Purshouse, R. and Brennan, A. (2010) Model based appraisal of alcohol minimum pricing and off-licensed trade discount bans in Scotland: A Scottish adaptation of the Sheffield alcohol policy model v2 – an update based on newly available data. Sheffield University.

Meng, Y., Hill-McManus, D. and Brennan, A. (2012) Model-Based Appraisal of Alcohol Minimum Pricing and Off-Licensed Trade Discount Bans in Scotland (v2) second update. Sheffield University.

Meng, Y., Brennan, A., Purshouse, R., Hill-McManus, D., Angus, C., Holmes, J. and Meier, P. (2014) Estimation of own and cross price elasticities of alcohol demand in the UK—A pseudo-panel approach using the Living Costs and Food Survey 2001–2009. *Journal of Health Economics* 34: 96–103.

Mill, J. S. (1987) *On Liberty*. London: Penguin.

Moodie, C. and Hastings, G. (2010) Plain packaging: a time for action. *European Journal of Public Health* 20(1): 10–11.

Moodie, C., Stead, M., Bauld, L., McNeill, A., Angus, K., Hinds, K., Kwan, I., Thomas, J., Hastings, G. and O'Mara-Eves, A. (2012) Plain tobacco packaging: A systematic review. Public Health Research Consortium.

Moodie, C., Angus, K., Stead, M. and Bauld, L. (2013) Plain tobacco packaging research: an update. Centre for Tobacco Control Research, Institute for Social Marketing. University of Stirling.

Moodie, C. and MacKintosh, A. (2013) Young adult women smokers' response to using plain cigarette packaging: a naturalistic approach. *BMJ Open* 3: e002402.

Moodie, C., Angus, K. and Stead, M. (2019) A systematic review of research exploring the response of consumers, retailers and tobacco companies to standardised packaging in the United Kingdom. University of Stirling/Public Health Research Consortium.

Munafò, M., Roberts, N., Bauld, L. and Leonards, U. (2011) Plain packaging increases visual attention to health warnings on cigarette packs in non-smokers and weekly smokers but not daily smokers. *Addiction* 106(8): 1,505–10.

Moskalewicz, J., Garretsen, H. and Room, R. (2022) A half-century of the Kettil Bruun Society: A history against a backdrop of global developments. *Alcoholism and Drug Addiction* 35(4): 293–306.

Mytton, O., Gray, A., Rayner, M. and Rutter, H. (2007) Could targeted food taxes improve health? *Journal of Epidemiology and Community Health* 61: 689–94.

Mytton, O., Clarke, D. and Rayner, M. (2012) Taxing unhealthy food and drinks to improve health. *British Medical Journal* 344: e2931.

Nakamura, R., Suhrcke, M., Pechey, R., Marciano, M., Roland, M. and Marteau, T. (2013) Impact on alcohol purchasing of a ban on multi-buy promotions: a quasi-experimental evaluation comparing Scotland with England and Wales. *Addiction* 109(4): 558–67.

National Institute for Health and Care Research (2017) Evaluation of the health impacts of the UK Treasury Soft Drinks Industry Levy (SDIL). Award ID 16/130/01. https://web.archive.org/web/20230401170547/https://fundingawards.nihr.ac.uk/award/16/130/01

National Institute of Clinical Excellence (2010) Alcohol-use disorders: Preventing the development of hazardous and harmful drinking.

National Institute of Public Health of Mexico (2015) Why it is not possible to make determinations on the usefulness of the tax on sugar sweetened beverages in Mexico during 2015 using raw sales data. https://www.insp.mx/epppo/blog/4063-tax-sugar-sweetened-beverages.html

NERA Economic Consulting (2014) The Stake of the Nation – Balancing the Bookies: Review of the Association of British Bookmakers' Impact Assessment. April.

Niskanen, W. (1968) The peculiar economics of bureaucracy. *American Economic Review* 58(2): 293–305.

Oakley, B. (2013) Concepts and implications of altruism bias and pathological altruism. *Proceedings of the National Academy of Sciences* 110(supp. 2): 10,408–15.

Obama, B. (2009) President Barack Obama's Inaugural Address. White House: https://obamawhitehouse.archives.gov/blog/2009/01/21/president-barack-obamas-inaugural-address

Office for National Statistics (2022) E-cigarette use in Great Britain.

Okrent, D. (2010) *Last Call: The Rise and Fall of Prohibition*. New York: Scribner.

Olson, M. (1971) *The Logic of Collective Action: Public Goods and the Theory of Groups*. Cambridge, Mass.: Harvard University Press.

Orford, J., Wardle, H. and Griffiths, M. (2012) What proportion of gambling is problem gambling? Estimates from the 2010 British Gambling Prevalence Survey. *International Gambling Studies* 12(1): 4–18.

Overman, E. S. and Simanton, D. F. (1986) Iron Triangles and Issue Networks of Information Policy. *Public Administration Review* 46 Special Issue: 584–9.

Parke, A. J., Harris, A., Parke, J. and Goddard, P. (2014) The Role of Stake Size in Loss of Control in Within-Session Gambling: Impact of Stake Size on Reflection Impulsivity, Response Inhibition and Arousal when Gambling on a Simulated Virtual Roulette Gambling Task: Implications for Gambling Related Harm. London: Responsible Gambling Trust.

Parkhurst, J. (2016) Appeals to evidence for the resolution of wicked problems: the origins and mechanisms of evidentiary bias. *Policy Sciences* 49: 373–93.

Parkhurst, J., Hawkins, B. and Ettelt, S. (2018) Conclusion: Reflecting on Studying Evidence Use from a Public Policy Perspective in Parkhurst et al. (eds) *Evidence Use in Health Making.* International series on public policy. Palgrave Macmillan.

Parsons, W. (2002) From Muddling Through to Muddling Up– Evidence Based Policy Making and the Modernisation of British Government. *Public Policy and Administration* 17(3): 43–60.

Patt, A. and Zeckhauser, R. (2000) Action bias and environmental decisions. *Journal of Risk and Uncertainty* 21(1): 45–72.

Pechey, R., Spielgelhalter, D. and Marteau, T. (2013) Impact of plain packaging of tobacco products on smoking in adults and children: an elicitation of international experts' estimates. *BMC Public Health* 13:18.

Peev, G. (2013) Ministers refuse to act on 'crack cocaine' high stakes gambling machines. *Daily Mail,* 11 January.

Pell, D. Mytton, O., Penny, T. et al. (2021) Changes in soft drinks purchased by British households associated with the UK soft drinks industry levy: controlled interrupted time series analysis. *British Medical Journal* 372: n254.

Peltzman, S. (1976) Toward a More General Theory of Regulation. *Journal of Law & Economics* 19(2): 211–40.

Pierce, J. P., Kealey, S., Leas, E. C. et al. (2022) Effect of Graphic Warning Labels on Cigarette Pack-Hiding Behavior Among Smokers: The CASA Randomized Clinical Trial. *JAMA Network Open* 5(6): e2214242.

Pryce, R., Hollingsworth, B. and Walker, I. (2018) Alcohol quantity and quality price elasticities: quantile regression estimates. *European Journal of Health Economics* 20: 439–54.

Public Health England (2015a) Sugar Reduction: The evidence for action. October.

Public Health England (2015b) Sugar Reduction: The evidence for action – Annexe 2: A mixed method review of behaviour changes resulting from experimental studies that examine the effect of fiscal measures targeted at high sugar food and non-alcoholic drink. October.

Public Health England (2016) The Public Health Burden of Alcohol and the Effectiveness and Cost-Effectiveness of Alcohol Control Policies: An evidence review. 2 December.

Public Health Scotland (2023) Evaluating the impact of minimum unit pricing for alcohol in Scotland: Final report. 27 June.

Purshouse, R., Meng, Y., Rafia, R. and Brennan, A. (2009a) Model based appraisal of alcohol minimum pricing and off-licensed trade discount bans in Scotland: A Scottish adaptation of the Sheffield alcohol policy model v2. Sheffield University.

Purshouse, R., Brennan, A., Latimer, N., Meng, Y. and Rafia, R. (2009b) Modelling to assess the effectiveness and cost-effectiveness of public health related strategies and interventions to reduce alcohol attributable harm in England using the Sheffield Alcohol Policy Model version 2.0. Sheffield University.

Purshouse, R. C., Meier, P. S., Brennan, A., Taylor, K. B. and Rafia, R. (2010) Estimated effect of alcohol pricing policies on health and health economic outcomes in England: an epidemiological model. *Lancet* 375(9723): 1,355–64.

Quit Victoria, Cancer Council Victoria (2011) Plain packaging of tobacco products: a review of the evidence. May.

Rafia, R. and Brennan, A. (2010) Modelling methods to estimate the potential impact of lowering the blood alcohol concentration limit from 80 mg/100ml to 50mg/100ml in England and Wales. University of Sheffield. 12 January.

Ramesh, R. (2013) Betting terminals 'being used to make huge profits from vulnerable people'. *Guardian*, 11 February.

Ramunno, S., Mandeville, K. L. and Yarrow, K. (2012) The effect of plain cigarette packaging on attention to health warnings. *Lancet* 380 (November Suppl.): S5.

Raninen, J. and Livingston, M. (2020) The theory of collectivity of drinking cultures: how alcohol became everyone's problem. *Addiction* 115(9): 1,773–76.

Rayner, M. (2012) Why I am no longer a Minister in Secular Employment. Mike Rayner Sermons (blog): https://web.archive.org/web/20190705221053/http://mikeraynersermons.blogspot.com/2012/01/why-i-am-no-longer-minister-in-secular.html

Record, C. and Day, C. (2009) Britain's alcohol market: how minimum alcohol prices could stop moderate drinkers subsidising those drinking at hazardous and harmful levels. *Clinical Medicine* 9(5): 421–5.

Reed, H. (2015) The Economic Impact of Fixed Odds Betting Terminals: 2015 update. Landman Economics. November.

Rehm, J., O'Donnell, A., Kaner, E., Llopis, E. J., Manthey, J. and Anderson, P. (2022) Differential impact of minimum unit pricing on alcohol consumption between Scottish men and women: controlled interrupted time series analysis. *BMJ Open* 12: e054161.

Responsible Gambling and Strategy Board (RGSB) (2017) Advice in relation to the DCMS review of gaming machines and social responsibility measures. 31 January.

Rizzo, M. J. and Whitman, G. (2020) *Escaping Paternalism: Rationality, Behavioural Economics and Public Policy*. Cambridge: Cambridge University Press.

Roche, A. (1997) The shifting sands of alcohol prevention: rethinking population control approaches. *Australian and New Zealand Journal of Public Health* 21(6): 621–5.

Rodríguez-Pose, A. and Gill, N. (2005) On the 'Economic Dividend' of Devolution *Regional Studies* 39(4): 405–20.

Roerecke, M. and Rehm, J. (2013) On the evidence of a cardioprotective effect of alcohol consumption. *Addiction* 108(2): 429–31.

Rogers, N. T., Cummins, S., Forde, H., Jones, C. P., Mytton, O., Rutter, H., Sharp, S., Theis, D., White, M. and Adams, J. (2023a) Associations between trajectories of obesity prevalence in English primary school children and the UK soft drinks industry levy: An interrupted time series analysis of surveillance data. *PLOS Medicine* 20(1): e1004160.

Rogers, N. T., Conway, D., Mytton, O., Roberts, C., Rutter, H., Sherriff, A., White, M. and Adams, J. (2023b) Estimated impact of the UK soft drinks industry levy on childhood hospital admissions for carious tooth extractions: interrupted time series analysis. *BMJ Nutrition, Prevention & Health* 0: e000714.

Rogers, N., Pell, D., Mytton, O. et al. (2023c) Changes in soft drinks purchased by British households associated with the UK soft drinks industry levy: a controlled interrupted time series analysis. *BMJ Open* 13: e077059.

Room, R. (2004) Disabling the public interest: alcohol strategies and policies for England. *Addiction* 99: 1,083–9.

Room, R. (2014) A Book of Letters for Robin Room. Celebrating Fifty Years of Research and Service (festschrift).

Rowell, A., Evans-Reeves, K. and Gilmore, A. (2014) Tobacco industry manipulation of data on and press coverage of the illicit tobacco trade in the UK. *Tobacco Control* 23: e35–43.

Rudd, K. (2008) Reforming the Australian Public Service. 30 April. https://web.archive.org/web/20210225165931/https://kevinrudd.com/2008/04/30/reforming-the-australian-public-service/

Sample, I. (2020) Face masks cannot stop healthy people getting Covid-19, says WHO. *Guardian*, 7 April.

Sanchez-Romero, L. M., Penko, J., Coxson, P. et al. (2016) Projected Impact of Mexico's Sugar-Sweetened Beverage Tax Policy on Diabetes and Cardiovascular Disease: A Modeling Study. *PLOS Medicine* 13(11): e1002158.

Savell, E., Gilmore, A. and Fooks, G. (2014) How Does the Tobacco Industry Attempt to Influence Marketing Regulations? A Systematic Review. *PLOS One* 9(2): e87389.

Savell, E., Fooks, G. and Gilmore, A. (2016) How does the alcohol industry attempt to influence marketing regulations? A systematic review. *Addiction* 111(1): 18–32.

Scarborough, P., Adhikari, V., Harrington, R. A. et al. (2020) Impact of the announcement and implementation of the UK Soft Drinks Industry Levy on sugar content, price, product size and number of available soft drinks in the UK, 2015–19: A controlled interrupted time series analysis. *PLOS Medicine* 17(2): e1003025.

Schmacker, R. and Smed, S. (2023) Sin Taxes and Self-Control. *American Economic Journal: Economic Policy* 15(3): 1–34.

Schoenfeld, J. and Ioannidis, J. (2013) Is everything we eat associated with cancer? A systematic cookbook review. *American Journal of Clinical Nutrition* 97(1): 127–34.

Scollo, M., Zacher, M., Durkin, S. and Wakefield, M. (2014) Early evidence about the predicted unintended consequences of standardised packaging of tobacco products in Australia: a cross-sectional study of the place of purchase, regular brands and use of illicit tobacco. *BMJ Open* 4: e005873.

Scollo, M., Bayly, M. and Wakefield, M. (2015) Availability of illicit tobacco in small retail outlets before and after the implementation of Australian plain packaging legislation. *Tobacco Control* 24(e1): e45–51.

Scottish Government (2008) Changing Scotland's relationship with alcohol: a discussion paper on our strategic approach. June.

Scottish Government (2018) Final Business and Regulatory Impact Assessment – Alcohol (Minimum Pricing) (Scotland) Act 2012, The Alcohol (Minimum Price per Unit) (Scotland) Order 2018. March.

Scottish Government (2023) Minimum Unit Pricing has 'positive impact' on health. 27 June https://web.archive.org/web/20230627040851/https://www.gov.scot/news/minimum-unit-pricing-has-positive-impact-on-health/ (Updated 21 August: https://web.archive.org/web/20230830122558/https://www.gov.scot/news/minimum-unit-pricing-has-positive-impact-on-health/)

Scottish Parliament (2012) Health and Sport Committee 2nd Report, 2012 (Session 4) Stage 1 Report on the Alcohol (Minimum Pricing) (Scotland) Bill. 7 March.

Simpson, D. (1998) 'ASH: Witness on Smoking' in Lock, S., Reynolds, L. and Tansey, E. (eds) *Ashes to Ashes: The History of Smoking and Health*. Amsterdam: Brill Rodopi.

Skog, O-J. (1985) The Collectivity of Drinking Cultures: A Theory of the Distribution of Alcohol Consumption. *British Journal of Addiction* 80(1): 83–99.

Smith, E. and Malone, R. (2020) An argument for phasing out sales of cigarettes. *Tobacco Control* 29: 703–8.

Smith, K. E. (2013) Understanding the Influence of Evidence in Public Health Policy: What Can We Learn from the 'Tobacco Wars'? *Social Policy & Administration* 47(4): 382–98.

Snowdon, C. (2025a) Bootlegging Baptists: The Logic of Paternalistic Collective Action. *Journal of Public Finance and Public Choice* 41(1): 27–48.

Snowdon, C. (2025b) *The People vs Paternalism*. IEA Discussion Paper 134. London: Institute of Economic Affairs.

So, V., Millard, A. D., Katikireddi, S. V. et al. (2021) Intended and unintended consequences of the implementation of minimum unit pricing of alcohol in Scotland: a natural experiment. *Public Health Research* 9(11).

Sousa, J. (2014) Estimation of price elasticities of demand for alcohol in the United Kingdom. HMRC Working Paper 16.

Stevely, A. K., Mackay, D., Alava, M. H., Brennan, A., Meier, P., Sasso, A. and Holmes, J. (2023) Evaluating the effects of minimum unit pricing in Scotland on the prevalence of harmful drinking: a controlled interrupted time series analysis. *Public Health* 220: 43–49.

Stigler, G. J. (1971) The Theory of Economic Regulation. *Bell Journal of Economics and Management Science* 2(1): 3–21.

Stockwell, T. (2015) Minimum unit pricing for alcohol. *British Medical Journal* 49: g5617.

Stockwell, T., Auld, M. C., Zhao, J. and Martin, G. (2012a) Does minimum pricing reduce consumption? The experience of a Canadian province. (2012) *Addiction* 107(5): 912–20.

Stockwell, T., Zhao, J., Giesbrecht, N., Macdonald, S., Thomas, G., and Wettlaufer, A. (2012b) The Raising of Minimum Alcohol Prices in Saskatchewan, Canada: Impacts on Consumption and Implications for Public Health. *American Journal of Public Health* 102(12): e103–10.

Stockwell, T., Zhao, J., Martin, G., Macdonald, S., Vallance, K., Treno, A., et al. (2013) Misleading UK alcohol industry criticism of Canadian research on minimum pricing. *Addiction* 108(6): 1,172–3.

Stockwell, T. and Thomas, G. (2013b) Is alcohol too cheap in the UK? The case for setting a Minimum Unit Price for alcohol. Institute of Alcohol Studies. April.

Stockwell, T., Zhao, J., Marzell, M., Gruenewald, P. J., Macdonald, S., Ponicki, W. R. et al. (2015) Relationships Between Minimum Alcohol Pricing and Crime During the Partial Privatisation of a Canadian Government Alcohol Monopoly. *Journal of Studies on Alcohol and Drugs* 76(4): 628–34.

Strong, D. R., Pierce, J. P., Pulvers, K. et al. (2021) Effect of Graphic Warning Labels on Cigarette Packs on US Smokers' Cognitions and Smoking Behavior After 3 Months: A Randomised Clinical Trial. *JAMA Network Open* 4(8): e2121387.

Sutton, S., and Hallett, R. (1988) Smoking intervention in the workplace using videotapes and nicotine chewing gum. *Preventive Medicine* 17: 48–59.

Thom, B., Herring, R., Thickett, A. and Duke, K. (2016) The Alcohol Health Alliance: The emergence of an advocacy coalition to stimulate policy change. *British Politics* 11: 301–23.

Thompson, K., Stockwell, T., Vallance, K., Giesbrecht, N. and Wettlaufer, A. (2013) Reducing Alcohol-Related Harms and Costs in British Columbia: A Provincial Summary Report. CARBC Bulletin 10. August.

Truman, D. (1951) *The Governmental Process: Political Interests and Public Opinion*. New York: Alfred A. Knopf, Inc.

Tullock, G. (1984) A (partial) rehabilitation of the public interest theory. *Public Choice* 42: 89–99.

Uhl, A. (2015) Evidence-based research, epidemiology and alcohol policy: a critique. *Contemporary Social Science* 10(2): 221–31.

Ulucanlar, S., Fooks, G., Hatchard, J. and Gilmore, A. (2014) Representation and Misrepresentation of Scientific Evidence in Contemporary Tobacco Regulation: A Review of Tobacco Industry Submissions to the UK Government Consultation on Standardised Packaging. *PLOS Medicine* 11(3): e1001629.

University of Cambridge (2021) Improving health through reductions in population sugar consumption. REF2021 (Public Health, Health Services and Primary Care): Research Excellence Framework.

University of Oxford (2021) Making the case for sugar taxes: UK, Ireland and Mexico. REF2021 (Public Health, Health Services and Primary Care): Research Excellence Framework.

University of Sheffield (2014) The impact of the Sheffield Alcohol Policy Model on alcohol policy. REF2014 (Public Health, Health Services and Primary Care): Research Excellence Framework.

Uppal, N., Shahab, L., Britton, J. and Ratschen, E. (2013) The forgotten smoker: a qualitative study of attitudes towards smoking, quitting, and tobacco control policies among continuing smokers. *BMC Public Health* 13: 432.

Vis, B. (2019) Heuristics and Political Elites' Judgment and Decision-Making. *Political Studies Review* 17(1): 41–52.

Voigt, K. (2012) Ethical Concerns in Tobacco Control Nonsmoker and "Nonnicotine" Hiring Policies: The Implications of Employment Restrictions for Tobacco Control. *American Journal of Public Health* 102(11): 2,013–18.

Walker, J. L. (1983) The Origins and Maintenance of Interest Groups in America. *The American Political Science Review* 77(2): 390–406.

Wakefield, M. (2011) Welcome to cardboard country: how plain packaging could change the subjective experience of smoking. *Tobacco Control* 20(5): 321–22.

Wakefield, M., Germain, D. and Durkin, S. J. (2008) How does increasingly plainer cigarette packaging influence adult smokers. Perceptions about brand image? An experimental study. *Tobacco Control* 17: 416–21.

Wakefield, M., Hayes, L., Durkin, S. and Borland, R. (2013) Introduction effects of the Australian plain packaging policy on adult smokers: a cross-sectional study. *BMJ Open* 3: e003175.

Wang, Y.C., Coxson, P., Shen, Y-M, Goldman, L. and Bibbins-Domingo, K. (2012) A Penny-Per-Ounce Tax on Sugar-Sweetened Beverages Would Cut Health and Cost Burdens of Diabetes. *Health Affairs* 31(1): 199–207.

Wansink, B., Hanks, A., and Just, D. (2012) From Coke to Coors: A field study of a fat tax and its unintended consequences. *Social Science Research Network.*

Wardle, H., Sproston, K., Orford, J., Erens, B., Griffiths, M., Constantine, R. and Pigott, S. (2007). British Gambling Prevalence Survey 2007. National Centre for Social Research, prepared for the Gambling Commission.

Wardle, H., Excell, D., Ireland, E., Ilic, N. and Sharman, S. (2014a) Gambling machines research programme - Report 2: Identifying problem gambling – findings from a survey of loyalty card customers. London: NatCen.

Wardle, H., Seabury, C., Ahmed, H., Payne, C., Byron, C., Corbett, J. and Sutton, R.(2014b) Gambling behaviour in England and Scotland: Findings from the Health Survey for England 2012 and Scottish Health Survey 2012. London: NatCen.

Wardle, H., Fuller, E., Maplethorpe, N. and Jones, H. (2017) Follow-up study of loyalty card customers: Changes in gambling behaviour over time. London: NatCen.

Wardle, H., Reith, G., Langham, E., and Rogers, R. (2019) Gambling and public health: we need policy action to prevent harm. *British Medical Journal* 365: l1807.

Waterlander, W. E., Ni Mhurchu, C. and Steenhuis, I. (2014) Effects of a price increase on purchases of sugar sweetened beverages. Results from a randomized controlled trial. *Appetite* 78: 32–9.

Webb, T. and Sheeran, P. (2006) Does Changing Behavioural Intentions Engender Behaviour Change? A Meta-Analysis of the Experimental Evidence. *Psychological Bulletin* 132(2): 249–68.

Weiss, C. (1977) Research for Policy's Sake: The Enlightenment Function of Social Research. *Policy Analysis* 3(4): 531–45.

Weiss, C. (1978) 'Improving the linkage between social research and public policy' in Lynn (1978) (see above): 23–81.

Weiss, C. (1979) The Many Meanings of Research Utilisation. *Public Administration Review* September/October: 426–31.

White, C. M., Hammond, D., Thrasher, J. F. and Fong, G. F. (2012) The potential impact of plain packaging of cigarette products among Brazilian young women: an experimental study. *BMC Public Health* 12(737).

White, V., Williams, T. and Wakefield, M. (2015) Has the introduction of plain packaging with larger graphic health warnings changed adolescents' perceptions of cigarette packs and brands? *Tobacco Control* 24 (Suppl 2): ii42–ii49.

Whiteley, P. F. (1995) Rational Choice and Political Participation – Evaluating the Debate. *Political Research Quarterly* 48(1): 211–33.

WHO Europe (2024) *Commercial determinants of noncommunicable diseases in the WHO European Region*. Copenhagen: WHO Regional Office for Europe.

Widerquist, K. (2003) Public choice and altruism. *Eastern Economic Journal* 29(3): 317–37.

Williams, L. V., Page, L., Parke, J. and Rigbye, J. (2008) British Gambling Prevalence Survey 2007: Secondary Analysis. London: Gambling Commission.

Wintour, P. (2013) Plans for minimum alcohol pricing reportedly dropped after cabinet revolt. *Guardian*, 13 March.

Wyatt, A. (2002) Evidence Based Policy: The View from a Centre. *Public Policy and Administration* 17(3): 12–28.

Wyper, G. M. A., Mackay, D., Fraser, C. et al. (2023) Evaluating the impact of alcohol minimum unit pricing on deaths and hospitalisations in Scotland: a controlled interrupted time series study. *Lancet* 401(10385): 1,361–70.

Yandle, B. (1983) Bootleggers and Baptists: The Education of a Regulatory Economist. *Regulation* May/June: 12–16.

Young, J., Stacey, I., Dobbins, T., Dunlop, S., Dessaix, A. and Currow, D. (2014) Association between tobacco plain packaging and Quitline calls: a population-based, interrupted time-series analysis. *Medical Journal of Australia* 200(1): 29–32.

Zacher, M., Bayley, M., Brennan, E., Dono, J., Miller, C., Durkin, S., Scollo, M. and Wakefield, M. (2014) Personal tobacco pack display before and after the introduction of plain packaging with larger pictorial health warnings in Australia: an observational study of outdoor café strips. *Addiction* 109(4): 653–62.

Zarb-Cousin, M. (2019) How to Campaign for Social Change – and Win. *Tribune*, 15 January: https://tribunemag.co.uk/2019/01/fixed-odds-betting-terminals-fobts

Zhao, J., Stockwell, T., Martin, G. et al. (2013) The relationship between minimum alcohol prices, outlet densities and alcohol-attributable deaths in British Columbia, 2002–09. *Addiction* 108(6): 1,059–69.

Zingales, L. (2017) Towards a Political Theory of the Firm. *Journal of Economic Perspectives* 31(3): 113–130.

ABOUT THE IEA

The Institute of Economic Affairs is a research and educational charity (No. CC 235 351). Its mission is to improve understanding of the fundamental institutions of a free society by analysing and expounding the role of markets in solving economic and social problems.

The IEA achieves its mission through:

- a high-quality publishing programme
- conferences, seminars, lectures and other events
- outreach to school and university students
- appearances across print, broadcast and digital media

The IEA, established in 1955 by the late Sir Antony Fisher, is an educational charity, not a political organisation. It is independent of any political party or group and does not carry on activities intended to affect support for any political party or candidate in any election or referendum, or at any other time. It is financed by sales of publications, conference fees and voluntary donations.

In addition to its main series of publications, the IEA publishes the academic journal *Economic Affairs* in partnership with the University of Buckingham.

The IEA is aided in its work by an Academic Advisory Council and a panel of Honorary Fellows. Together with other academics, they review prospective IEA publications, their comments being passed on anonymously to authors. All IEA papers are therefore subject to the same rigorous, independent refereeing process as used by leading academic journals.

IEA publications are often used in classrooms and incorporated into school and university courses. They are also sold throughout the world and often translated and reprinted. The IEA supports and works with a global network of like-minded organisations, through its Initiative for African Trade and Prosperity, EPICENTER and other international programmes.

Views expressed in the IEA's publications are those of the authors, not those of the Institute (which has no corporate view), its Managing Trustees, Academic Advisory Council members or senior staff. Members of the Institute's Academic Advisory Council, Honorary Fellows, Trustees and Staff are listed on the following page.

The Institute gratefully acknowledges financial support for its publications programme and other work from a generous benefaction by the late Professor Ronald Coase.

The Institute of Economic Affairs
2 Lord North Street, Westminster, London SW1P 3LB
Tel: 020 7799 8900
Email: iea@iea.org.uk
Web: iea.org.uk

Other books recently published by the IEA include:

The Henry Fords of Healthcare … Lessons the West Can Learn from the East
Nima Sanandaji
ISBN 978-0-255-36788-2; £10.00

An Introduction to Entrepreneurship
Eamonn Butler
ISBN 978-0-255-36794-3; £12.50

An Introduction to Democracy
Eamonn Butler
ISBN 978-0-255-36797-4; £12.50

Having Your Say: Threats to Free Speech in the 21st Century
Edited by J. R. Shackleton
ISBN 978-0-255-36800-1; £17.50

The Sharing Economy: Its Pitfalls and Promises
Michael C. Munger
ISBN 978-0-255-36791-2; £12.50

An Introduction to Trade and Globalisation
Eamonn Butler
ISBN 978-0-255-36803-2; £12.50

Why Free Speech Matters
Jamie Whyte
ISBN 978-0-255-36806-3; £10.00

The People Paradox: Does the World Have Too Many or Too Few People?
Steven E. Landsburg and Stephen Davies
ISBN 978-0-255-36809-4; £10.00

An Introduction to Economic Inequality
Eamonn Butler
ISBN 978-0-255-36815-5; £10.00

Carbon Conundrum: How to Save Climate Change Policy from Government Failure
Philip Booth and Carlo Stagnaro
ISBN 978-0-255-36812-4; £12.50

Scaling the Heights: Thought Leadership, Liberal Values and the History of The Mont Pelerin Society
Eamonn Butler
ISBN 978-0-255-36818-6; £10.00

Faith in Markets? Abrahamic Religions and Economics
Edited by Benedikt Koehler
ISBN 978-0-255-36824-7; £17.50

Human Nature and World Affairs: An Introduction to Classical Liberalism and International Relations Theory
Edwin van de Haar
ISBN 978-0-255-36827-8; £15.00

The Experience of Free Banking
Edited by Kevin Dowd
ISBN 978-0-255-36830-8; £25.00

Apocalypse Next: The Economics of Global Catastrophic Risks
Stephen Davies
ISBN 978-0-255-36821-6; £17.50

New Paternalism Meets Older Wisdom: Looking to Smith and Hume on Rationality, Welfare and Behavioural Economics
Erik W. Matson
ISBN 978-0-255-36833-9; £12.50

An Introduction to Taxation
Eamonn Butler
ISBN 978-0-255-36836-0; £12.50

Imperial Measurement: A Cost–Benefit Analysis of Western Colonialism
Kristian Niemietz
ISBN 978-0-255-36839-1; £10.00

The Quantity Theory of Money: A New Restatement
Tim Congdon
ISBN 978-0-255-36842-1; £15.00

Unions Resurgent? The Past, Present and Uncertain Future of Trade Unions in Britain
J. R. Shackleton
ISBN 978-0-255-36845-2; £15.00

An Introduction to Schools of Economic Thought
Eamonn Butler
ISBN 978-0-255-36848-3; £12.50

The Welfare State Myth: How Low-Tax Countries Offer the World's Best Welfare
Stefan Fölster and Nima Sanandaji
ISBN 978-0-255-36851-3; £10.00

Other IEA publications

Comprehensive information on other publications and the wider work of the IEA can be found at www.iea.org.uk. To order any publication please see below.

Personal customers

Orders from personal customers should be directed to the IEA:

IEA
2 Lord North Street
Westminster
London SW1P 3LB
Tel: 020 7799 8911
Email: accounts@iea.org.uk

Trade customers

All orders from the book trade should be directed to the IEA's distributor:

University of Buckingham Press
51 Gower Street
London
WC1E 6HJ
Tel: +44(0)1256302692
Email: info@unibuckinghampress.com

IEA subscriptions

The IEA offers a subscription service. For £350 a year, UK-based subscribers will receive every book the IEA publishes along with invitations to IEA events – while also supporting the IEA's charitable mission. You can subscribe online by becoming a 'Founding Insider' at insider.iea.org.uk. Otherwise, please contact:

Subscriptions
IEA
2 Lord North Street
Westminster
London SW1P 3LB
Tel: 020 7799 8911
Email: accounts@iea.org.uk

www.ingramcontent.com/pod-product-compliance
Lightning Source LLC
La Vergne TN
LVHW100251210926
848480LV00003B/897